Joshua L Bearden

Revolutionary Backlash

EARLY AMERICAN STUDIES

Daniel K. Richter and Kathleen M. Brown, Series Editors

Exploring neglected aspects of our colonial, revolutionary, and early national history and culture, Early American Studies reinterprets familiar themes and events in fresh ways. Interdisciplinary in character, and with a special emphasis on the period from about 1600 to 1850, the series is published in partnership with the McNeil Center for Early American Studies.

A complete list of books in the series is available from the publisher.

Revolutionary Backlash

Women and Politics in the Early American Republic

ROSEMARIE ZAGARRI

PENN

University of Pennsylvania Press

Philadelphia

10   9   8   7   6   5   4   3   2   1

Published by
University of Pennsylvania Press
Philadelphia, Pennsylvania 19104–4112

A Cataloging-in-Publication record is available from the Library of Congress

ISBN-13: 978–0-8122–4027–6
ISBN-10: 0–8122–4027–8

To Bill, with love

Contents

Figure 1. *Liberty Displaying the Arts & Sciences [or The Genius of America Encouraging the Emancipation of the Blacks]* (1792), by Samuel Jennings. This image shows the goddess Liberty, portrayed as a modern woman, holding a staff with a liberty cap on top. She is surrounded by the artifacts of learning and refinement—books, a globe, scientific instruments, an artist's palette, a musician's lyre, a sculptor's bust. In the foreground, a group of African Americans bow in front of these symbols of advancement. In the background, African Americans dance around a liberty pole. For women and for blacks, the post-revolutionary era offered a brief moment of hope for improvement in their status. (The Library Company of Philadelphia.)

Introduction

More than three decades after the American Revolution ended, a Maryland newspaper published an article with the reassuring headline "Revolutions Never Go Backward." Expressing the hope that the world had "wearied" of revolutions, the author maintained that people throughout the world were now ready to "settle down in quiet, for the purpose of enjoying what little good there may be, mingled with the evil in this naughty world." Yet, if American women and men felt that the gains of their political Revolution had been secured, its effects on women were less certain. In the immediate wake of the Revolution, women's prospects seemed promising. Writing in 1798, Massachusetts author Judith Sargent Murray congratulated her "fair country-women" on what she called "the happy revolution which the few past years has made in their favour." At long last, she said, "'the Rights of Women' begin to be understood; we seem, at length, determined to do justice" to women. Such was her "confidence" that she expected even more changes to be forthcoming. "Our young women," Murray declared, are "forming a new era in female history."[1]

Just a few years later, however, the effects of the French Revolution and the upheavals of domestic political strife seemed to be taking a toll. A male writer viewed the situation, particularly with respect to women, with alarm. "That revolutionary mania," he maintained, "which of late has so forcibly extended its deleterious effects to almost every subject" had infected women as well. "Blind to the happiness of their present situation and seized with a revolutionary phrenzy, [women] feel themselves highly wronged and oppressed. . . . They seem ardently to wish for a revolution in their present situation." Yet both the threat and the promise of a new era for women seem to have come quickly to an end. In 1832 the historian Hannah Adams observed, "We hear no longer of the *alarming*, and perhaps justly obnoxious din, of the 'rights of women.' Whatever [women's] capacity of receiving instruction may be, there can be no use in extending it beyond the sphere of their duties." Why had just a few short decades produced such a changed perception of women's rights, roles, and responsibilities?[2]

This is a book about the transformation of American politics from the

American Revolution to the election of Andrew Jackson. It is not the typical story of the rise of democracy and the emergence of the common man. It is a tale about how the Revolution profoundly changed the popular understanding of women's political status and initiated a widespread, ongoing debate over the meaning of women's rights. It shows how the Revolution created new opportunities for women to participate, at least informally, in party and electoral politics and how these activities continued into the era of the Federalists and Jeffersonian Republicans. Yet this opening for women soon closed. By 1830 a conservative backlash had developed. The recognition of women's political potential, as much as actual changes in their role, unleashed this reaction. At the same time, the broadening of political opportunities for white males, especially the growth of political parties and the expansion of the franchise, diminished the importance of nonvoters, including women, in the electoral process and led to an increasing focus on a more restricted group, white male electors. The era of democratization for men thus produced a narrowing of political possibilities for women.

For a long time it was assumed that the American Revolution had not created a corresponding revolution for women. Because the new nation did not grant women political rights, their status was thought to have changed little. The pathbreaking works of Linda Kerber and Mary Beth Norton, published in 1980, demolished this belief. By expanding the definition of "politics" beyond the formal realm of voting and holding public office, it became apparent that women had indeed been active participants in the nation's formative event, the American Revolution. Women talked, wrote, and thought about political ideas, and they expressed their sentiments in political action. Through the making and wearing of homespun, participation in economic boycotts, and sacrifices made in the course of the war, women contributed to the success of the revolutionary cause. In the process they also became politically aware and engaged. During and after the war, men not only acknowledged women's political role but also encouraged and praised their contributions.[3]

Historians such as Catherine Allgor, Susan Branson, Cynthia Kierner, Simon Newman, David Waldstreicher, and Jan Lewis have more recently demonstrated the continuation of women's political involvement during the first years of the new republic. Borrowing from the social sciences, they define politics to include not only the formal institutions of government but also a wide variety of informal norms, symbolic actions, and everyday behaviors. In addition to studying the behavior of women, they also examine assumptions about gender roles and the power relations between the sexes. This approach expands the possibilities for understanding the extent to which political institutions either reflect, reinforce, or subvert the existing gender hierarchy.[4] What these historians have found is that even as conflict between Federalists and Democratic Republicans was transforming the country's political landscape, many middle-class and elite white women embraced a political role for themselves. The wheels of government would have turned less effectively without their presence.[5]

There has nonetheless been some resistance to this approach. Despite important exceptions, political historians and women's historians of the early American republic sometimes still write as if the two fields had no common ground. Traditional political historians portray women as peripheral to the central political events of the time, excusing themselves from taking women seriously because of women's lack of formal political rights. Their focus remains on the great white men who shaped national politics and policies—the presidencies of larger-than-life figures such as George Washington and Thomas Jefferson; the conflict between intellectual titans such as James Madison and Alexander Hamilton; the idiosyncrasies of John Adams or Aaron Burr. When they broaden the scope of discussion to include the middling or lower classes, the focus of the story, as in Sean Wilentz's *The Rise of American Democracy: Jefferson to Lincoln* (2005), often continues to be on white males.[6] If they do mention women, they tend to do so in a separate discussion, parallel to the main narrative.

Early American women's historians, on the other hand, often depict developments in male politics as tangential to women's lives. Some inveigh against privileging white male politics. Others want to scrap the political narrative altogether, seeking instead to recover the substance of women's daily lives and allow women to speak in their own voices. By studying women of all social classes and races, their works have fruitfully revealed, among other things, a thriving female domestic economy, sophisticated social reform movements, and diverse notions of womanhood in the early republic. Yet minimizing the importance of women's relationship to the state has a cost. The period between the American Revolution and the Seneca Falls Convention of 1848 appears to be nothing more than a frustrating hiatus in the development of women's rights. Important changes in the popular discourse about women's rights have been overlooked or ignored.

This study, then, operates at the intersection of political history, women's history, and gender history. Its long-term origins begin in the late seventeenth century, when thinkers such as François Poulain de la Barre, John Locke, Mary Astell, and others began to challenge the notion of women's inherent intellectual inferiority. In eighteenth-century England, Scotland, and France, Enlightenment philosophers began to promote a theory of historical change that placed women at the center of social progress. Other authors popularized a new genre, the earliest women's histories, celebrating women's literary, philosophical, and political achievements in past times and far-flung places throughout the world. All of these developments challenged the notion that women were inherently inferior to men. Women's potential was limited not by innate feminine characteristics but by society's customs, habits, and traditions. Under the right circumstances and with the proper education, women, it seemed, might well equal men in a wide range of arenas that had been closed to them.

The American Revolution accelerated this reevaluation of women's role and gave it a specifically political valence. By celebrating the principles of equality and natural rights, the Revolution established universal ideals as the benchmark by which American society would subsequently judge the fairness and equity of its policies. Although not initially intended to apply to women, these ideals were not, in theory, limited to any particular nation, group, race, or sex; they extended to all people. Americans soon had to decide whether they meant what they said. In many ways the story of postrevolutionary America is the story of how American women and men sought to define—and ultimately to limit and restrict—the expansive ideals they had so successfully deployed against Britain. The new nation had opened a Pandora's box, unleashing consequences that were only dimly understood at the time.

For a few brief decades, in fact, significant changes in women's status appeared possible. This was a world in which much political activity of importance occurred out of doors and in the streets. Nonvoters as well as voters, blacks as well as whites, and women as well as men, had a place in a capacious, informal political realm. Building on the precedent set by the American Revolution, male politicians encouraged, and even welcomed, women's participation in party politics and electoral activities. In New Jersey women actually gained a more formal role. Legislators in that state extended the principle linking taxation and representation to include women. Beginning in 1776, qualified women, usually wealthy widows, voted in both state and federal elections. Although the experiment ended in 1807, for a time the unimaginable had become a reality. Women shared in exactly the same political rights and privileges as men did.

The publication in 1792 of Mary Wollstonecraft's *A Vindication of the Rights of Woman* raised the stakes and transformed the debate. Her work introduced the term "women's rights" into widespread popular usage. In periodicals, speeches, novels, and private letters American men and women pondered, probed, and fought over what it meant for women to possess rights and whether those rights included voting and holding public office. Although they were socially and legally subordinate to men, white women, it became clear, enjoyed a privileged status. Unlike slaves or free blacks, white women were distinct individuals who shared certain rights with white men. Wollstonecraft's formulation also exposed a more troubling issue. A contradiction lay at the heart of the new republican experiment. How could the United States reconcile its commitment to equality and natural rights with the exclusion of women from government and politics?

It was both the promise and the threat of these possibilities that made the concept of women's rights so explosive. Beginning with the American Revolution, white women had gained public sanction to act politically in the role of what historians have called the "republican wife" or the "republican mother."[7] This notion carved out a significantly new understanding of women's political status. As wives and mothers, it was said, women had contributed to the success of the revolutionary cause. In the future, their contributions would help determine the success or failure of the new republic. Even without leaving their traditional feminine roles, women would have an important political role to play. Republican motherhood, however, also limited the scope of women's political possibilities. It did not expand their role beyond that of wives and mothers or extend their potential as independent political beings. Their actions had efficacy primarily because of women's influence over their husbands and sons—the future soldiers, voters, and statesmen of the republic—rather than by means of women's own agency. Republican motherhood thus represented a moderate, non-threatening response to the challenge of the Revolution for women. It was a formulation that kept the gender status quo intact.

A highly visible, if relatively small, number of women, however, embraced a more radical alternative. They assumed their political role with an independence of spirit and an intellectual assertiveness that impressed some people and alarmed others. These women even gained their own designation: "female politicians." Although such women neither sought nor held public office, they were known for their deep interest in and passion about party and electoral politics. In contrast to "republican wives" and "republican mothers," female politicians saw themselves—and were seen by others—as political actors in their own right. For their supporters, the women's intense politicization represented a means of extending the political opportunities opened up by the American Revolution. Their actions reflected women's increasing competence in a realm that had previously been closed to them. For their detractors, however, female politicians represented a threat. Such women violated the bounds of feminine modesty, challenged male authority, and eroded the essential distinctions between the sexes. Like

Mary Wollstonecraft and the female voters of New Jersey, their actions might undermine the country's political order, social hierarchy, and gender status quo—all of which presumed a male monopoly on power.

Over time, women's increasing politicization, along with the threat posed by women's rights, produced a backlash. As party conflict between Federalists and Republicans intensified, women allied themselves with one party or the other and took sides in bitter partisan struggles. Party conflict began to threaten not only the country's political future but also its social fabric. Families split apart, communities divided, and the nation repeatedly went to the brink of civil war. In this context, women's political participation, especially that of "female politicians," took on a new and more ominous significance. Instead of serving the good of the entire nation, women were now advancing the interests of a particular party. At a time when factionalism threatened to rend the nation in two, women were behaving as partisans, not as patriots. In response, a new discourse emerged. Women, it was said, could best serve the nation not by engaging in politics but by withdrawing to the domestic realm. As wives and mothers, they could mitigate party passions by acting as mediators between warring male partisans and inculcate in their husbands and children a spirit of openness to dissenting views. If women removed themselves from party and electoral politics, then it might be possible for men to engage in party warfare without wrecking communities, destroying sociability, or undermining the stability of the republic. Women, moreover, would still have a political role to play. Like the republican mothers of the American Revolution, they would exercise their political influence indirectly, by means of their husbands and sons, rather than in the more overt manner practiced by female politicians.

By the time of Andrew Jackson's election, a combination of factors led to a further narrowing of the political possibilities for women. First were structural changes in American laws and institutions. Despite their claims to support the universal "rights of man," Republicans made it clear during debates over the expansion of the franchise that they did not include women in their demands. In fact, even as the Republicans became more successful in broadening the franchise for men, states increasingly began to exclude women from the vote, explicitly limiting suffrage to "free, white males." Whereas women's previous exclusion had mostly been on the basis of custom, the new restrictions had the force of law. Moreover, with each passing year both the Republicans and the Federalists systematized, regularized, and institutionalized the operations of their party organizations. The growth of party caucuses for nominating candidates, the development of more sophisticated electioneering techniques, and the use of a ticket system at elections became more common. As a result, over time both Jeffersonians and Federalists turned their attention away from public activities meant to gain the support of the masses and concentrated their efforts on building party loyalty and getting out the vote among their followers. A politics out of doors and in the streets which had included both women and men gave way to more selective gatherings of the party faithful, who were all men. Political leaders now cultivated those who mattered most: white male electors.

Cultural changes occurring after the turn of the century solidified and reaffirmed women's exclusion. Thinkers of the transatlantic Enlightenment had promoted a notion that attributed variations between the sexes to custom, education, or upbringing. With sufficient education and opportunity, it was said, women might accomplish as much as men. By the early nineteenth century, however, a more essentialist view of human nature was gaining prominence. Slowly and erratically, in a variety of venues ranging from scientific literature to medical textbooks to popular periodicals, distinctions between the sexes came to be seen not in terms of custom or tradition but as the result of innate, biological differences. Women's bodies were not just different from men's; they were inferior. As a result, the exclusion of women from the polity came to be considered not as unfair, arbitrary, or capricious but as the recognition of scientific "fact."

This is not to say that all the gains for women from the revolutionary era were lost. Here, however, it is crucial to differentiate between various meanings ascribed to the concept of "politics." At its most restrictive, "politics" refers primarily to formal institutions of government and the activities related to governing. In the early United States, these activities included voting, electioneering, passing legislation, and the functions of party organizations. At another extreme is a definition offered by the feminist historian Joan Scott. In the early 1980s, Scott maintained that a broader, and less restrictive, definition of politics would make it easier to incorporate women more fully into the historical narrative. Urging historians to move beyond "studying power as it is exercised by and in relation to formal governmental authorities," she suggested that they see "all unequal power relationships as somehow 'political' because [they] involv[e] unequal distributions of power." Useful as this definition may be for some purposes, it is also so broad as to include almost every kind of relationship that exists in society. If the focus is to be on women's relationship to the state, then a more delimited understanding of politics is useful. Here the work of Mary Kelley, building on the framework offered by John Brooke, is pertinent. Kelley offers the concept of "civil society" as a descriptive term to clarify the nature of women's activities in early America. As she defines it, civil society includes "any and all publics except those dedicated to the organized politics constituted in political parties and elections to local, state, and national office." Civil society thus provides a conceptual middle ground between the extremes of party and electoral politics, on the one hand, and politics defined as all unequal power relations, on the other.[8]

At various times, this study deploys all these various notions of politics in order to explain women's relationship to the early American state. It attempts to do so, however, with some degree of analytical rigor and consistency. This work also seeks to analyze politics in the terms in which people at the time understood the concept. The effort is complicated by the fact that in the period under investigation the structure of politics was itself in flux. From 1789 to approximately 1830, the focus of legitimate political activity shifted from a more informal and capacious politics of the street to a more organized set of norms centered around voting and political parties. At the same time, the American Revolution created a new environment for women's participation in politics. Because of the nature of revolutionary politics and the rise of print culture, new opportunities arose that allowed women to participate, albeit informally, in partisan affairs and electoral politics. Although resistance to women's politicization never completely disappeared, many American men and women affirmed women's political involvement and validated their political contributions. Just as important, the spread of an ideology celebrating equality and natural rights gave women a heightened status as the possessors of natural rights. A widespread popular debate ensued that explored the possibility that women, too, might one day enjoy the same political rights and privileges as men. For a few brief decades, a comprehensive transformation in women's rights, roles, and responsibilities seemed not only possible but perhaps inevitable.

By the time Andrew Jackson became president, however, this atmosphere had dissipated. An almost universal belief prevailed which claimed that women had no place in either party or electoral politics. This does not mean that women no longer engaged in politics of any sort. Here, too, however, the precise definition of "politics" is at issue. As dozens of recent studies have shown, throughout the entire era from the American Revolution to the Civil War women continued to read about politics, write about partisan affairs, engage in political discussions, and influence men's political choices. Perhaps even more importantly, they were vital players in what Kelley calls "civil society." Charitable societies, benevolent organizations, and social reform movements, including temperance and abolitionism, allowed women to contribute to the polity in different ways than party and electoral politics had. Through these organizations women continued to influence the nation's political ideas and shape its political institutions. Thus at the

same time that women's ability to participate in party politics and electoral affairs began to decrease, women began to find venues for participating in politics by another means. In this sense, then, the Revolution's
legacy persisted for women.[9]

Nonetheless, a sea change had occurred. By the middle decades of the
nineteenth century, women were actively discouraged from participating in any activity that smacked of "politics." Women who did so openly
were disparaged or vilified. Even the female reformers of the Antebellum era who themselves sought to change the American political system
vehemently denied the political nature of their activities and distanced
themselves from party politics and electoral affairs. Unlike the women
of the postrevolutionary generation, these women made their contributions not because they were encouraged to participate in politics but in
spite of rampant hostility and discrimination against them. The rapid
shift in perceptions, and self-perceptions, of women's political role is, in
some measure, what this study hopes to explain.

In the end, the soundness of all works of history depends on their
faithfulness to what people actually wrote, thought, said, and did in the
past. We can know this only through the sources that have survived.
Records by and about women's political activities in the distant past are
much less voluminous, less accessible, and more scattered than those of
men. To take a case in point: while many archives preserved the correspondence of even the most minor members of Congress, they much
less frequently retained the letters from their wives. In fact, only recently
has the correspondence of Martha Washington and Dolley Madison,
wives of major political figures, been published in scholarly editions. In
order to study the political role of women in postrevolutionary America,
then, we must look to the traditional sources of male political history,
including newspapers, legislative records, political pamphlets, and correspondence among political elites. Read with a sensitivity to issues concerning gender, these documents do have something to tell us about
women and politics; in fact, they have much more to say than most people assume they do. At the same time, we must expand our scope to
include other kinds of sources: popular periodicals and ladies' magazines; Fourth of July orations; fiction; satire; and the writings of women
contained in letters to their husbands, friends, and relatives. These
sources get us closer to the actual experiences of women and to the
thinking of the wider public at the time. It is also true that the sources
primarily reflect the thinking of white, middle-class, and elite Americans
rather than that of black people, lower-class people, or other marginal-
ized groups. Nonetheless, it is in this expanded public arena that the
ferment about women's political rights was occurring. What these documents say about women may not seem so surprising today. Yet in the

decades following the American Revolution the issue of women's rights was so explosive that after a brief moment of receptivity, American women and men chose to foreclose the debate rather than pursue it to its logical conclusion.

Despite, or perhaps because of, these constraints, Americans confronted—perhaps for the first time—the limits of their revolutionary ideology with respect to women. Women were excluded from government not because they lacked sufficient knowledge, intellect, or virtue but simply on the basis of their sex—because they were women. This also suggests the darker side of the democratic process: how the broadening of political opportunities for white males meant the increasing exclusion of white females. Rather than a straightforward march toward progress ending in women's achievement of full political equality with men, this story involves many false starts, much resistance, and many detours. Women had agency, but there were limits to their agency. Just as we can no longer think about the rise of American liberty during the American Revolution without also considering its underside, the role of slavery, so we should also understand that democratization for white males in the early republic resulted in the more deliberate exclusion of women from politics and governance. The consequences of this development continue to bedevil us even to the present day.

Chapter 1
The Rights of Woman

In 1798, less than ten years after the ratification of the U.S. Constitution, the writer Charles Brockden Brown, often considered the country's first professional man of letters, published an article on a controversial topic in his periodical, the Philadelphia *Weekly Magazine*. Entitled "The Rights of Woman," the piece depicted a dialogue between a young man, Alcuin, and his female acquaintance, Mrs. Carter. At one point Alcuin, the namesake of a medieval monk, posed a question to his companion, asking the woman about her preferences in terms of political parties. Instead of deferentially refusing to discuss such an unfeminine topic, Mrs. Carter went on the offensive. "What have I, as a woman, to do with politics?" she asked. "Even the government of our country, which is said to be the freest in the world, passes over women as if they were not [free]. We are excluded from all political rights without the least ceremony. Lawmakers thought as little of comprehending us in their code of liberty, as if we were pigs, or sheep. That females are exceptions to their general maxims perhaps never occurred to them. If it did, the idea was quietly discarded, without leaving behind the slightest consciousness of inconsistency or injustice."[1]

Charles Brockden Brown had gone straight to the heart of a fundamental contradiction in postrevolutionary American society. Although the Revolution had been fought in the name of equality and natural rights, the American political system failed to embody those ideals for substantial portions of its population. It denied equal rights to all black people and to nearly one-half of the white population: women. Although the first organized resistance to slavery began to emerge at this time, there was no comparable movement for women's rights. Most historians, in fact, assume that the first widespread debates about women's rights did not occur until the decade or so preceding the Seneca Falls Convention of 1848. Yet, as Brown's tirade suggests, the first agitation about women's rights can actually be traced to the years immediately following the Revolution, or even earlier, to Enlightenment discussions about the role of women in history and society. Although the American Revolution was not fought in an effort to promote women's rights, the commitment to equality and natural rights created an unexpected conundrum. Would American women share in what the author Judith Sargent Murray called "the blessings of liberty"?[2] Or would the new country treat its women, as Brown claimed, merely like "pigs, or sheep"?

Women, Custom, and History

The relationship of women to the polity is part of the ongoing, long-term *querelle des femmes* that began during the Renaissance, continued through the Enlightenment, and gained new momentum after the American and French Revolutions. The Enlightenment, in particular, produced important shifts in the understanding of women's role and status. In 1673 François Poulain de la Barre published a work in France called *The Equality of the Two Sexes*. Building on the Cartesian belief in the centrality of reason, Poulain argued that women's physical traits did not impair their mental faculties. Men's and women's minds were essentially the same; the differences between their bodies were incidental to this more fundamental fact. Over the course of the eighteenth century, Poulain's dictum "The mind has no sex" became widely accepted among the educated classes throughout the transatlantic world. If both men and women had the ability to reason, then women were as capable as men in the arena that mattered most: the realm of the intellect. John Locke's *Essay on Human Understanding* provided a different kind of support for the possibility that men and women might have equal intellectual faculties. He proposed that the mind is a tabula rasa, a blank slate shaped by the environment and education rather than by innate ideas. This explanation helped explain women's apparent intellectual inferiority. Their deficiencies were the result not of inherent incapacity but of the failure to receive adequate educational opportunities. Embracing this notion, the English writer Mary Astell attacked men for their complicity in keeping women in ignorance. "Instead of inquiring why all Women are not wise and good," wrote Astell in 1694, "we have reason to wonder that there are any so. Were the Men as much neglected, and as little care taken to cultivate and improve them, perhaps they wou'd be so far from surpassing those whom they now dispise, that they themselves wou'd sink into the greatest stupidity and brutality." The "Incapacity" of the female mind, "if there be any," she concluded, "is acquired, not natural." Given the same opportunities as men, women would be able to match their male counterparts in intellectual achievement.[3]

Around the same time, other thinkers also began to challenge the belief in women's inherent inferiority. They recounted women's roles and accomplishments in distant times and places. The very earliest women's histories appeared during the Renaissance, beginning with Giovanni Boccaccio's *Concerning Famous Women* (1355–59) and Christine de Pisan's *Book of the City of Ladies* (1404). During the late seventeenth and eighteenth centuries a whole new profusion of women's histories appeared. Usually consisting of a series of biographical sketches, these works listed the accomplishments of notable "female worthies" from ancient times to modern, including women from the Old Testament, Roman matrons, Greek poetesses, famous queens, and female writers and thinkers. Significantly, these women succeeded in areas that were typically thought to be the province of men, such as literature, politics, government, and warfare. Playing to the tastes of an increasingly literate female audience, the women's histories intended to set the historical record straight by recovering a story that had been lost, ignored, or suppressed. Conventional histories focused on men and "Eclipsed the brightest Candor of Female perfection." Their purpose, according to one author, was to enlighten women as to "the history of their own sex." Women, said another, would receive "a valuable proportion of the praise [they have] merited." Women would have their own past. This would be nothing less than "An Historical Vindication of the Female Sex."[4]

Judging by the pace of publication, the publishers were correct. Readers, especially women, seemed to have a voracious appetite for these works. Thomas Heywood's *Generall History of Women*, published in England in 1657, was followed in 1686 by John Shirley's *Illustrious History of Women, or A Compendium of the Many Virtues that Adorn the Fair Sex*. Others appeared in quick succession: Richard Burton's *Female Excellency or the Ladies Glory* in 1688; and Nahum Tate's *A Present for the Ladies: Being an Historical Account of Several Illustrious Persons of the Female Sex* in 1693. After the turn of the century, the genre gained momentum. James Bland issued his *Essay in Praise of Women* in 1735, while in 1752 the Oxonian George Ballard published *Memoirs of several Ladies of Great Britain, who have been celebrated for their writings and skill in the learned languages, arts, and science*. In 1766 *The Biographium Foemineum: or, Memoirs of the Most Illustrious Ladies of All Ages and Nations* appeared. French authors turned out similar works, some of which were translated into English.[5]

North American British colonists shared the motherland's enthusiasm for women's history. Not only did Americans import a substantial number of volumes, which were quite expensive, but they also began to print their own, cheaper editions. In 1774 a Philadelphia publisher issued William Russell's translation of Antoine-Léonard Thomas's *Essay on the Character, Manners, and Genius of Women in Different Ages*, which had been issued the previous year in London and was originally printed in France in 1772. In 1796 and 1800 Philadelphia editions of the anonymous work *Sketches of the History, Genius, Disposition, Accomplishments, Employments,*

Customs and Importance of the Fair Sex in All Parts of the World appeared. In addition, popular periodicals and literary magazines often excerpted portions of the histories, enabling the works to reach a larger audience.[6]

One of the most popular and influential works was William Alexander's two-volume *History of Women, From the Earliest Antiquity, to the Present Time; Giving an Account of Almost Every Interesting Particular Concerning that Sex, Among All Nations, Ancient and Modern*. (See Figure 2.) The work was first issued in London and Dublin in 1779, and excerpts were published in the *Boston Magazine* from December 1784 through July 1785. *The History of Women* appeared in two American editions, one in 1795 and another a year later. The 1796 printing alone listed more than 450 subscribers, including sixty-four women, booksellers such as Matthew Carey, and eminent personages such as General Thomas Craig, Governor Thomas Mifflin, and Supreme Court Justice James Wilson. References to the work abounded. Many American writers, including Judith Sargent Murray and Hannah Mather Crocker, explicitly cited Alexander's history of women in their own writings.[7]

Then as now, however, the lessons of the past were not self-evident or unambiguous. Different readers took away different lessons. For some, the histories provided proof that women could equal men in their intellect and achievements. The past provided a trove of evidence that could be marshaled in women's defense. In 1806, for example, the *Literary Magazine* proclaimed that Sappho, the poetess of ancient Lesbos, "soared above her sex in the wonderful endowments of her mind." Semiramis of Nineveh, it was said, ruled an empire in the ancient Middle East. Queen Christina of Sweden, observed the *New York Weekly Museum*, was noted for her prodigious learning and relinquished her crown rather than marry and "resign [her] liberty." More recently, England and America produced famous women authors, including Hannah More, Susanna Rowson, Charlotte Rowe, and Mercy Warren. Laura Bassi earned a doctorate in mathematics at the Institute of Bologna. Throughout history, it seemed, women had demonstrated the capacity to excel in the same areas as men did.[8]

Other readers, however, came to different conclusions. These observers criticized women from the past who displayed traits that they deemed masculine, such as leadership or learning. An article in the *Weekly Museum*, for example, condemned the female ruler of ancient Assyria, Semiramis, for her "cruelty" in power as well as her hideous murder of her husband. Another author unfavorably compared Elizabeth of England, who exhibited "the foibles of a weak woman," to her sister, Mary, Queen of Scots, who combined "the merit of a literary character [with] every female accomplishment." Their praise was reserved for women who most nearly conformed to contemporary feminine ide-

VIRTUE

Dispelling *the Clouds of* Ignorance.

Figure 2. "Frontispiece: Virtue Dispelling the Clouds of Ignorance," from vol. 1 of *The History of Women, from the Earliest Antiquity, to the Present Time*, by William Alexander (Philadelphia, 1796). Alexander's *History of Women* was one of the most popular works in this genre that recovered women's achievements from the past. Although the caption below the figure suggests that Virtue dispels "the Clouds of Ignorance" surrounding women's past, the figure's scroll says "History of Women," suggesting that knowledge is as important as virtue. (Courtesy, American Antiquarian Society, Worcester, Massachusetts.)

als of beauty, purity, modesty, or self-sacrifice. *Port Folio* magazine, for example, celebrated the French writer Madame de Sevigne because she was "always a woman; never an author, never a pedant, never a literary female. . . . A woman always loses by attempting to be a man." Another author claimed that although "we admire the masculine mind of Elizabeth, we love Mary Queen of Scots." Although women might have the ability to succeed in the same arenas as men did, they should not necessarily aspire to such goals. "It will generally be found," said the *New York Weekly Museum*, "that woman is better calculated to tread in softer and smoother paths; to leave the tumultuous bustle of public life, to spread light, cheerfulness, and felicity in less splendid circles." Thus the early women's histories could be read either to critique the gender status quo or to affirm it.[9]

Whether or not women's past actions gained approval, the histories presented irrefutable evidence of women's past accomplishments and, hence, of their current untapped potential abilities. Even if one believed that women should not aspire to achieve the same accomplishments as men, the histories demonstrated that women were capable of doing so. "The history of women," asserted the *Female Advocate*, "is forever intruding on our unwilling eyes, bold and ardent spirits, who no tyrant could tame, no prejudice enslave." Despite resistance, women in the past had overcome innumerable obstacles in order to succeed. In her *Gleaner* essays, Judith Sargent Murray noted that there were over 845 women "writers of eminence" in the past. "If the triumphs and the attainments of THE SEX, under the various oppressions with which they have struggled, have been thus splendid," she said, "how would they have been augmented, had not ignorant or interested men . . . contrived to erect around them almost insurmountable barriers." The "distinction" between men and women "was artificial, and not *natural*," insisted another author, and "there have always been instances of female intelligence and female merit to prove [it]." Women would not be deterred.[10]

Perhaps most important, the early histories of women revealed the bankruptcy of the belief in women's inherent inferiority. As William Alexander pointed out, women in the eighteenth century had failed to accomplish as much as their forebears had not because they were incapable but because of "all the disadvantages they are laid under by the law, and by custom." This meant that society had developed norms that limited women's role and restricted their choices. "Why," demanded an author writing in the *New-York Magazine*, "are the ladies condemned to remain in ignorance?" The answer, at least to this writer, seemed apparent: "It is because the majority of men have an interest in concealing knowledge from them." Custom and tradition, not nature, limited women's roles and possibilities.[11]

This was a key insight. While inherent differences were immutable, custom could be changed. Hence, as Judith Sargent Murray put it, women "were *naturally* as susceptible of every improvement, as those of men." If women took responsibility for their own condition, they could change society. Women, proclaimed a young woman graduating from a female academy, should throw off "the shackles of custom, and dispel from our minds those clouds of ignorance and darkness, in which our sex has been too long involv'd." Once freed from customary restrictions, women's prospects seemed almost limitless. "The greatest concerns," declared the *Gentleman and Lady's Magazine*, "are not beyond their capacity." Although custom might be what Murray called a "tyrant," it was an oppressor that could be overthrown. Even those who disparaged women's past achievements as "masculine" would have to admit that.[12]

At the same time that the early histories of women were challenging the notion of women's inherent inferiority, Enlightenment thinkers posited a new conception of history, sometimes called "conjectural history," that moved women from the margins of the historical process to the center. Philosophers as diverse as Henry Home (Lord Kames), John Millar, David Hume, the baron de Montesquieu, and Condorcet all employed some version of this approach in their writings. In their view, societies progressed through a series of predictable stages along a continuum from savagery to civilization. Although the precise number of stages, ranging from four to twelve, varied according to each philosopher, the trajectory was similar.

In the first stage, the primitive or savage phase, life was simple, hard, and brutal. Men were hunters who spent most of their time mired in the basic struggle for subsistence. Over time, some societies moved beyond this basic level into the more auspicious pastoral phase of existence. Large numbers of people herded sheep and kept cattle. With their basic needs taken care of, life lost some of its brutality and harshness. An even smaller number of societies moved beyond this point into the agrarian phase. For people living in these societies, material existence became more secure. Inhabitants enjoyed a certain amount of comfort and leisure. Society began to shed some of its rusticity; people became more refined and cultivated. An even smaller number of societies moved into the final phase, the mercantile stage. Having escaped the demands of mere subsistence, commercial societies allowed people to escape the crudities of their earlier existence and cultivate their higher interests and pleasures. Inhabitants could spend time in learning, leisure, or the refined arts. These stages were not regarded merely as abstract theories. The natives of North America represented the primitive end of the spectrum, while modern Britain exemplified the other extreme, a nation that had reached the pinnacle of civilization, refinement, and achievement.[13]

Significantly, conjectural historians portrayed women as key agents in the development of society and civilization. In their schema, women represented both an index to and an instrument of social advancement. The more a society progressed, the better it treated its women. In the lowest stage of civilization, women were regarded as nothing more than men's slaves, suitable primarily for sexual congress and physical labor. There was, according to William Robertson, "a cruel distinction between the sexes, which forms the one to be harsh and unfeeling, and humbles the other to servility and subjection." As society moved into the pastoral and agrarian phases, however, men treated women with more dignity and respect. "That women are indebted to the refinements of polished manners for a happy change in their state," commented Robertson, "is a point which can admit of no doubt." At the same time, women furthered social progress by cultivating men's higher instincts, refining their manners, and helping them discipline their more unruly passions. "The gentle and insinuating manners of the female sex," said Kames, "tend to soften the roughness of the other sex; and where-ever women are indulged with any degree of freedom, they polish sooner than men." Eventually women gained greater status and better treatment. They emerged from their status as chattel or as simple objects of lust and rose, according to Kames, "out of slavery to possess the elevated state they are justly entitled to by nature." In the highest stage of development, the mercantile phase, women enjoyed "that nearness of rank, not to say equality," as Hume put it, "which nature has established between the sexes." They now took their place as men's friends and companions. According to Millar, women were "encouraged to quit that retirement which was formerly esteemed so suitable to their character, to enlarge the sphere of their acquaintance, and to appear in mixed company, and in public meetings of pleasure." They became the social—though not political—equals of men.[14]

Conjectural histories helped American men and women appreciate women's contributions to society. Women had a crucial role in inculcating virtue, fostering manners, and promoting the civilizing process. "Female manners," observed John Cosens Ogden of New Hampshire, "must and ever will, form those of men. The latter are rude and savage, polished and refined, in proportion as the former are cultivated and softened." Society's treatment of its women would, in turn, reflect its degree of progress toward civilization. "There is no truth more generally admitted," noted the Reverend Samuel Miller, "than that every step in the progress of civilization brings new honour to the female sex, and increases their importance to society." American men and women knew that their own society would be judged by these standards. "It is a fact," the *Weekly Museum* declared, "that in all ages of the world, in proportion as mankind have advanced in civilization, in the same proportion have the softer sex been esteemed and treated with respect." As men's friends and companions, women gained dignity, respect, and a modicum of equality.[15]

Acknowledging women's centrality to society made it easier to envision the possibility that women might contribute to the polity as well. In a monarchy women's place was primarily ornamental. In a republic where the people governed themselves, women could shape the values and ideals of the populace. "[Although] the men possess the more ostensible powers of making and executing the laws," observed an Independence Day speaker, "the women, in every free country, have an absolute control of manners: and it is confessed, that in a republic, manners are of equal importance with laws." In their role as wives and mothers, women could instill virtue and inculcate patriotism in their children, husbands, and neighbors. Addressing the women attending his lectures on the law in 1790, the lawyer James Wilson emphasized the significance of women's contributions. "To protect and to improve social life," he said, "is, as we have seen, the end of government and law. If, therefore, you [women] have no share in the formation, you have a most intimate connexion with the effects, of a good system of law and government." Through their influence over men, women could have a crucial, if indirect, influence on the polity. They might have a political role to play.[16]

Women and the American Revolution

The new Enlightenment histories of women and stage theories of social change created new perceptions of women's roles and possibilities. Writing in 1803, the American Presbyterian minister Samuel Miller noted, "One of the most striking peculiarities of the eighteenth century . . . is the change of opinion gradually introduced into society, respecting the importance, capacity, and dignity of the *Female Sex*." The effect, as he saw it, amounted to nothing less than "a revolution radical and unprecedented with respect to [women's] treatment and character."[17]

Yet this was a revolution of a certain kind—a change in the understanding of women's intellectual capacity and social contributions rather than the achievement of political rights and privileges. Before the American Revolution the popular perception remained that politics and government were exclusively male realms. Although women had certain rights, their status was inferior to that of men. Only men could vote and hold public office. Only men could attend meetings of the colonial assemblies, hold positions of power at court, serve in the military, collect customs duties, or be appointed governor. Men so thoroughly monopolized government and politics that the prevailing belief was that women either had no opinions about these subjects or, if they did, should not express them.

Yet even before the American Revolution, small numbers of elite women in both England and America had already begun to express an interest in politics and a desire to participate in government. Aristocratic women in England attended balls, salons, and court ceremonies, which gave them access to and influence over political figures. The English civil war and Glorious Revolution produced a torrent of works written by women on political subjects ranging from the state of the monarchy, succession, and republican government to the prospect of foreign war. By the early eighteenth century some British women had grown dissatisfied with their inferior legal status and had begun to protest publicly against the system's inequities. In a 1735 petition to Parliament, one group of women condemned the "Hardship of English Laws in Relation to Wives," which, they said, "put us in a worse Condition than Slavery itself." Claiming their privilege as "Free-born Subjects of *England,*" they sought redress of their grievances, requesting more equitable treatment in terms of property rights, widows' portions, and physical safety at the hands of their spouses. Writing a few years later, a woman calling herself "Sophia, A Person of Quality," produced the published tract, *Vindication of the Natural Right of the Fair-Sex to a Perfect Equality of Power, Dignity, and Esteem, with Men.* Not only did the author maintain that women were men's intellectual equals, she also claimed that women were as fit as men to govern and hold public office. "I think it evidently appears," she declared, "that there is no science, office, or dignity, which Women have not an equal right to share with Men: Since there can be no superiority but that of brutal strength shewn in the latter, to entitle them to engross all power and prerogative to themselves; nor any incapacity proved in the former to disqualify them of their right, but what is owing to the unjust oppression of the Men, and might be easily removed." Continuing this line of investigation, the 1758 pamphlet called *Female Rights Vindicated* protested against women's exclusion from government and probed the nature of women's "Obligations to civil Society." According to the tract's female author, "women in general are as fit for the offices of state, as those who commonly fill them." By the 1780s and 1790s British radicals such as John Gale Jones, William Hodgson, Thomas Cooper, and Jeremy Bentham, associated with clubs such as the London Corresponding Society and the Manchester Literary and Philosophical Society, were advancing propositions supporting women's equality and natural rights, including women's right to vote.[18]

Women in colonial British North America also experienced political stirrings. Two editions of the British tract *Female Grievances Debated* were printed in the colonies between 1731 and 1758. In fact, the Custis family of Virginia—Martha Washington's family of origin—owned the original English edition. Colonial newspapers sometimes printed pieces that satirized men's treatment of women or challenged women's subordinate status. A poem published in Virginia in 1736 and South Carolina in 1743 declared,

> Then equal Laws let Custom find,
>   And neither Sex oppress;
> More Freedom give to Womankind,
>   Or to Mankind give less.

Other pieces picked up on the theme of women's subjugation. A poem from 1743, subsequently reprinted in other publications, described marriage as woman's "wretched" fate, a condition that changed the man into a "tyrant" and the woman into a creature bound by a "Slave's Fetters." The Englishwomen's 1735 petition to Parliament was reprinted in 1788 in Philadelphia's *Columbian Magazine* under the heading "A Tract on the Unreasonableness of the Laws of England, in regard to Wives." Though it appeared without editorial comment, the implication seemed to be clear.[19]

As in Britain, however, the predominant norm in colonial British America held that women should neither interest themselves in politics nor involve themselves in the business of government. Nonetheless, a long-term growth in women's literacy and the increasing availability of political information, particularly newspapers, meant that more women in British America could read about politics and form their own opinions. In 1734 during the controversy over the prosecution of the printer John Peter Zenger for seditious libel, a reader of the *New-York Weekly Journal* complained to the editor that women in the colony were "contending about some abstruce Point in Politicks, and running into the greatest Heats about they know not what." Hoping to quell the outburst, he dismissed their comments, saying, "Politicks is what does not become them." Yet some women apparently continued to express political views. "The Men," reported Esther Edwards Burr in 1755, "say . . . that Women have no business to concern themselves about [politics] but [should] trust to those that know better." Although men complained, women did not always defer to their judgment.[20]

By and large, however, most women remained reluctant to transgress into what was understood to be male territory. Even Mercy Otis Warren, who would become one of the most accomplished women authors of her generation, responded timidly when her friend John Adams first spoke to her about the subject of politics. In a letter written in 1776, Adams asked Warren what form of government she would prefer for the newly independent United States. In reply, she expressed her hesitancy to speak to the issue, fearing that a discussion of "war, politicks, or anything relative thereto" was off-limits to women. She wondered whether his query was "designed to ridicule the sex for paying any attention to political matters." Only after she received his explicit reassurances did she dare "approach the verge of any thing so far beyond the line of my sex."[21]

This state of affairs could have persisted indefinitely if not for the American Revolution. The American Revolution marked a watershed in the popular perceptions of women's relationship to the state. Almost as soon as the controversy began in the 1760s, Whig leaders realized that the effectiveness of their resistance to Britain depended on their ability to mobilize popular support. This included women. Women's support, they knew, would be critical to the resistance movement against Britain and could affect the course of the war. Significantly, patriot leaders did not presume that American women would automatically follow their husbands' lead. Schooled in Enlightenment theories about women, many men believed that women had an equal capacity to reason. Just as skeptical farmers, merchants, artisans, and mechanics would have to be persuaded to aid the resistance movement, women too would have to be won over to the cause.

It is plausible, even likely, that women had played some role, direct or indirect, in determining the outcome of previous wars, conflicts, and rebellions throughout history. What was different about the American Revolution was the nature and extent of the appeals to women. The more extensive use of print media made this change possible. Newspapers, magazines, and broadsides reached out to women in a direct, widespread, and public fashion. Using poems, essays, plays, and orations, male political leaders urged women to join in the effort. During the 1760s they asked women to boycott imported luxury goods, produce homemade textiles and clothing, and give up drinking British tea. Once armed resistance began, they asked them to sacrifice the conveniences of life, take over their husbands' duties at home in their absence, and, if necessary, be willing to offer their men's lives for their country on the field of battle. Printed appeals drew women to the cause.

Women responded with a widespread outpouring of support. During the 1760s women in Boston, Massachusetts, and Edenton, North Carolina, signed formal agreements to abide by the boycotts forbidding the importation of British goods. In other places women organized local chapters of the Daughters of Liberty as female counterparts to the Sons of Liberty, held patriotic spinning bees, or wore homespun as a sign of symbolic sacrifice. Soon after declaring independence, New Yorkers toppled a leaden statue of George III on the Bowling Green. Seizing the opportunity, the women of Litchfield, Connecticut retrieved the statuary and transformed the broken pieces into over forty-two thousand cartridges to supply the Continental Army with ammunition. Once the war began, some women sewed shirts or knit stockings for Washington's desperately needy troops. Still others took even more direct action. In 1780 Esther DeBerdt Reed spearheaded a drive in Philadelphia to collect funds for the Continental Army. In towns throughout Pennsylvania, Maryland, New Jersey, and Virginia, women went door to door soliciting funds to assist the wavering war effort. Participating in the revolutionary movement in their own ways and on their own terms, women made themselves a political force.[22]

At the grassroots level, women came to realize that their personal response to the Revolution could have an impact on the course of the war itself. The new nation needed thousands of men, year after year, to fill offices in the new state and federal governments, to serve in the militia or the Continental Army, and to represent the country as ambassadors abroad. When men left home to take up arms or serve in government positions, they depended on women to take over their duties on the farm, in business, and within the family. Women often had little prior training or experience in supervising these matters. Economic conditions were difficult; war-time shortages and inflation made matters worse. The trials of family life without a father present caused untold emotional strains.

Women's willingness to shoulder men's burdens and become what Laurel Ulrich has called, in another context, a "deputy husband" gave men the freedom to participate in the war effort. Yet women were well aware of the personal costs. Helen Kortright Brasher of New York City recalled that although she supported the Revolution, she resented her husband's absences from home. "He had formerly been a most domestick man; now he was forever out of his house surrounded with gentlemen conversing on politicks; every evening out at some meeting or other haranguing his fellow citizens, writing for the public prints; in short the whole city experienced the unhappy change and every family was more or less in the same painful situation."[23]

Not all women responded equally willingly to the calls for sacrifice. Differences in women's responses suggest important ways in which women could influence their husbands' political choices and ultimately affect the course of the war. While some women rose to the new challenges, or at least accepted the responsibilities grudgingly, others refused or resisted. This was true even among families of the leaders of the revolutionary cause. Abigail Adams represented a paragon of female revolutionary patriotism. Her husband John was, of course, a stalwart of the resistance movement. Beginning as a young lawyer, he quickly moved into a leadership position in the Massachusetts Assembly and then during the early years of the Revolution became one of the central figures in the new Continental Congress. Beginning in 1778 he went abroad for several years to negotiate treaties, first with France and then with Britain. During these long separations Abigail bore the full burden of managing the house, farm, and family without her husband. Although Abigail proved to be a skillfull "farmeress," as she called herself, she always grieved her husband's absence. Anticipating John's arrival for a quick trip home in 1775, she poured out her despair to her friend Mercy Otis Warren: "I find I am obliged to summon all my patriotism to feel willing to part with [John] again. You will readily believe me when I say that I make no small sacrifice to the publick." Warren sympathized with her plight as her own husband was often gone for long periods on public business. "The frequent Absence of the best of friends," she wrote to Abigail, "prevents to you and to me the full injoyment of the Many Blessings providence has kindly showered Down upon us. . . . But while the sword and the pestilence pervade the Land, and Misery is portion of Millions, why should we expect to feel No interruption of Happiness." Abigail Adams nonetheless repeatedly gave her blessing to her husband's choices and supported his decision to serve the public.[24]

In contrast, Mercy Otis Warren chose not to be as self-abnegating as Abigail Adams was. Both were avid patriots. In the 1770s, Mercy, in fact, had written several satirical plays and numerous poems attacking British tyranny and, in particular, the treachery of Massachusetts lieutenant governor Thomas Hutchinson. Her husband, James, began his political career in the mid-1760s and served for over ten years in the Massachusetts General Court. An early leader of the resistance movement in his hometown of Plymouth, he also served during the war as a member of the state constitutional convention, as an officer in the Massachusetts militia, on the federal navy board, and in various other offices. These duties frequently entailed absences from home lasting anywhere from several weeks to several months. By 1780 Mercy had had enough. She urged her husband to retire from public service and return home to be with her. "I am sometimes Ready," she wrote to James, "to think you could serve the public better unencumbered by anxieties for me, but I am not Hipocrite Enough to conceal the secret Regrets that pray upon my mind and Interrupt my peace." Her entreaties convinced him. Despite the fact that the war had not yet been won and the business of state building had just begun, he essentially withdrew from public service. As Warren's case demonstrates, patriotic appeals to women were not simply rhetorical exercises. If women were unwilling to sacrifice for the cause, their husbands might be less likely to participate as well. Women needed to subordinate their own private happiness for the sake of the common good—and act more like Abigail Adams than Mercy Warren.[25]

Aware of their dependence on women, men realized that they would ignore "the sex" at their peril. Throughout the war, patriot leaders publicly praised women's sacrifices and stoked the fires of female patriotism. By recognizing women's political efforts and contributions, they politicized women, acknowledging their capacity as political agents. Women felt a new sense of empowerment. In a poem on the Townshend boycotts against the British goods, Warren highlighted the importance of women to the plan's success: by "quit[ting] the useless vanities of life," women would "at once . . . end the great political strife." Their actions would "bless, or ruin all mankind." Similarly, Milcah Martha Moore of Pennsylvania emphasized the ability of women to provide leadership during the crisis over the Tea Act:

Let the Daughters of Liberty, nobly arise,
And tho' we've no Voice, but a negative here,
The use of the Taxables, let us forbear. . . .
That rather than Freedom, we'll part with our Tea.

Instead of being simply followers, women would lead the way and "point out their Duty to Men." Having suffered numerous adversities, they came to believe that their patriotism equaled any man's. Carrying on while her husband was a British prisoner, Mary Fish of Connecticut declared, "I have the vanity to think I have in some measure acted the heroine as well as my dear Husband the Hero." American women were, as Esther DeBerdt Reed put it, "Born for liberty."[26]

Once independence was achieved, men reinforced women's newfound sense of themselves as political actors. In public speeches and published articles, they repeatedly acknowledged women's support and praised their contributions to the revolutionary cause. Like men, women had felt the scourge of British tyranny and suffered through a multitude of deprivations and hardships. "Though ruin and desolation pervaded your country, and those to whom you [women] were bound by the dearest ties were insulted, outraged and imprisoned," proclaimed John Fauchereaud Grimké, "still you remained firm and undismayed in the conscientious discharge of your duty." Celebrating women's cooperation, they acknowledged their contribution in achieving victory over Britain. Both sexes, noted Richard Dinsmore, "gloried in the appellation rebel." Although female patriotism was, as Keating Lewis Simon noted, more "of a kind entirely suited to their sex," women had fully earned the country's esteem. "Our heroines, in their place," concluded Solomon Aiken, "were not a whit behind our foremost heroes."[27]

These appeals had effects that lasted well beyond the war. Print culture established a vehicle through which patriot leaders might reach out to large numbers of women and involve them in the revolutionary cause. Women received public recognition for their activities. In acknowledging women's importance to the cause, men affirmed women's capacity to act as political agents. Their actions not only affected the fates of individual families but also had an impact on the course of the war, politics, and society. Although the Revolution did not necessarily radicalize women, it did politicize them in ways and to an extent that had never before occurred. They started to see themselves—and were seen by others—as political beings. No longer were they politically invisible.

Rights and Revolution

Before the Revolution, the notion of women's subordination to men permeated American society. The doctrine of coverture assumed that women were not independent legal agents. Before they were married, they were under the guardianship of their fathers. Once married, their husbands acted in their stead. Without a separate legal identity, women could not sue or be sued in court, make contracts, or own property. In addition, the assumption that they lacked an independent identity extended far beyond statutory prescriptions. Young women were supposed to defer to their fathers' opinions; married women, to their husbands. Their lives were defined with reference to home and family. Women were not supposed to travel alone, speak in public to audiences that included men, or become too learned. Their exclusion from political rights was an assumed given, seldom questioned or discussed.[28]

It is undeniably true that at the beginning of the war for independence, most American leaders would never have dreamed that their struggle against Britain would turn into an attack on the gender status quo. Yet, like all revolutions, the American Revolution produced its share of unintended consequences. No single person or group could control the direction of events or the flow of ideas. This was especially true with regard to ideas about women's relationship to the state, their involvement with politics, and their political rights and privileges.

The most crucial development was the growing centrality of the principles of equality and natural rights. Originally, of course, these ideas were meant to pertain primarily, if not exclusively, to men. During the 1760s and 1770s American colonists found themselves in an ongoing political struggle with Britain. Initially they protested against British policies by insisting on their rights as Englishmen. As British subjects, they claimed to share in a long tradition of English rights that included the right to trial by jury, the right to petition, the right to freedom of speech, and a right to be taxed only when they were properly represented in their legislatures. When Britain repeatedly dismissed or ignored Americans' protests, the colonists realized that they must seek other grounds on which to justify their claims. By 1776 many Americans believed that Britain had violated not only their rights as Englishmen but also their God-given natural rights, inscribed in nature. The Declaration of Independence justified independence by asserting men's natural equality and by invoking the "Laws of Nature and of Nature's God." Natural rights commanded assent because they were said to be inalienable, immutable, and universal—possessed by virtue of one's personhood rather than as a result of citizenship, parentage, or wealth. Such claims were hard to refute.

Yet unbeknownst to the revolutionaries, these concepts could take on a life of their own.[29] Equality and natural rights had an elastic quality, capable of almost infinite expansion and extension. If these principles were universal in nature, as was contended, why did they not apply to other dispossessed groups, such as poor white men, black people, or women? One of the first areas to be challenged was the property qualification for voting. As was the case in Britain, the North American British colonies allowed only those who met certain property qualifications to vote for members of their colonial assemblies. Colonists assumed that those who owned property had a greater stake in society and a greater interest in the deliberations of the legislature than those who did not. Property owners, moreover, were believed to be more independent and virtuous than the propertyless masses, who might be susceptible to bribery, manipulation, or corruption. In England electors had to own a forty-shilling freehold to vote for members of Parliament. In most of the colonies a similar requirement was established, sometimes based on acreage rather than land value. In practice, however, the same principle had very different implications in the two places. Whereas in England, due to the shortage of land, no more than 20 percent of adult males could vote, in the colonies, because of the widespread cheapness and availability of land, between 50 percent and 80 percent of all white males could vote. What had been a restrictive requirement in Britain was inconsequential in America. Even before the Revolution, then, a majority of white men were enfranchised.[30]

Even so, once the Revolution began, the very existence of property qualifications for voting started to bother some members of society. As states began to write their first constitutions, agitation for lowering or eliminating property qualifications became a subject of debate. Some commentators pointed out the inconsistency in allowing men to fight and die for their country but not allowing them to vote. Others pointed out that by expanding the franchise, state governments would broaden their base of popular support. Still others noted that if Americans believed that those who paid taxes should be represented, then all taxpayers, not just owners of real property, should be enfranchised. The most powerful argument, however, was that if all men were truly created equal and shared the same natural rights, then all men should be entitled to vote.[31]

Inspired by these sentiments, William Sullivan wrote a letter in May 1776 to his friend John Adams in which he made the case for universal suffrage. Responding with alarm, Adams pointed out that all societies operate on the basis of "general rules," or commonly agreed-upon conventions. These conventions may or may not have a rational basis. With regard to voting, Adams said, many groups were excluded from the franchise, including women, children, and those who were not mentally sound. Some of these exclusions were somewhat arbitrary. He pointed out, for example, that while a twenty-one-year-old man could vote, an equally qualified man who was only "twenty years eleven months and twenty-seven days old" could not. Such norms and distinctions, Adams claimed, were necessary for society to maintain order and prevent chaos. He defended the property qualification because, among other things, it represented a clear and distinct line of demarcation. Those who possessed enough property could vote, and everyone else was excluded; there was no ambiguity. Adams, however, had a bigger fear—a suspicion that revolutionary ideology might produce a larger movement to eradicate distinctions between the social classes. Without property qualifications, he believed, there would be no sound basis for excluding other groups in society from the franchise, including women. The elimination of property qualifications, he said, would "confound and destroy all distinctions, and prostrate all ranks to one common level." Significantly, Adams instinctively grasped what many other people at the time did not: that the rationale for excluding women from government rested on certain agreed-on social conventions rather than any inherent reason. Thus even before women agitated for the vote, Adams perceived the direction in which revolutionary ideology might lead.[32]

Before the Revolution, questions had seldom arisen about whether women could or should be able to vote. At the same time, although all voters were men, voting itself was not necessarily defined as an exclusively male prerogative. In fact, fewer than half of the colonies—Pennsylvania, Delaware, Georgia, Virginia, and South Carolina—used the word "male" in their election statutes or otherwise specifically excluded women. Women's exclusion may have been regarded as so self-evident that it did not require a specific prohibition. Because of the legal doctrine of coverture, married women, under the guardianship of their husbands, could not own property. Although widows and single women could own property, they constituted just a small fraction of the population. Hence the question of women voting did not often arise. Even so, it is significant that women were not alone in their disfranchisement. Substantial numbers of white males (from 20 percent to 50 percent) and in most colonies all free black males also did not meet the property qualifications and thus were excluded from the franchise. Thus, while it is true that women did not have the right to vote, neither did a lot of men. Class, not sex, represented the primary basis for inclusion or exclusion.[33]

The issue of female suffrage did not receive a great deal of public attention during the War for Independence itself. A few writers, such as James Otis and Thomas Paine, published articles that mentioned the notion of women voting, but they did not take up the issue in a sustained fashioned. In 1790 in the *Massachusetts Magazine,* Judith Sargent Murray published an essay called "On the Equality of the Sexes," which demanded greater educational opportunities for women. She did not, however, address the question of women's political rights. In private letters and discussions, the issue of female suffrage did start to surface. Individuals such as Rachel Wells, and Mary Willing Byrd, and others began to broach the subject in letters to friends, family, and spouses. Hannah Lee Corbin of Virginia, for example, challenged her brother, the revolutionary leader Richard Henry Lee, as to why she, as a taxpaying woman, was not allowed to vote even though she met the state's property qualifications to do so. Having recently asserted the principle of "no taxation without representation" against the British, Lee was put on the defensive. He admitted that neither "wisdom" nor "policy" offered valid reasons "to forbid widows having property from voting." The best he could offer was to point to custom and tradition: it had "never been the practice either here or in England." Though he promised that he "would at any time give my consent to establish their right of voting," the issue went no further.[34]

Today many historians cite Abigail Adams's letter of March 31, 1776, to her husband as a plea for woman suffrage. In this letter Adams reflected on the imminence of independence and contemplated what that meant for the country. She then proposed to John, who was at that time a member of the Continental Congress, that the members of the new assembly "Remember the Ladies" when they prepared a new code of laws for the nation. "Be more generous & favourable to [women] than your ancestors," she said. "Do not put such unlimited power into the hands of the Husbands. Remember all Men would be tyrants if they could." John responded with a combination of patronizing condescension and weak humor. "As to your extraordinary Code of Laws," he said, "I cannot but laugh. . . . We know better than to repeal our Masculine systems. Altho they are in full Force, you know they are little more than Theory. . . . We have only the Name of Masters." If "we give up this," he continued, men "would be completely subject" to the "Despotism of the Peticoat." In fact, despite the playfully defiant tone of her remarks, Abigail probably was not demanding the vote. She was more concerned with married women's lack of property rights and lack of protection against abusive husbands. Moreover, while the letter is well-known today, it was a private missive intended for John's eyes only. Although Abigail did mention her concerns at the time to her good friend Mercy Otis Warren, her ideas did not reach a larger public audience at the time. Whatever the case, John's reply indicated that he was resistant even to discussing the issue.[35]

Abigail Adams's letter, however, did make an important point: women understood the principles of the American Revolution and could apply them to their own situation. Thus when John Adams received William Sullivan's letter shortly thereafter raising the question of expanding the male franchise he could clearly see the ultimate implications of the proposal. In fact, in his response to Sullivan, Adams admitted that many women were as intelligent and well-informed about politics as some men were. They possessed "as good judgments, and as independent minds, as those men who are wholly destitute of property." Their abilities raised the stakes for abolishing the property qualifier among males. If women had as much wisdom and virtue as men, then on what basis could women be excluded? John Adams wanted to foreclose such possibilities before they ever became real threats. Unlike Abigail's letter to John, the letter to Sullivan did not remain private; it was published in 1792 in a popular Philadelphia magazine.[36] More than most of his contemporaries, Adams understood the fragile assumptions that underlay the social order and gender hierarchy. Ironically, he was uncannily accurate in predicting how the logic of the debate over both universal male suffrage and the female franchise would ultimately unfold.

The New Jersey Exception

At the very time that Adams was ruminating about the dangers of women voting, one state actually experimented with that possibility. In May 1776, anticipating the coming of independence, the Continental Congress sent out instructions ordering each state to devise a new framework for governing. Meeting in convention, the legislature of New Jersey wrote a new state constitution. Describing who would be entitled to vote, the document stipulated that "all inhabitants of this colony of full age, who are worth fifty pounds . . . shall be entitled to vote for Representatives in Council and Assembly; and also for all other public officers, that shall be elected by the people of the county at large." The use of gender-neutral language—"all inhabitants"—was not in and of itself significant. In fact, only five of the first state constitutions—those of New York, Georgia, South Carolina, Pennsylvania, and Massachusetts—specified that the vote be limited to men, by using the word "male," or inserting a reference to "sons." Since voting had customarily been a male prerogative, there probably was little need to be more specific.[37]

It soon became clear, however, that the New Jersey legislators had more radical intentions. Their initially ambiguous formulation gave way to more unequivocal assertions. Although in 1777 and 1783 the legislature enacted laws regarding election procedures that used only the male pronoun, beginning in 1790 the assembly passed an election statute, pertaining to seven of the thirteen counties in the state, that explicitly enfranchised women. It said, "No Person shall be entitled to Vote in any other Township or precinct, than that in which *he or she* doth actually reside at the time of the Election" (emphasis added). A 1797 law extended these privileges to all qualified women throughout the state. Voters, the law stated, should "openly and in full view deliver *his or her* ballot." Seldom has the use of a single pronoun effected such a radical change in political practices.[38] (See Figure 3.)

In actuality, the New Jersey law applied only to a small proportion of the women in the state. Because married women could not own property, and voting required ownership of a substantial amount of property, widows who had inherited their deceased husbands' estates were the women most likely to vote. Although single women who had never been married could theoretically exercise the franchise, they were less likely to have accumulated enough wealth to meet the property qualification that the constitution required. As a result, female suffrage in New Jersey never pertained to more than a small proportion of the state's female population. In any given election, it was likely that not more than a few hundred cast ballots. Nonetheless, among those who qualified, women could vote—and did vote—in both state and federal elections for a time.[39]

Due to the lack of documentary records, we do not know why New Jersey legislators were willing, when no other state was, to extend the vote to women. There is no indication that New Jersey women actively demanded the vote. They did not send petitions to the legislature, hold rallies, or mount campaigns on their own behalf. Some historians speculate that Quaker delegates, grounded in their religion's more egalitarian ideas about women, may have been behind the initial efforts to enfranchise women. Other historians argue that by the 1790s partisan Federal-

Figure 3. Women voting in New Jersey (n.d.). This rare depiction of women casting ballots in a New Jersey election was probably printed in a periodical in the mid- to late nineteenth century but portrays events occurring in New Jersey from 1776 to 1807. (The Library of Congress.)

ists believed that enfranchising women would give them an edge over their Republican opponents. It is true that the 1790 law applied only to the seven southern New Jersey counties, which were heavily populated by Quakers and more politically conservative. By 1797, however, the legislature had expanded the privilege to all qualified women throughout the state.

In fact, New Jersey legislators seem to have given women the vote because they followed their revolutionary beliefs to their logical, if unexpected and untraditional, conclusion. Reviewing the history of female voting in New Jersey, a Trenton newspaper from the time maintained that the assembly had acted "from a principle of justice, deeming it right that every free person who pays a tax should have a vote." If those who paid taxes should be allowed to vote, there was on the face of it no logical reason why taxpaying women should be excluded. Other newspapers confirmed this rationale. Discussing a debate over a proposed election law in 1800, the *Newark Centinel of Freedom* published a letter that reported, "A motion was made to amend the bill by adding that 'it is the true intent and meaning of this act that the inspectors of elections . . . shall not refuse the vote to any widow or unmarried woman of full age.'" As it turned out, the legislators defeated the motion—not because they objected to women voting but rather because they found it superfluous: "The House unanimously agreed that this section would be clearly within the meaning of the Constitution and as the Constitution is the guide of inspectors it would be entirely useless to insert it in the law." The conclusion seemed obvious: "Our Constitution gives this right to maids or widows, black or white."[40]

Others outside of New Jersey understood the experiment in similar terms—as an extension of revolutionary ideals. "Single Females in the State of New Jersey, possessed of a certain property, and having paid taxes, are entitled to vote at elections," reported a Boston newspaper in 1800. "We understand that at a late election, there were many [who] exercised this privilege." Abigail Adams also was aware of these developments. Discussing a recent election held in her sister's home parish, Adams declared mischievously, "Tell [your friend that] if our State constitution [in Massachusetts] had been equally liberal with that of New Jersey and had admitted the females to vote, I should certainly have exercised it on his behalf." Adams's plea for women had found an unexpected fulfillment in New Jersey's experiment in female suffrage.[41]

The practice remained extremely controversial. Many people at the time believed that female voting degraded the political process, masculinized women, and undermined male authority. Even critics, however, understood the rationale behind the innovation. At a Fourth of July oration at the local Presbyterian church in Morristown, New Jersey, Henry Ford of Morristown remarked, "Our constitution requires a voter to be possessed of 50 pounds. The prevailing theory is that taxation and representation should go together." Yet he believed that the theory had gone too far and said, "Our practice outstrips them both, in its liberality, and makes no invidious exceptions. It admits to the pole people of all sexes, colors, tongues, characters, and conditions. In our unbounded generosity, we would admit to a participation in our choicest rights the lame, and the halt, and the blind [as well as] . . . the worthless and the penniless;—as motley a group as the day of Pentecost or the pool of Bethesda ever witnessed." Another critic, William Griffith, admitted the legality of the practice: "If we were to be guided by the letter of the charter, it would seem to place [women] on the same footing in this particular [with men]—." Nonetheless, he insisted that "it is perfectly disgusting to witness the manner in which women are polled at elections. Nothing can be a greater mockery of this invaluable and sacred right, than to suffer it to be exercised by persons, who do not even pretend to any judgment on this subject." Another skeptic concluded, "The petticoat faction's a dangerous thing." Even as they attacked the practice, however, opponents of female suffrage had conceded the validity of the principle.[42]

Whatever their reservations or objections, members of both political parties in New Jersey courted female voters and sought their support for their candidates. Especially in close elections, women might provide the margin of victory for one side or the other. Because only women who owned a substantial amount of property were entitled to vote, women voters, much to the dismay of the Republicans, tended to favor Federalist candidates. Yet neither side in New Jersey ever lost its doubts about the wisdom of enfranchising women. A poem published in 1797 in a Newark newspaper captures the conflicting feelings surrounding the New Jersey experiment. Called "The Freedom of Election," the poem was to be sung to the tune of "The Battle of the Kegs," which suggests its satirical purpose.[43] The opening stanza appears to celebrate New Jersey's liberality for enfranchising women:

> In freedom's cause you gain'd applause,
>   and nobly spurn'd subjection;
> You're now the *Oracle of Laws,*
>   and *Freedom of Election!*

A subsequent stanza appears to support women's new opportunities and condemn the "narrow-minded" policies that promoted women's subordination. It even suggests that men's freedom was linked with women's liberty:

> That tho' we read, in days of yore,
>   The woman's occupation,
> Was to direct the wheel and loom,
>   Not to direct the nation;
> This narrow-minded policy
>   By us hath met detection;
> While woman's bound, men can't be free,
>   Nor have a *fair Election.*

Later stanzas, however, disclose the author's true beliefs. The poem portrays an election scene in which women voters "parade" to the poll, "some marching cheek by jole [jowl], sir!" Women voting presented a sight so "strange" and so unnatural that it seemed a "*Milennial* state was near, sir!" There were other problems as well. While the deluded women went off to vote, predatory men subjected the women who stayed behind to their unwanted sexual advances:

> While men of rank, who play'd this prank,
>   beat up the widows' quarters;
> Their hands they laid on every maid,
>   And scarce spar'd wives, or daughters!

Allowing women to vote, then, was nothing more than a sexual "prank" played on women by "men of rank." Yet the practice had opened up the possibility of further trouble. Women would not be satisfied merely with the vote; they would soon seek to pursue other male prerogatives:

> To Congress, lo! Widows shall go,
>   Like metamorphos'd witches!
> Cloth'ed in the dignity of state,
>   And eke! in coat and breeches!

Women who sought political privileges abandoned their femininity and literally became like men. "Cloth'ed in the dignity of state," they would dress like men, "in coat and breeches." In the process they would become "metamorphos'd witches," repugnant aberrations of their true feminine selves.

The final stanza appears once again to celebrate female suffrage and proclaim the end of men's oppression of women:

> Then Freedom hail—thy powers prevail
>   O'er prejudice and error
> No longer shall man tyrannize
>   And rule the world in terror.

Although the poem recognizes women's claims to political equality with men, its hostility is even stronger. The closing lines reveal the poem to be a vicious satire:

> Open wide your throats
> And welcome in the peaceful scene
> Of Government in petticoats!

Female suffrage would be accepted only if it were literally shoved down people's throats.

Continuing ambivalence meant that the female franchise was constantly under attack from one quarter or another. In session after session the New Jersey legislature considered proposals that would abolish female voting. For a time a sufficient number of members rallied, out of either principle or interest, to preserve the experiment, but this would soon end. The precipitating cause was a local election in 1807 in which the voters of Essex County were to decide on a new location for their county courthouse. Citizens of Newark and Elizabeth each hoped that their town would prevail. A courthouse, they believed, would bring business, economic development, and prestige to their locale. On election day boosters on each side beat the bushes to turn out the vote. Voting was heavy. After the votes were counted, Newark claimed victory. Charging fraud and corruption, the citizens of Elizabeth demanded a recount. When they investigated, state officials found that more votes had been cast than the number of legal voters in the county. Observers claimed that men and young boys had dressed up as women in order to cast multiple ballots for their side. "Their dress favouring disguise," reported one commentator, "it is said that some have repeated the vote without detection."[44]

In the ensuing scandal, the legislature voided the election results. Claiming an opportunity to eliminate voter fraud, Federalists and Republicans in the legislature joined together to make a Faustian bargain. Federalists, who had benefited from the women's vote, and Republicans, who had enjoyed the support of free blacks, each agreed to relinquish the votes of the group that the other considered suspect. The assembly passed a law disenfranchising both women and free blacks, the groups that were least well represented and least able to defend themselves. Significantly, there is no evidence that either free blacks or women publicly protested their loss.[45]

Perhaps, given the circumstances, women may have suspected that any kind of public protest would be fruitless. For women, however, voting presented a host of problems that had never been satisfactorily resolved. At the most practical level, it was inconvenient. Women often lived substantial distances from their polling places. Because respectable women did not travel alone, they always needed male family members or friends to accompany them to the polls. The atmosphere at the election site may have also represented a deterrent. It was not uncommon for voting to occur at taverns or other public places. Riotous drinking was typical. Groups of drunken or disorderly men often mulled about outside. Fights, or even riots, were common. Investigating a 1794 election, one congressman noted casually, "If the committee are to break up every election where persons were seen drunk, they will have a great deal of work upon hand." At every stage women would have felt uncomfortable and out of place, subjected to unwanted scrutiny and possible ridicule.

Responding to his sister's query about voting rights for widows, Richard Henry Lee noted that while he supported the idea in principle, he "thought [it] rather out of character for women to press into those tumultuous assemblages of men where the business of choosing representatives is conducted." Only the most determined women—or women goaded on by ambitious male politicians—would have braved such obstacles. Many may have been relieved once they no longer had to do so.[46]

There may have been other reasons as well why women did not object to the loss of the vote. It was understood that New Jersey had pioneered female suffrage by extending to women the principle of no taxation without representation. At this time, voting was considered a privilege of private property. In colonial Anglo-America this was the common and widely accepted understanding of the franchise. In fact, north of the border in lower Canada, from 1791 until 1834 unmarried women with property also were allowed to vote.[47] In neither place did women object when their legislatures reversed this decision and withdrew their privilege. Women may have reasoned thusly: because members of the assembly granted women the vote, they also had the authority to take it away. In later decades, once voting came to be seen as a natural right belonging to all people, the consequences of denying the vote to individuals or groups would be much more severe.

Despite the reversal, New Jersey had taken a profound step. Allowing women to vote had made the unimaginable a reality. Women could behave politically in the same ways and on the same terms as men. Perhaps even more important, the New Jersey legislators appear to have acted out of principle. Those in power—white males—understood that if they took their revolutionary ideals seriously, then they must, in the interest of fairness and consistency, allow women to vote. What had started out as a justification for rebelling against Britain ended in a critique of gender inequality.

Women as Rights Bearers

Citizenship at this time was understood to encompass privileges much broader than simply the ability to vote. With the coming of independence, all free white inhabitants who had been subjects of the Crown, including white women, were presumed to be citizens. Yet the precise meaning of "citizenship" was vague, subject to changing legal and popular definitions. At various times in American history, "citizen" could refer to all inhabitants, all white inhabitants, all legal nonaliens, white male residents, or just to male voters. Significantly, the language in the new United States Constitution tended to be gender-neutral, employing the term "person" rather than "male" or "men." No provision explicitly excluded women from voting or holding federal office. In fact, only in 1868, with the passage of the Fourteenth Amendment, did the Constitution employ the phrase "male citizen" and explicitly exclude women from certain political rights.[48]

It is not clear whether the earlier use of gender-neutral language was deliberate or accidental. Nonetheless, some people at the time believed that at least some provisions of the Constitution were meant to encompass women. In particular, Article I, Section IV describes who should be counted in the census in order to determine the ratio of people to congressional representatives for each state. While it was clear that only three-fifths of the total number of slaves would be represented, white women were to be counted on an equal basis with white men. Explaining the significance of this point to his wife, Sen. Samuel Mitchill of New York noted, "In the theory of our Constitution women are calculated as political beings. They are numbered in the census of inhabitants . . . and the Representatives are apportioned among the people according to their numbers, reckoning the females as well as the males. Though, therefore, women do not vote, they are nevertheless represented in the national government to their full amount." As part of the enumerated population, women thus were members of the body politic. They were, as Mitchill said, nonvoting "political beings." In this sense, women were represented "virtually" in much the same way that the North American British colonists were represented in Parliament before the Revolution.[49]

Even if they could not vote, women actually did enjoy many specific rights and liberties. Widows and single women received the same protections for their property as men did. More importantly, to the extent that the Constitution, and especially the Bill of Rights, shifted the focus away from the rights of property owners and toward the rights enjoyed by all human beings, women were included and protected. They could practice their religion freely, assemble to protest governmental actions, and exercise free speech. If accused of a crime, a woman, like a man, had the right to receive a trial by jury—though the jury would be composed exclusively of men. As the president of Harvard College pointed out in 1798, every citizen, female as well as male, enjoyed "the right to life and personal security, . . . the right to liberty of action, the right to reputation, the right to liberty of opinion, of speech, and of religious profession and worship." If citizenship was understood to encompass rights besides voting, the Constitution did indeed guarantee a broad array of civil liberties to women as well as men.[50]

For women of the early republic, one of the most important of these liberties was the right to petition. Petitioning the legislature represented a crucial means for women, who lacked the vote, to express their political sentiments directly to their legislators. Petitioning was a powerful and time-honored tradition in the Anglo-American political tradition. For centuries women in both England and the colonies had petitioned their colonial assemblies on a variety of matters. After the Revolution, American women, inspired by notions of popular government, seemed to have seized on the petition as a preferred means of expressing their grievances and asking for redress from their legislators. In Massachusetts, as the historian Nancy Cott has shown, the number of women petitioning the legislature for divorce increased at a far greater rate than the population growth would suggest. In North and South Carolina, as Cynthia Kierner has demonstrated, the number of women's petitions increased tenfold in the last quarter of the eighteenth century. These women were often asking for compensation of some sort: restitution of property, military pensions for widows, payment for confiscated land, or requests for husbands' back pay as the result of military service. Women also believed that the new national legislature should be responsive to their needs. Between 1789 and 1820 at least 246 women submitted petitions to the new U.S. Congress. Among these, the vast majority (83 percent) sought compensation for losses or payment of military pensions related to the American Revolution.[51]

Whether or not their petitions were granted, the very fact that women petitioned their governments revealed the extent to which they felt a stake in or a connection with the formal institutions of governance. Their actions implied that women believed that the government was, in some real sense, their own and accountable to them. Janet Spurgin, for example, had a husband who had been a loyalist during the American Revolution. Afterward his property was confiscated and he fled to Britain, leaving his wife and eight children behind in North Carolina. Asserting her status as a loyal American, Janet Spurgin petitioned the North Carolina Assembly in an effort to recoup some of the property. She had, she asserted, "always behaved herself as a good Citizen and well attached to the government" and believed it "extreamly hard to be deprived of the Common rights of Citizens."[52] Like Spurgin, many women saw themselves as good citizens, a part of the government, not apart from it. In subsequent decades women would frequently turn to petitioning as a vehicle of social reform, appealing to the federal government on a variety of moral, social, or religious issues. Long before that time, however, women had begun to use the petition in order to act as "political beings" in their own right.

The acknowledgment of women's civil liberties also implied something even more significant. Women were understood to be autonomous beings who possessed rights. By recognizing that women had rights, the state acknowledged that it also had a responsibility to protect women—not as adjuncts to their husbands or fathers but as separate and distinct individuals. The fuller meaning of this idea became apparent after the publication in 1792 of Mary Wollstonecraft's incendiary tract *A Vindication of the Rights of Woman*. Wollstonecraft was an unlikely revolutionary. A self-educated young woman who traveled in radical literary circles in London, she followed the early years of the French Revolution with great interest and anticipation. When the French proposed a system of national education for men but ignored the education of women, Wollstonecraft penned her treatise. Deliberately echoing the title of Thomas Paine's *Rights of Man*, published the previous year, Wollstonecraft's work exposed the gendered assumptions behind the revolutionaries' thinking. While Paine had argued that all human beings shared certain basic rights, the specific rights he mentioned—the rights to own property, to vote, to participate in government—were, in fact, limited only to men. Typically for his time, Paine did not even consider whether women had rights or what those rights might be.[53]

In contrast, Wollstonecraft explicitly applied the concept of natural rights to women. Given by God, these rights were universal, inherent in the condition of being human, and they applied to all people, regardless of sex. Women's rights were thus irrevocable and undeniable. "If the abstract rights of man will bear discussion and explanation," she insisted, "those of woman, by parity of reasoning, will not shrink from the same test." Yet while only some men had been denied their rights, all women had been excluded from enjoying their rights simply because of their sex. "The *rights* of humanity have been . . . confined to the male line from Adam downwards." The greatest social inequity, she claimed, did not exist between or among males but between men and women. The result was that half of the population had been kept from realizing its full human potential. "The tyranny of man" and the perpetuation of a "male aristocracy" had oppressed women in all aspects of their lives, retarding the development of their intellect, hindering the growth of their virtue, and preventing them from making a full contribution to society.[54]

Significantly, Wollstonecraft mentioned but did not emphasize the question of women's political rights. She raised the issue of female suffrage only once, and then only briefly and tentatively. "I may excite laughter," she noted, "by dropping a hint, which I mean to pursue at some future time, for I really think that women ought to have representatives." She never took up the issue again. It was more important, she believed, that women gain greater educational and economic opportunities than to participate in what she considered to be a deeply flawed and corrupt political system. The franchise would presumably come in the wake of other gains.[55]

As in Britain, many Americans at first responded favorably to Wollstonecraft's work. Excerpts from *A Vindication* appeared almost immediately in American periodicals and magazines such as the *Ladies Magazine* published in Philadelphia and the *Massachusetts Magazine* published in Boston. By 1795 three American editions of the volume had been issued. A modern study indicates that Wollstonecraft's treatise appeared in more American libraries of the era than Paine's *Rights of Man* did.[56]

Personal scandal, however, soon tarnished her reputation. In 1798, soon after Wollstonecraft's death, her husband, the freethinking radical philosopher William Godwin, published a memoir of his wife. Committed to an unflinchingly honest portrayal, Godwin mentioned details about Wollstonecraft's life that had not been widely known. During the French Revolution, he said, Wollstonecraft had had an affair with an American man, Gilbert Imlay, and gave birth to an illegitimate child. Subsequently she tried to kill herself not once but twice. After taking up with Godwin, but before they married, she conceived their daughter (who, as Mary Shelley, would later author the classic work *Frankenstein*), whose birth resulted in her death. These actions represented an assault on the conventional Christian morality of the time and provided ample ammunition for Wollstonecraft's critics. Her "licentious practice," railed the minister Samuel Miller, "renders her memory odious to every friend of virtue."[57]

Despite the scandal, Wollstonecraft's tract popularized the notion of women's rights and introduced the phrase into widespread usage. Whereas the American Revolution had raised the question of women's rights indirectly, Wollstonecraft's work raised the issue directly, in a way that could not be avoided. Numerous pieces of poetry, fiction, humor, and prescriptive essays bore the title "The Rights of Woman" or contained allusions to women's rights. Songs were written on the subject. In 1795, for example, several different periodicals published the same piece "Rights of Woman," written by a "Young Lady" of Philadelphia. Sung to the tune of "God Save America," the piece began:

> God save each Female's right,
> Show to her ravish'd fight
>   Woman is Free;
> Let Freedom's voice prevail,
> And draw aside the veil,
> Supreme Effulgence hail,
>   Sweet Liberty.

The poem continues,

> Let Woman have a share,
> Nor yield to slavish fear.
> Her equal rights declare,
>   And well maintain.[58]

Although the precise meaning of "women's rights" remained ambiguous Wollstonecraft was claimed as "a friend."

In subsequent years the concept of women's rights took on a life of its own. A widespread public debate ensued over what it meant for women to have rights and whether women shared the same rights, including political rights, as men. Occurring outside of formal legal channels, in venues such as novels, essays, periodicals, and public speeches, the phrase became a staple of popular discourse. As early as 1793 Congressman Elias Boudinot could announce, "The Rights of Women are no longer strange sounds to an American ear; they are now heard as familiar terms in every part of the United States." A 1799 article noted that Wollstonecraft's work had "quickly became a staple commodity at the circulating libraries, saw two editions in the year of its publication, was the manual and vademecum of every romantic Miss." An 1818 article declared that "there are to be found, some females who delight to make the 'Vindication' . . . their text book."[59] Wollstonecraft became the chief symbol and enduring referent for the notion of women's rights in the United States.

So pervasive was Wollstonecraft's influence that even those who opposed her felt obliged to refute her in her own terms. An 1801 essay entitled "A Second Vindication of the Rights of Women" invoked Wollstonecraft—only to reject her central claims. Another adversary, a Maine orator, minced no words. Speaking to the women in his audience, he insisted, "You will not consult a Wollstonecraft for a code of 'The Rights of Women.' Do not usurp the rights of man; they are essentially distinct. Scorn her principles." In 1818 Hannah Mather Crocker, a descendant of the Puritan minister Cotton Mather, published her own refutation, entitled *Observations on the Real Rights of Women, with their Appropriate Duties, agreeable to Scripture, Reason, and Common Sense.* Although highly controversial and deeply contested, the concept of women's rights could no longer be ignored. By the first decade of the nineteenth century, even a hardened Wollstonecraft hater had to admit that her "ingenious vindication of the *Rights of Woman* [was] universally known."[60]

Acknowledging that women had natural rights opened up other possibilities. If women shared in the same constellation of God-given rights as men did, then women were what modern political theorists call "rights bearers." Implicit in this concept was an understanding that women were separate individuals who were distinct from men and who possessed their own rights and responsibilities. They were, in this sense, equal to men. As rights-bearing individuals, women gained the moral authority to demand that the state protect their God-given natural rights from infringement or usurpation. As Wollstonecraft herself pointed out, if men refused to recognize that women had rights, then "by the same rule, their duties vanish, for rights and duties are inseparable." White women, in particular, enjoyed a privileged status. They were unlike slaves, who were considered to be outside the social compact, and they were different from free blacks, whose race was often invoked to disqualify them from possessing the same rights and privileges that white men enjoyed.[61]

Even when the meaning of the phrase "women's rights" was vague or imprecise, it evoked a whole new world of possibility for women. In 1796 Harvard graduate William Boyd devoted his entire commencement address to the subject of "Woman." After hailing women's contributions throughout world history, he pointed out how little women's status had changed over time: "Still lives this truth, by savage man confess'd / *Woman belov'd, yet Women the oppres'd.*" Ending his speech with a solemn vow, another commentator concluded, "I shall always be found among the foremost to contribute my feeble efforts to defend THE RIGHTS OF WOMAN." This insight led some commentators to acknowledge men's role in oppressing women. In 1800 the *National Magazine* quoted the English radical Thomas Cooper, declaring, "Let the defenders of male despotism answer (if they can) *The Rights of Woman*, by Miss Wollstonecraft." To Americans, the analogy was clear. Just as England had stifled America's freedom, so men repressed women. "It appears ever to have been the policy of our sex," a Boston man said, "to arrogate to themselves a superiority over the other, and to treat them with all the spirit of a petty tyranny." Acknowledging the fragile basis of male authority, he noted, "We seemed to have claimed a prescriptive right for calling them our inferiors, and we can give no better account of our authority for treating them as such, than that custom has so established it." Although the solution was vague, the problem was now widely acknowledged.[62]

Others found the prospect of women's rights more troubling. Women's assertion of rights might subvert the gender hierarchy and threaten the subordination of women to men. Even the terminology itself seemed to open up dangerous prospects. Discussions of "equality of right," worried "A Lady," might "excit[e] an insurrection in the female world." A man calling himself "Ignotus" agreed: "If once a man raises his wife to an equality with himself, it is all over, and he is doomed to become a subject for life to the most despotic of governments." Nothing, he decided, "was more dangerous to the rights of man [than] when it took possession in *the home department.*" Not only would the relations between the sexes be affected, but the whole family structure might suffer as well. A satirical poem called "The Rights of Both Sexes," originally published in England and republished several times in the United States, warned of the possibility of ludicrous role reversals. Men would "reside at the tea-table, regulate the household, and rule the nursery; while all the offices of state and business of commerce should pass into the hands of the ladies." Men might even end up, the poem warned, as a "wet-nurse" to the baby. As each sex took over the other's "employments, amusements, and cares," the whole world would be turned upside down. What was good for women, then, might be bad for men. "These *Rights of Woman,*" concluded a Massachusetts newspaper, "would become the *wrongs* of man."[63]

Long before the American Revolution, Enlightenment conjectural histories and the earliest histories of women challenged the notion of women's inherent incapacity and raised the possibility that custom and tradition explained their apparent inferiority to men. Changed circumstances, it was said, would allow women to achieve as much as men could, perhaps even in traditionally masculine arenas such as philosophy, literature, government, and politics. Over the course of the eighteenth century, these ideas elevated women's status and focused public attention on their standing in society. Women, it seemed, might well be men's social and intellectual equals.

The coming of the American Revolution gave these ideas a political salience and created new opportunities for women to participate in politics. Responding to men's appeals, women engaged in a variety of actions in support of the revolutionary cause, which led women to experience a greater sense of connection to and involvement with the polity. After the war their political contributions were praised, celebrated, and remembered. Instead of political ciphers, women now were seen as political beings who had the capacity to influence the course of war, politics, and history.

Even more important, Wollstonecraft's *A Vindication of the Rights of Woman* changed the terms of the debate, suggesting that women shared in the same natural rights enjoyed by men. As rights-bearing individuals, women were independent beings who enjoyed certain rights simply because they were human. Unlike slaves or free blacks, white women were also understood to have the moral authority to demand that the state protect their rights. Wollstonecraft's work appeared when women in New Jersey were actually casting ballots. Ultimately, it was less significant that New Jersey women lost the franchise than that the experiment in female suffrage had been tried. These developments raised the stakes for women immensely. Whereas the Revolution had addressed the question of women's rights obliquely, now the question arose directly, in a way that could not be avoided. Whether they wanted to or not, American men and women had to confront the meaning of their revolutionary principles for women.

Chapter 2
Female Politicians

In 1821 former president John Adams wrote a letter to his grandson admonishing him for his enthusiasm over expanding the franchise. Always the social conservative, Adams feared that abolishing property qualifications among white men might open the door to new challenges, particularly from women. "You make very light of the argument for the ladies," he told his grandson, "& evade it by a twin of wit and gallantry." This, he insisted, "is not argument. Upon what principle of liberty, justice, equality and fraternity would you exclude [women]?" Women, he pointed out, were already growing restive with the restrictions placed on them. In the 1790s in Virginia, he recalled, Nelly Parke Custis, the step-granddaughter of George Washington, had once mounted her steed and "galloped to the hustings & demanded her right to vote as a free-holder." Even Adams had to admit that she had valid grounds for doing so. As an unmarried property owner, she was "a freeholder . . . to a large amount." The lesson was clear. "Once [you] let [women] know they have rights," he warned, "you will find them as fond of displaying them . . . in public as the men and as ardently aspiring to offices and dignities."[1]

Nelly Custis's ride to the hustings was but one example of women's desire to claim a new political role for themselves in postrevolutionary America. At the same time that Mary Wollstonecraft was opening up the public debate about women's rights, women were becoming increasingly active in and engaged with politics. Growing female literacy and increasing access to printed materials allowed them to form their own political opinions. As readers and writers, they felt freer to express their views in private conversations, letters, and in print. As more men came to serve in government at both the state and federal levels, more women became partners in serving the public good. The nature of politics in postrevolutionary America also facilitated women's involvement. Conducted out of doors and in the streets, this kind of politics enabled nonvoters as well as voters to participate in activities and events of importance. As a result, middle-class and elite white women found more ways to involve themselves in politics than ever before.

Widely observed and reported, these changes provoked a variety of responses among American women and men. Some supported the innovations, others resisted. Highly politicized women even gained a name for themselves: female politicians. In contrast to republican wives and mothers, who affected politics indirectly by influencing their sons and husbands, female politicians saw themselves as independent political beings. Like Nelly Custis, they demanded that their political views be heard and sought out opportunities to express themselves. Along with Mary Wollstonecraft and female suffrage in New Jersey, these "female politicians" came to symbolize both the perils and the possibilities of women's rights in the early republic.

Debating Women's Rights

Historians have often commented on the apparently limited impact of the American Revolution on women's political rights. Women did not organize collectively to demand their rights. Except in New Jersey, no state allowed women to vote. Even in the *Vindication of the Rights of Woman*, Mary Wollstonecraft presented only a brief and tentative discussion of women's political rights. Even so, the postrevolutionary era did witness a widespread, vigorous, and often heated debate on the subject of whether women should vote and hold public office. By and large this debate occurred not because an organized group or formal institution demanded it but because the idea raised issues that Americans needed to answer for themselves. A subject that had once seemed too obvious to warrant discussion was now open to scrutiny and subject to public debate.

Significantly, the phrase "women's rights" did not always or necessarily refer to the issue of women's political rights. The term had a wide variety of meanings. One common interpretation focused on women's spiritual equality with men and their right to achieve salvation. For centuries, many Christians had placed the entire burden of original sin on women and attributed their inferiority to this transgression. Under the influence of Enlightenment principles, more liberal theologians began to blame Adam as well as Eve for the sin in the Garden of Eden. Others insisted that whatever the original fault, Christ's death and resurrection had absolved women of their responsibility. According to one commentator, women were now "entitled to the same rights, capable of the same enjoyments, and expectants of the same immortality" as men were. Men and women were truly spiritual equals.[2]

Another understanding of "women's rights" drew on the stage theories of historical progress. According to Enlightenment conjectural histories, women achieved a certain kind of equality, and attained certain kinds of rights, through the process of historical evolution. By the time societies reached the highest stage of development, the mercantile or commercial phase, women were no longer to be considered men's slaves or playthings but were regarded as their friends and companions. This elevated social status gave women equal social standing with men. "The RIGHTS OF WOMEN, as well as OF MEN, are acknowledged," proclaimed the *American Spectator,* "and . . . [women] are caressed as the first and dearest friends of their partners." As men's social equals, women gained the right to be protected and respected by men.[3]

Perhaps the most common usage of "women's rights" was in the context of discussions about women's intellectual equality with men and their right to an adequate education. An 1825 article entitled "The Natural Rights of Woman" called for women to enjoy "the extrinsic advantages of education, and the opportunities for cultivating the[ir] mental faculties." If women had the same mental capacities as men, then they should enjoy the same opportunities as men to improve their intellects. Yet this sentiment did not necessarily imply that women's education should be identical with that of men. As the *Mercury and New-England Palladium* succinctly put it, "The proper purpose of women's education is to make women rational companions, good wives and good mothers." Their education would be equal to, but different from, that of men.[4]

The allusiveness—and elusiveness—of "women's rights" thus opened the phrase up to multiple meanings and interpretations. It is clear, however, that many American women and men *did* understand the notion of women's rights in political terms. Wollstonecraft's assertion that both sexes enjoyed the same natural rights implied that their rights might well extend to the political realm. The fact that women were actually voting in New Jersey proved that women could indeed exercise the franchise. As a result, a widespread public debate erupted in both public and private venues about what it meant for women to have rights and whether those rights included the right to vote and hold public office.

Neither women nor men shared a single point of view on the subject of women's rights, roles, and responsibilities. In a graduation speech at the Philadelphia Ladies Academy, one young woman took the opportunity to denounce what she perceived as women's growing interest in politics. Women who discussed politics, she declared, were often unladylike, "loud," and "ignorant of the meaning of the terms" they employed. "I do not think," she concluded, "we [women] are or ought to be capable of judging on political questions." When Priscilla Mason graduated from the same institution in 1793, however, she took a very different position. Railing against women's exclusion from positions of power in government and society, she proclaimed, "The Church, the Bar, and the

Senate are shut against us. Who shut them? *Man*; despotic man, first made us incapable of the duty, and then forbid us the exercise." Anticipating the day when women would participate more fully in the nation's political life, she urged the creation of a "senate of women," which, she said, "would fire the female breast with the most generous ambition, prompting [them] to illustrious actions. It would furnish the most noble theatre for the display, the exercise and improvement of every faculty. It would call forth all that is human—all that is *divine* in the soul of woman; and having proved them equally capable with the other sex, would lead to their equal participation of honor and office." Despite opposing views, the fact that women felt the need to address the question indicated that they took the issue seriously.[5]

Young men too felt compelled to address the subject. In college debating societies and private clubs, they explored what must have seemed like a shocking proposition to their elders: that women might be men's equals and hence entitled to share certain political privileges. On at least three occasions in the 1780s and two times in the 1790s, the Brothers in Unity at Yale College discussed variations on the question of "Whether Women ought to have a share in Civil Government" or "Whether Females ought to be excluded from a share in Civil Government." At least five times between 1788 and 1800, the Belles-Lettres Society of Dickinson College discussed issues relating to women, including: "Ought women to participate in the government of a state or not?"; "Whether it is the design of nature that women be entirely excluded from civil and ecclesiastical preferments"; and whether "women ought not to be legislators." A University of North Carolina debating organization, the Dialectic Society, asked its members in 1803 and 1804 to consider whether "females ought to be upon equal footing with us in education and power." It is perhaps not surprising that when these propositions were put to a vote, they usually failed. More surprising, however, is the fact that the men discussed the issue at all. In the postrevolutionary era men began to pay attention to the issue of women's rights and regard female political power as a realistic possibility.[6]

Raising the question of women's rights opened up a deeper and more troubling issue: the contradiction between the American commitment to equality and natural rights and the exclusion of women from government. A 1790 article on "The Ladies" in the *New-York Daily Advertiser* rendered a firm judgment on the issue: "The present custom in the world, especially in America, of excluding women from any share in legislation is both unjust and detrimental. It is certainly unjust to exclude from any share in government one half of those who considered as equals of the males, are obliged to be subject to laws they have no share in making!" More than a decade and a half later, "A Lady" writing in the *New-York*

Weekly Museum made a similarly critical remark. It is a "curious fact," she said, "that a republic which avows equality of right as its first principle, persists in an ungenerous exclusion of the female sex from its executive department."[7]

Philadelphia writer Charles Brockden Brown made perhaps the most sustained case against the injustice of women's exclusion. In a fictional dialogue, first published in 1798, between Mrs. Carter and her male companion, Alcuin, the woman noted, "I shall ever consider it, as a gross abuse that we are hindered from sharing with you in the power of chusing our rulers, and of making those laws to which we equally with yourselves are subject." Such a situation reflected a contradiction at the heart of the American experiment. "Even the government of our country, which is said to be the freest in the world, passes over women as if they were not [free]. We [women] are excluded from all political rights without least ceremony." As a result, the American system not only fell far short of that ideal; it "annihilat[ed] the political existence of at least one half of the community." The conclusion seemed inevitable. "This constitution," Mrs. Carter declared, "is unjust and absurd."[8]

Although Brown's opinion may not have been widely shared, even those who opposed the possibility of women's rights now found that they had to consider the issue. Speaking in 1798, Harvard president John Thornton Kirkland distinguished between "the right to protection, and the right to govern the state." Women possessed the former; men, the latter. Yet he too was aware of the contradictions implicit in his argument. "Had the new theory of the *Rights of Women* enlightened the world at the period of the formation of our constitution," he remarked sarcastically, "it is possible that the framers, convinced of its arguments, might have set aside the old system of exclusion, upon which the world has always proceeded till this reforming age, as illiberal, and tyrannical." To Kirkland, the notion that anyone could imagine the Constitution, the great bulwark of the people's liberty, as "illiberal" or "tyrannical" seemed self-evidently absurd. Yet he did admit that the American system could be considered one "of exclusion." Whatever their positions, American women and men found the subject of women's rights up for grabs. What had once been taken for granted now required public consideration and active refutation.[9]

Women, Literacy, and Politics

Thanks to increasing literacy and the growth of print media, the debate over women's rights spread beyond a narrow elite to encompass white, middle-class men and women. Like men at the time, women of the post-revolutionary era were being swept into a new political world mediated by print. Newspapers, books, magazines, and other materials printed in the United States helped extend the reach of political ideas and events to a mass audience. As a result, more and more people—not just educated white males—were reading about politics, hearing about politics, and talking about politics. Conservative Federalists, who viewed these developments with a wary eye, inveighed against them. One critic decried the growing tendency of ordinary people to "talk politics," calling it unfortunate evidence of the spread of "the new-fangled creed of 'Equality.'" Another was equally acerbic about the trend. "I verily believe," despaired a haughty Bostonian, "there is not a country on the whole globe where politics are so thrashed over as in this. Every body is wise enough to be secretary of state." Nonetheless, whether they liked it or not, the democratization of information was democratizing politics.[10]

Women as well as men joined in the conversations. In the colonial era, most females received little formal education. Many girls learned to read from their mothers. Elite girls might benefit from the instruction of private tutors, but their studies were often more ornamental than substantive in nature. Nonetheless, female literacy rose over the course of the eighteenth century. By the American Revolution, a surprisingly large proportion of white women could read. More than half of all New England women and at least one-third of all white southern women were literate. Interestingly, writing was taught as a separate skill from reading, so the number of women who could write was much smaller. Afterward the proportion of women who could both read and write rose rapidly. By 1800 approximately 80–90 percent of all New England women and nearly half of southern white women had these skills. In fact, by 1818 several periodicals ran articles that mentioned the purported formation of a young men's society in Connecticut that prohibited its members from marrying illiterate women. The very appearance of such an article indicated the increasing premium that society now placed on women's ability to read and write.[11] (See Figure 4.)

In addition to becoming more literate, more women also received some kind of formal education. At this time few states outside of New England had publicly supported grammar schools; even fewer allowed girls to attend. Nonetheless, in the decades after the Revolution over four hundred private "ladies academies" and female seminaries were founded throughout the country. In these institutions girls learned to read, write, and do arithmetic. They also moved beyond ornamental skills such as music, dancing, and embroidery to learn about higher intellectual pursuits such as history, geography, mathematics, natural science, and public speaking. Among the goals listed in an 1821 article for a girl's education was "That she should understand the nature, design and kinds of governments and the reciprocal duties of the gover-

Figure 4. *Mrs. Elias Boudinot IV* (1784), by Charles Willson Peale (1741–1827). Oil on canvas. Hannah Stockton Boudinot (1736–1808) was the wife of Elias Boudinot, a three-term congressman from New Jersey and a supporter of women's rights. Hannah Boudinot indicated her literacy and pride in learning by having her portrait painted showing her holding an open book. A majority of white women in the North could read by 1800. (The Art Museum, Princeton University. Gift of Mr. and Mrs. Landon K. Thorne for the Boudinot Collection.)

nor and governed." As the first teachers of children, women could use their education to instill patriotism and virtue in the younger generation; as helpmates and facilitators, they could encourage their husbands and sons to make sacrifices for their country's sake. "By her precept and example," declared one young lady, a woman "inspires her brothers, her husbands, or her sons, with such love of virtue, such just ideas of the true value of civil liberty, and how for a proper exertion of martial ardour may be necessary for its support and defence." Education, then, might have benefits that extended well beyond the specific purposes for which it was intended.[12]

As the proportion of literate women rose, the number, kinds, and quality of print materials available to women also increased at an exponential rate. The number of newspapers jumped from nearly 50 at the end of the Revolution, to over 100 in 1790, to over 250 by 1800, and to over 575 by 1820, an increase that far outstripped the rate of population growth. Advocating an explicitly partisan point of view, the papers abounded in political information. Usually under ten pages in length and often published only once or twice a week, newspapers carried both foreign and domestic news along with letters to the editor, advertisements, and at times poetry, satire, or topical essays. These publications increasingly carried features designed to appeal to female readers, including advertisements for consumer goods, poetry addressed to women, and articles about wives, mothers, and relationships between the sexes.[13]

Another genre, the popular periodical, also came into its own at this time. Before the Revolution, colonists had imported most of their magazines from England. In 1784 the first American periodical the *Gentleman and Lady's Town and Country Magazine,* appeared. Hundreds more emerged in subsequent decades. Distinguished from newspapers by a less explicit focus on current events, the American periodicals borrowed heavily from one another and from their English counterparts and included articles on politics, culture, history, and society as well as poetry, humorous essays, and fiction. Because of the variety of genres, the general-interest periodicals were meant to appeal to both women and men. Yet some publishers, realizing the growing potential of a literate female audience, began to appeal specifically to women. With a British model in mind—Joseph Addison and Richard Steele's *Spectator*—a Philadelphia printer in 1792 issued a periodical directed toward women, the *Ladies' Magazine and Repository of Entertaining Knowledge.* Its stated purpose: to enhance "the province of female excellence alone, with the beams of intellectual light, which illuminates the paths of literature." Many other ladies' magazines soon followed. Like the general-interest periodicals, these magazines contained a wide variety of genres, including fiction, history, poetry, and prescriptive essays, as well as articles about contemporary moral, social, and sometimes political issues. More than one hundred titles specifically geared toward women appeared in the United States before the Civil War. Women, in fact, actually edited a handful of these publications, which included Mary Clarke Carr's *Intellectual Regale; or Ladies Tea Tray*, published in Philadelphia; *Mrs. A. S. Colvin's Weekly Messenger*, published in Washington, D.C.; and most famously, Sarah Josepha Hale's *Godey's Lady's Book*.[14]

Although most magazines were published in the North, the publications reached a wide geographic area. Subscription lists included the names of women and men, southerners and northerners. The Federalist organ the *Port Folio*, which was published in Philadelphia, included paying customers from at least fifteen states, two territories, and Canada. While 80 percent of *New-York Magazine*'s readers resided in New York City, others lived as far away as Nova Scotia and Antigua. The *Ladies Literary Miscellany* and the *Intellectual Regale*, both issued in Philadelphia, reached people up and down the eastern seaboard from New Hampshire to Virginia. In 1789 Matthew Carey claimed that his magazine, the *American Museum*, published in Philadelphia, had over 140 subscribers in the southern states. As Cynthia Kierner has shown, southern women at this time saw themselves as part of the national republic of letters and actively participated in the intellectual exchange fostered by these new print media. Mrs. Mehatable Mumford of Fayetteville, North Carolina, for example, sent her payment to Boston for the *Euterpeiad* magazine along with an enthusiastic note to the editor, commenting, "I consider your Paper, Sir, as one of the most *interesting* publications which I receive." Despite their extensive circulation, many of the journals were continually short on funds and ceased publication after a short time. Although existing magazines constantly disappeared, new ones were always being founded.[15]

A wide cross section of white women had access to these publications. Although subscriptions remained rather expensive, the circulation of the magazines was more extensive than their subscription lists might indicate. Individuals often had access to such items even when they did not buy them. It was common practice after reading a publication for one individual to pass the item on to neighbors, friends, and relatives. As a result, one copy of any given book or periodical was often read by many different people. Moreover, beginning in the 1760s more and more towns throughout the country began to open lending libraries where, for a small annual fee, people would be able to borrow a broad range of printed materials. At least 376 libraries existed by 1790. In some cases women could become members. Even when they could not, their husbands could—and often did—borrow items for them.[16]

The political content of these publications varied. Some periodicals shunned political news for fear of arousing controversy. The *Ladies Visitor* of Boston, for example, asserted, "The pages of the *Visitor*, is open to everything which is entertaining or instructing—but closed against *Politics* and *Obscenity*." The linkage of politics with obscenity perhaps says it all. In contrast, many other periodicals often included political material. Sometimes the attention to politics was explicit, such as in articles about the French Revolution, the actions of Congress, or discussions about wars, past and present. In 1791, for example, the *New York Magazine; or, Literary Repository* published a resolution from the *Journals of Congress* that awarded a military pension to Margaret Corbin, a woman who had fought in the Revolutionary War and was wounded at the battle of Fort Washington. The female editor of a Washington, D.C., publication insisted that her magazine was "chiefly Literary" in nature but routinely included news on party politics. In many cases the line between what was considered political and what was nonpolitical was not clear-cut. The *Lady's Miscellany*, reporting on a "Singular Custom in the Isle of Man," reported without comment that when a man was convicted of rape, the woman was allowed her choice of punishment: "to have him hanged, or beheaded, or to marry him." The editor of the *Lady's Miscellany* justified the inclusion of a piece about slavery, maintaining that the topic was "not connected with *party politics*, and is, on that account, as well as its moral tendency, entitled to a place in our paper." Thus even in publications that were not overtly political, women often found themselves reading about political ideas and events.[17]

Printed materials did not, of course, reach all women equally. Reading patterns varied according to region, race, social class, and marital status. Not surprisingly, white women of means were more likely to be literate, and better able to afford to buy publications, than their lower-class counterparts. Most slaves could not read, and literacy among free black women was rare. Phillis Wheatley, who became a published poet during the American Revolution, was an unusual exception. Even among well-off white women, marriage and children often cut into reading time. When Margaret Bayard contemplated her impending marriage to Samuel Harrison, she noted that she expected to have less leisure for reading: "I expect every hour is to be so entirely occupied by household duties," she said. Yet a substantial proportion of the female population could and did read a wide variety of printed materials.[18]

It is often assumed that much of the reading that women did at this time was of a religious or devotional nature or was confined to novels.[19] While many women may have conformed to this pattern, many others did not. After the American Revolution women expanded the range of their reading to include a wide variety of genres. In fact, the reading diary of an obscure southern woman, Maria Margaret Martini De Rieux, offers a glimpse into an ordinary woman's reading material. From 1806 to 1823 De Rieux kept what appears to be a complete list of each book she read, year by year. A married woman who began her diary at age forty-four, she lived in various locales during this time, including Raleigh, North Carolina, and various places in Virginia, such as Augusta County, Petersburg, and Richmond. De Rieux was a voracious reader, having perused almost four hundred books in thirteen years. Like many other women at the time, she read a wide variety of novels, including William Hill Brown's extremely popular, *The Power of Sympathy*. Only occasionally did she read books of a religious nature or devotional tracts. Most significantly, she was a voracious consumer of nonfiction, especially biography, history, philosophy, and travel literature.[20]

De Rieux's choices in reading material reveal important clues about women's access to political information and ideas. Although she lived in the rural South, far from major publishing centers, she had a diverse reading portfolio. She seems to have preferred nonfiction over fiction and religion. Instead of novels or devotional tracts, she sought out works about her own country, its history and political leaders, and periodical literature that provided political information and ideas. During the time she kept her list, De Rieux read a two-volume *History of the American Revolution*. In addition, she devoured biographies of various Revolutionary War figures such as George Washington, Thomas Paine, Patrick Henry, and Francis Marion. Her periodical tastes were quite extensive, ranging from the highly partisan Federalist periodical, the *Port Folio,* to the more literary *Town and Country Magazine,* to those aimed primarily at a female audience, such as the *Lady's Museum,* the *Lady's Miscellany,* and the *Lady's Cabinet.* Although it is impossible to say how typical De Rieux was, Mary Kelley's study of reading practices in the early republic suggests that there were many other women who made similar choices.[21]

The expansion of literary societies and reading circles also offered new occasions for women to discuss their political ideas and interests with other women. One such group could be found in Norwich, Connecticut. From 1800 to 1805 a group of thirty-nine women, calling themselves the Ladies' Literary Society, met from time to time "for the Special Purpose of Enlightening our Understanding, expanding our Ideas, and promoting useful Knowledge among our Sex." At one meeting they discussed an article, "Address to Females," in the *Massachusetts Magazine* that led them to speculate on "the influence [women's] manners and example have on society" and on the "profligate [manners] (of the other sex)." Another time, after reading David Ramsay's *History of the American Revolution*, the group discussed women's contributions to the patriot cause. Their conclusion revealed a nascent protofeminist sentiment: "We . . . females are of importance in the scale of beings—let us then enquire what we can do toward securing those rights & privileges so nobly gained." Throughout the country hundreds of women's reading circles and literary clubs appeared, drawing thousands of women into organizations that sharpened their critical-thinking skills, provided a forum for speaking and writing, and gave them an opportunity for continuing intellectual engagement. These groups allowed women to explore current political ideas and events while being shielded from public scrutiny or criticism.[22]

More generally, access to print media increased women's political literacy and sophistication. During the 1790s, for example, Elizabeth Drinker of Philadelphia read newspapers almost every day that catered to her Federalist political sympathies, such as the *Gazette of the United States* and *Porcupine's Gazette*. During a stay in Norfolk, Virginia, in 1802 Ruth Bascom reported that she often made trips to the local lending library for the purpose of reading newspapers from her home state of Massachusetts, specifically to obtain news about state and local elections. Offhand references suggest that women were gaining increased comfort in discussing political events and ideas. During Jefferson's embargo of 1807–8, Rachel Mordecai of North Carolina complained that her brother had failed to write recently by slyly asking, "Pray has any one presumed to lay an *Embargo* on your ideas?" Catherine Byles of Massachusetts reported on the events of election day in Boston to a female friend, commenting that "all descriptions of inhabitants . . . are in constant motion in pursuit of happiness." Her choice of phrase, "in pursuit of happiness," reveals both her familiarity with the Declaration of Independence and her intuitive grasp of the idioms of American political discourse. Being well informed gave women the freedom to criticize the country or its leaders. Julia Anne Hieronymus Tevis noted that in 1815 she had been taken as a young girl to the Capitol to witness the debates in Congress. Although impressed with statements by men such as Henry Clay and John C. Calhoun, she was distinctly underwhelmed by others. "Even to the eye of the uninitiated," she noted, "many of our legislators were utterly unfit to be intrusted with the important duties that devolved upon them." Greater knowledge led to an awareness of the contradictions in American society. Frances Few, niece of Mrs. Albert Gallatin, voiced a horrified response to the existence of slavery in the nation's capital. "I was more shocked than I can express at seeing two droves of negrows pass—each drove contained eight or ten persons chained together. . . . What a sight for a country that boasts of being a land of liberty & an asylum for the oppressed," she remarked.[23]

Printed materials also gave women a sense of direct connection to the nation's political life and heightened sense of involvement in the polity.

The old taboos preventing women from speaking about politics began to dissipate. Although they might approach the subject of politics tentatively, women nonetheless forged ahead. In 1790 Pamela Dwight Sedgwick wrote to her husband, Congressman Theodore Sedgwick, berating Congress for its handling of a dispute over the temporary location of the national capital. Anticipating her husband's response, she said, "Do I write Treason[?] I hear you say yes and that I am medling with a Subject I am Totally Ignorant of." Feigning fear of rebuke, she then made a formulaic, and perhaps tongue-in-cheek, gesture of submission: "To my Lord & Master do I submit all my opinions on Politicks—to be corrected, amended and if he should please wholly expunged." Even women who were far less wealthy and educated felt a new sense of empowerment. In 1803, a barely literate woman named Susana Robson wrote a letter to President Thomas Jefferson. Aware that she was violating existing gender norms, she noted, "I am sencibel" that "I have broke throw those ruls subscrib[ed] to my sex." She nonetheless proceeded with her request and asked the president of the United States to send financial assistance to her widowed mother.[24]

Even women who might disparage other women in general for talking about politics often did so themselves without any sense of irony or self-contradiction. Ann Steele, daughter of a federal official, wrote to her father, "Though I like to hear how the wheels of Government move, I make it an invariable rule to be silent on political subjects. In my opinion they are altogether out of a Lady's sphere; they ought rather to suppress and stifle those boisterous passions which politics never fail to call forth." Yet in a letter shortly thereafter she violated her own "invariable rule." Unable to contain her curiosity, she asked, "Is it true[,] Papa, that Mr. Jefferson is going on as his enemies expected?" Similarly, Rosalie Stier Calvert of Maryland saw her own interest in politics as more valid than that of other women. Many women, she insisted, made "themselves ridiculous by discussing politics at random without understanding the subject." Although vowing "not to meddle in politics," she promptly and repeatedly discussed political affairs in numerous letters to family members and friends.[25]

Women and Print Culture

The expansion of print media in postrevolutionary America provided women with another, different kind of opportunity to express their political opinions. General-interest periodicals as well as ladies' magazines were often desperate for material. Working on a shoestring budget, printers usually did not pay authors; rather, they filled their pages by borrowing from other publications or soliciting contributions from their readers, including women. In a variety of ways, "scribbling" women helped shape the contents of these early magazines. The editor of the *Ariel and Ladies' Literary Gazette*, for example, announced his intention to be "more than commonly attentive" to "the Ladies." He continued, "The pages of the Ariel will be graced with the literary productions of able writers, and of either sex." Like male authors at the time, women usually wrote anonymously or under pseudonymns. This practice meant that the author's true identity was not known with certainty—either then or now. Nonetheless, there is strong evidence that women did write many pieces in the magazines, especially those signed with a female pseudonym or by "A Lady." The anonymity of the genre worked to women's advantage. If a woman wanted to write about politics, she could do so without fear of disapproval or dismissal simply on the basis of her sex.[26]

The two most prominent women to take advantage of this expanding print culture were Mercy Otis Warren and Judith Sargent Murray. Both were born in Massachusetts; both started their writing careers during the ferment of the revolutionary era. Warren's husband, James, and brother, James Otis, were leaders in the Massachusetts resistance movement. Over time John Adams, a family friend, recognized that although she was a woman, Mercy had a gift for writing. He urged her to use her gift to support the patriot cause. During the 1760s and 1770s Warren wrote political poems and satirical plays, published anonymously, that attacked British tyranny and rallied support for the American cause. In particular, *The Adulateur* and *The Group*, attacked the corruption of royal government in Massachusetts and called on the colonists to resist infringements on their liberties. Adams praised her contributions to the revolutionary movement, commenting, "[Her] poetical pen has no equal that I know of in this country." Despite Warren's official anonymity, in the close-knit world of patriot leaders she was known and celebrated.

After the Revolution, women continued to write about political affairs. During the debate over the ratification of the U.S. Constitution, she issued a stinging attack on the document under the pseudonym, "A Columbian Patriot." By 1790 she felt confident enough to issue a collection of her poems and plays under her own name. This work prompted Alexander Hamilton to remark that "in the career of dramatic compositions at least, female genius [in America] has outstripped the Male." In 1805 she issued her magnum opus, the three-volume *History of the Rise, Progress and Termination of the American Revolution*, which also came out under her name.[27]

It took time for Warren to grow comfortable in her role as a woman who wrote about politics, a subject that had previously been considered an exclusively male domain. In 1776 Adams attempted to draw Warren into a private correspondence about the country's future form of government. Though already a published author, Warren at first responded timidly, fearing that Adams was making fun of her interest in politics. Only with his explicit approval, she said, did she dare "approach the verge of any thing so far beyond the line of my sex." As Warren gained more confidence, she began to feel that she had as much right as any man to concern herself with the affairs of state. In the introduction to her history of the American Revolution she commented, "Recollecting that every domestic enjoyment depends on the unimpaired possession of civil and religious liberty, a concern for the welfare of society ought equally to glow in every human breast." Writing as both a woman and a historian, she assured her readers that she had "never laid aside the tenderness of the sex or the friend; at the same time," and had "endeavoured, on all occasions, that the strictest veracity should govern her heart, and the most exact impartiality be the guide of her pen." After the work was published, John Adams assailed Warren for her portrayal of him, which he thought was both too cursory and too negative. After enduring several scathing letters of rebuke, Warren responded: "Though I am fatigued with your repetition of abuse, I am not intimidated." She had come a long way from the person who feared to speak about politics to her male mentor.[28]

More than two decades younger than Warren, Judith Sargent Murray spent the American Revolution dealing with a series of personal crises, including the bankruptcy and death of her first husband. Inspired by revolutionary ideals, however, she penned one of the earliest American tracts asserting women's intellectual equality with men, "On the Equality of the Sexes," which was published in the *Massachusetts Magazine* in 1790. During the 1780s and 1790s Murray published various pieces of poetry, fiction, and essays—some on overtly political subjects. A strong Federalist, she supported George Washington and John Adams and attacked Jefferson's Democratic Republicans as the "misguided sons of liberty." Like Warren, Murray published her early works anonymously or under pseudonyms. In 1798, however, she published her collected writings under her own name in a work called *The Gleaner*. She also wrote three plays, some of which were performed onstage.[29]

Over the course of their careers, both Warren and Murray gained confidence in themselves as women who wrote about typically male subjects. When she revealed her true identity at the end of *The Gleaner*, Murray explained that she had not done so earlier because she feared that as a woman she would not be taken seriously: "Observing, in a variety of instances, the indifference, not to say contempt, with which female productions are regarded, and seeking to arrest attention, at least for a time, I was thus furnished with a very powerful motive for an assumption, which I flattered myself would prove favourable to my aspiring wishes." For both Murray and Warren, acknowledging their true identities represented a pivotal point in their lives. This move allowed both women to experience a taste of literary fame and gain financial compensation for their work. Even more important, each woman publicly proclaimed that she—as a woman—had something significant to say to a larger public. Doing so, however, opened them up to criticism, which could be scurrilous and vindictive. Unlike male authors, Warren and Murray could be attacked not just for the content of their works but also because their writings took them outside of their allotted female role. Reviewing Warren's history of the American Revolution, one critic remarked that the work was "the product of a mind that had not yet yielded to the assertion that all political attentions lay outside of the road of female life." Such attacks might wound even the most secure author.[30]

Despite potential fears, Murray and Warren were not the only women who began to express their views in print. In fact, a small number of women actually became printers, usually after their husbands had died. Many others simply began submitting their writings for publication. Sensing the growing presence of women, *Port Folio* magazine ran a piece in 1803 satirizing the pretensions of "literary ladies." Outraged at the insult, one woman dashed off a letter to the editor that highlighted the periodical's dependence on women writers. "In a periodical paper," she said, "you must so much depend on women's support both in the reading and writing way, that I am surprised you should there introduce such a satire." Pressing the editor for a response, she pointedly asked, "How could you for a moment lose sight of your own interest, and of the duty you owe to your female correspondents?" Print provided women with a venue for expressing their political views to a wider audience. In 1809, for example, a woman calling herself "Julia Francesca" voiced her views on American foreign policy. Almost ritualistically she expressed her reluctance to write about political matters for fear that she did not "possess talents equal to the support of a subject so abstruse and intricate as that of politics." She also worried that it was "unbecoming" to "the feminine character to interfere in matters so totally beyond their sphere or limit of action." Nonetheless, she then proceeded to explain her views in full. She called on the United States to support Britain in its war against France, and she maligned France's leader, Napoleon Bonaparte, as a "tyrannical usurper of France's diadem." Unlike generations of women before them, "Julia Francesca" and her cohorts had both the means and the opportunity to make their political views known to a broader public.[31]

Partners in Public Service

The emergence of new institutions of governance not only created new demands on men but also placed additional burdens on women. During the Revolution women's cooperation had been critical to the war effort. Their assistance would now be essential for the new government to succeed. By lowering the property qualifications for holding office, states opened up the possibility of public service to larger numbers of individuals. Many states also increased the size of their legislatures and required annual elections for representatives. More men would be needed to serve in more offices. By 1790 state legislatures averaged ninety-five members in each of their lower houses and twenty-one members in each of their upper houses. This meant that over 1,700 men would be needed each year to represent the people in their state assemblies alone.[32]

The creation of the new federal government added a whole new layer of office holding to the mix. In 1802 there were over 2,500 individuals who held nonmilitary positions as customs officials, revenue collectors, postmasters, federal judges, and district attorneys in the small but growing federal bureaucracy. Although the number was tiny compared with the number of federal workers today, the jobs required many public servants to be away from their homes for extended periods. This was especially true of the men who served in Congress. Between 1789 and 1828 the Senate increased from 26 to 48 members as each new state admitted to the union received its requisite two members. The House of Representatives, reapportioned every ten years to adjust for changes in the states' populations, grew from 65 members in the first Congress to 202 members by 1828. The cast of characters too was constantly changing. In the period from 1789 to 1828 the vast majority of members usually served in Congress for less than five years. In effect, republican government meant that more people would spend more time serving the public.[33]

This was especially true at the federal level. Before 1830 most congressmen came by themselves to the seat of government, leaving their wives and children back home. In 1807–8, for example, of 130 representatives and 34 senators, only 9 men brought their wives to the capital with them. In 1814 Dolley Madison reacted with surprise at the large number of women in the capital. "We have Ladies from almost every State in the Union," she wrote to Martha Jefferson Randolph, "and the City was never known so thronged with strangers." When the wives did come, they often left after the social season, especially if they had young children back home. When women were there, they had a dramatic impact on the character of the nation's political life. As Catherine Allgor has shown, women played a critical role in Washington society and politics. A savvy woman might arrange patronage appointments for friends and family members, serve as an intermediary between feuding partisans, or advance the political career of her husband. Political wives were often skilled operatives, capable of manipulating social relations for their own political ends.[34]

For most congressmen, however, moving the whole family to the nation's capital simply did not make sense. The difficulties of transportation, the cost of supporting two households, and the need for someone to maintain the family farm or business made removal seem unnecessary, undesirable, or impractical. Moreover, as difficult as it may have been to move to New York or Philadelphia, the shift of the national capital to Washington in 1800 made relocation of the whole family seem even more untenable. Created from wilderness, the new capital would be for many decades a skeletal city, lacking even in the basics of a comfortable existence. Houses were scarce, rudimentary, and expensive. Servants were difficult to obtain. Rain and snow turned the wide streets into muddy rivulets, making transportation cumbersome. Built on low-lying land, the place was a breeding ground for disease, especially malaria and dysentery. Even if they could afford it, congressmen hesitated to bring their families into such an environment.

Individual members usually lived in rented rooms or boardinghouses with other men. In 1807 over 50 percent lived in boardinghouses; by 1828 about 25 percent still lived in such accommodations. Conditions, according to John Randolph of Roanoke, resembled "a boarding school, or a monastery." Depending on the amount of business, Congresses met in sessions lasting anywhere from three to six months. The fifth Congress actually had three sessions lasting most of the year. During a twenty-two-month period from May 1797 to March 1799, Sen. Benjamin Hillhouse was away from his family in New Haven, Connecticut, for thirteen months. The longest session of Congress in the early national period actually lasted over eight months—245 days, to be precise—from early November 1811 to July 1812. Moreover, given the problems of transportation over long distances, most congressmen probably did not return home until the session was over. It could take at least a week to travel from Boston to Washington and even more time to points inland. Service to the federal government thus extracted a steep price from both husbands and wives. Men were often homesick; wives, lonely.[35]

Wives faced other problems besides loneliness. A husband's absence usually brought major changes to a wife's daily duties and responsibilities. Once the man went off to Congress, she had to assume the burdens of his role back home. Not only did she have the sole responsibility for rearing the children, she would also have to oversee the day-to-day management of the family farm or business. This might include overseeing land and financial transactions or managing laborers, servants, and slaves. Mary Stanford of North Carolina, for example, used the money sent by her husband in 1804 to purchase "grammers for the children, & leather for a band for the cotton machine." John Steele instructed his wife about when to slaughter the pigs, how much corn to put up, and whether to whip or sell certain slaves. Such responsibilities were, as one member acknowledged to his wife, "great and perplexing." While some wives thrived on the new challenges, others felt overwhelmed and inadequate. Yet without a wife's cooperation, it was difficult, if not impossible, for a man to be away from home for long periods.[36]

Not all wives were equally supportive. While her husband was in Washington, Hannah Gardner Bigelow referred to herself as being in a "Widowed State." Women did not necessarily acquiesce in their husbands' decisions to serve the public. After years of supporting her husband's political career, Catherine Few of Georgia concluded that the only real "means of enjoyment for this world" was to leave the political scene altogether. Writing to her sister, who was herself the wife of Secretary of the Treasury Albert Gallatin, Few lamented, "*We, our husbands* and our little ones should retire far from the vortex of politics." While the benefits of a husband's public career might seem distant and remote, the problems it caused were real and concrete. Beginning in 1792 Dwight Foster of Massachusetts set out on a career of public service that would eventually lead to the U.S. Senate. From the beginning, his wife actively tried to dissuade him. "I hope the time draws near when you will return to your family and enjoy the comforts of domestic life," she told him. "You have a dependant family that requires your attention at home." She did not like the long separations and found the burden of caring for her family alone too much to bear. "I [be]grudge the time you are absent," she told him bluntly. "Will you say I am too selfish?—I think I am not." Rebecca insisted that her priorities were just as valid as those of her husband and that they must be taken into account. To the extent that politicians depended on their wives, the new government depended on women for its success.[37]

In the most successful relationships husbands and wives acted as full partners in serving the public. In addition to maintaining the home front, many wives became their husbands' political advisers and trusted confidantes. Some members of Congress frequently consulted their wives on their own political positions and matters of public policy. Sen. Jeremiah Mason of New Hampshire sent his wife copies of his speeches on subjects such as the embargo law and diplomatic relations with

England and asked for her *"candid judgment."* He knew she would be interested and would provide him with an honest, informed evaluation of his position. Many politicians realized that their wives had their own political opinions that did not necessarily accord with their own views. Anticipating potential criticism from his wife, Elijah Brigham of Massachusetts remarked, "I have enclosed a newspaper which contains one of the speeches of your Husband. You will please to read it with that charity which hopeth all things and believeth all things and which will also cover my infirmities." Some wives provided unsolicited advice, whether their husbands wanted it or not. Phebe Hubbard warned her husband, who represented New York state in the House of Representatives, against abandoning his Democratic-Republican principles. He reassured her, saying, "You need not fear my changing my politicks. [T]ho' I think well of the federal delegation from the State of Connecticut, I can never approve their policy." Hubbard respected his wife's opinion and valued her judgment, even in the supposedly male realm of politics.[38] (See Figure 5.)

Congressmen often depended on their wives to be their eyes and ears in the community: to relay the latest gossip, to convey the tenor of public debate, and to transmit their views to their constituents. Soon after the approval of Jay's Treaty, for example, Rebecca Faulkner Foster reported to her Federalist husband about the rantings of a local "Antifederal" judge and local discontent with the new treaty. Catharine Carroll Harper sent her husband "the report of the town" that included the names of two men who proposed to stand for office in an upcoming election. In 1824 Kitty McLane told her husband what various individuals, including a local carpenter, thought about the relative prospects of William Henry Crawford and Andrew Jackson in the upcoming presidential election. Wives might also act as their husbands' representatives in the community—the representatives of the representatives, as it were. Congressmen sometimes asked their wives to express their views on particular issues to the people; the people relied on congressional wives to provide additional sources of information about the current political scene. Anticipating war with Britain, Jeremiah Mason told his wife in 1814, "You may tell anybody who inquires, that my opinion respecting the probability of peace seems very doubtful." At other times women actively endeavored to solicit opinions from community members or receive petitions, or written statements of grievances, which they would then transmit to their husbands in the capital.[39]

Wives might also alert their husbands to public criticism of their positions or doubts about their effectiveness in the community. Receiving reports that her husband might not be chosen as head of a local organization, Catharine Harper fumed to her husband, "There are a great

Figure 5. *Portrait of Oliver Ellsworth and Abigail Wolcott Ellsworth* (1792), by Ralph Earl. Oil on canvas. Abigail Wolcott Ellsworth and her husband, Oliver Ellsworth, a senator from Connecticut and framer of the U.S. Constitution, chose to have their portraits painted together. This suggests the close ties between the public servant and his wife, whose labors on the home front facilitated his career. Oliver Ellsworth holds a copy of the U.S. Constitution in his hand. The Connecticut landscape is in the background. (Wadsworth Atheneum Museum of Art, Hartford. Gift of the Ellsworth Heirs.)

number in Baltimore opposed to you, [a] selfish, mercenary, money making set of men. . . . I am provoked when I hear these men say you are not popular, that you ought not to be chosen. . . . It has put me in a passion, for I always thought you were popular among your own party." Politicians' wives, however, could be critical as well as loyal. In 1810 Hannah Gaston told her husband that he could enhance his chances for the U.S. House of Representatives if he spent more time back home, meeting and talking with the electors of Johnston County, North Carolina. In 1826 George Badger of North Carolina asked his fiancée, Mary Polk, whether she thought he was electable. "As to the *Congressional election*," Polk responded, "you know, I have often told you, it would mortify me amazingly to have you *beaten by a gentleman*, but the bare idea of *Genl Baringer's* representing this district in opposition to *you* is too outrageous to be endured." Because politicians spent so much time away from their home bases, their wives provided an essential link in the flow of political information between the representatives and their constituents.[40]

Men also understood that they should consult their wives when making the decision to continue to serve the public or return home. "I am yet withholding my letter declining a return to publick life, till I can come to an understanding with you on the subject," Louis McLane told Kitty in 1822. "I should like to have your deliberate and candid opinion of the matter." Wives assisted husbands in assessing the effects of public service on their private lives. "If you will give your consent," said Comptroller of the Treasury John Steele to his wife, "I will resign next summer." Both spouses together determined whether they could continue to function under the burden of the man's absence. Thinking about a future term in the Senate, Jeremiah Mason of New Hampshire told his wife, "My inclinations alone must not govern." If a man did make the decision without consulting his wife, he might find himself in for a rebuke. In 1801 Rebecca Faulkner Foster complained that she would have accepted her husband's decision to remain in Congress more easily if "we could have had opportunity to chat on the Matter before [it was] Determined on. . . . I am most heartily weary of these long seperations. It is attended with many inconveniences and causes a great Deal of anxiety which I find unavoidable." The expectation, then, was one of joint decision making about the husband's future public service.[41]

After her death, Abigail Adams gained fame as the prototypically good republican wife. Commentators praised Adams not only for her loyalty to her husband but also for her service to the country. They recognized that her personal sacrifices had a larger public significance. According to *Mrs. A. S. Colvin's Weekly Messenger*, Adams occupied a role at "the centre of a correspondence between the agents of the state and the nation, and a valuable and critical instrument in critical times, diminishing the political burden that pressed upon her husband and so far aiding him to promote the general welfare." Politicians' wives did more than just maintain the home front. By making their husbands' public service possible, they served the republic as well. As Hannah Mather Crocker observed, "By the mutual virtue, energy, and fortitude of the sexes, the freedom and independence of the United States were attained and secured. The same virtue, energy and fortitude, must be called into continual exercise, as long as we continue a free, federal, independent nation."[42]

Adams's experience was not altogether unique. As more men were drawn into the business of government, by serving in local, state, or federal offices, more women participated in the political process as well. Men sought women's advice and counsel. They depended on their ability to manage farms, families, and businesses without them. When the time came either to remain in office or retire, the decision was often a joint one. Together husbands and wives negotiated the terms of public life. What was true of politicians' wives was also true to a lesser extent of ordinary citizens. Good republican wives would help sustain an active male citizenry. As women became more informed and literate about politics, the subject of political service arose as a point of discussion, and sometimes contention, between spouses. Even if a husband was merely a juror, a justice of the peace, or a voter, a wife might have something to say about his activities. Ultimately, however, such women did not challenge the gender order; they affirmed it.

Politics out of Doors and in the Streets

Outside the official corridors of power, the American Revolution marked the coming-of-age of a new kind of politics. This was a politics conducted not by and among gentlemen elites but through a grassroots politics that involved the mass mobilization of people. As we have seen, during the revolutionary era the Whig elite realized that they could not successfully resist English tyranny without securing a broad base of popular support. Toward this end, many important political activities occurred out of doors and in the streets, including public demonstrations, peaceful protests, and symbolic crowd actions such as hanging effigies and marching around a liberty pole. These activities were understood to be legitimate expressions of political sentiment and valid forms of political expression.

After the Revolution, these new forms of popular politics helped solidify a sense of American nationalism. Throughout the country, people participated in what the historian David Waldstreicher has called "celebratory" politics, a diverse array of symbolic and ritualistic activities including patriotic parades, public festivals, and popular commemorations. Bound together through print culture, Americans knew that people in other parts of the country shared the same practices. These activities helped link a vast, heterogeneous, and loosely connected set of states into a cohesive nation and created a shared sense of American identity. Significantly, this notion of politics was broad and capacious, incorporating both voters and nonvoters, blacks as well as whites, women and men.[43]

In this political culture, men often desired and actively sought out, women's participation. Like men, women were considered patriotic citizens. According to author Hannah Mather Crocker, "Women may reasonably become equal with men in patriotism and disinterested love of country." In fact, because women could not vote, they could be seen as impartial patriots whose sentiments were beyond the taint of tawdry self-interest. Female patriotism, as Abigail Adams once put it, was "the most disinterested of all virtues." Unlike men, women loved their country without the expectation that they would directly benefit. Women's very presence, then, could confer a kind of validation or approval on men's activities. At a more general level, their participation reflected the more open and inclusive nature of politics conducted out of doors and in the streets.[44]

Observers saw women's presence in patriotic celebrations as a reflection of the unity and harmony of the new nation. During a procession in New York to celebrate the ratification of the U.S. Constitution, women rode atop a float that heralded the virtues of home manufacturing. When George Washington journeyed in 1789 from his home in Virginia to New York, where he would assume the presidency, women turned out in droves to greet him along the way. At Trenton women, dressed in white, gathered at an arch covered with laurel branches that bore the sign "The Defender of the Mothers will also Protect their Daughters." In a very visible way, women's presence suggested that Washington would not only unify different parts of the country but also provide a link between all Americans, regardless of their age or sex. Both women and men assented to the new government and would give it their full support.[45]

As rights-bearing individuals, many women also believed that they had a stake in the electoral process. They felt connected not only through their husbands' role as voters but also in their own capacity as citizens. In New England some towns marked the day with parades, public orations, and balls. While men went off to the polls, women would often bake a special treat called an "election cake." Election days were seen as special occasions—"a season," as Catherine Byles of Boston put it, "of *festivity* and *fun*." In the South, candidates standing for public office would often invite voters to enjoy their hospitality, "treating" prospective supporters to lavish barbecues that featured mounds of food and a prodigious supply of liquor. Women would help the candidates in their own ways. In Maryland, Rosalie Stier Calvert supported her brother-in-law's candidacy for the state legislature by hosting a feast in which "an entire ox [was] to be roasted for the support of *our cause.*" Calvert did not consider her actions a feminine responsibility but rather saw them as a political duty; it was "*our cause.*" Women followed local and national elections with eagerness and anticipation. While visiting relatives in Virginia, Ruth Bascom of Massachusetts commemorated election day by making an election cake for her southern relatives. Living away from home in Philadelphia during the hotly contested congressional elections of 1808, Maria Beckley of Virginia frequently questioned her friend Lucy Southall about electoral developments in her home state. Like Rosalie Calvert, these women considered elections not just a male concern but their own cause as well.[46]

More than any other occasion, however, the celebration of Independence Day offered women an opportunity to demonstrate both their patriotism and their sense of political commitment. In the years after 1776, the Fourth of July became a time of public commemoration. Towns and cities throughout the United States sponsored parades, military displays, feasts, and balls. Citizens punctuated the day with bell ringing, cannon firing, fireworks, or bonfires. Local eminences presented public orations that offered their reflections on the nation's history and ideals. During the first decade or so after independence, one of the day's most distinctive features was its inclusiveness. Rich and poor, young and old, black and white, men and women all came together to commemorate the nation's founding event. In 1797 in North Farms, New Jersey, for example, the townspeople lined up to form a procession, with "The Gentlemen" in the lead, followed by "The Ladies," who were followed by "The Youth." According to one report, "In this manner they proceeded round the Tree of Liberty, accompanied with music, both instrumental and vocal. The Ladies were decorated with white, . . . and were headed by a Lady near 80 years of age."[47] (See Figure 6.)

Communities placed a special premium on women's participation. In addition to marching in parades, women might sing patriotic songs, play instruments, or perform patriotic skits. At the day's oration, male speakers frequently acknowledged women's presence in the audience and reminded listeners of women's contributions to the revolutionary cause. Afterward citizens would celebrate with a lavish meal. Men would drink liquor; women, tea. Both would toast the people and ideals that made Independence Day special. It was, according to the citizens of Oswego, New York, "the duty of *both sexes equally to participate in [the day's] joys*." Women had suffered along with men to secure independence; they should be its beneficiaries in peace. "Who, then, have a better right to participate in the festivities of [Independence Day] than the fair daughters of Columbia?" asked a New York periodical. "Without their presence to grace the scene, it would lose half its charms, and be divested of more than half its interest." Women's participation represented a kind of affirmation of the day's larger meaning. "Our happiness can be but half completed," explained Elias Boudinot, "if you [women] refuse to

Figure 6. *Fourth of July in Centre Square* (1812), by John Lewis Krimmel. Oil on canvas. Krimmel's painting of an Independence Day celebration in Philadelphia, held on the grounds of the city's famous waterworks, suggests the inclusive nature of the day's festivities, which included white and black men, women, and children, during the early decades of the nineteenth century. (Courtesy of the Pennsylvania Academy of the Fine Arts, Philadelphia: Pennsylvania Academy purchase [from the estate of Paul Beck, Jr.].)

crown the whole with your kind approbation." The "public" was incomplete without them.[48]

In fact, Independence Day sometimes offered women a rare opportunity: a chance to speak in public. Public speaking had long been regarded as the exclusive domain of men. Biblical precepts warned against women addressing so-called "promiscuous" audiences made up of both sexes. Female speakers were thought to represent a challenge to male authority. During the colonial period, when a small number of female preachers set out to spread the Word of God, they continually faced the prospect of harassment and punishment. After the Revolution, however, certain new opportunities to speak in public began to emerge. In 1806 the English evangelist Dorothy Ripley was allowed to preach a sermon at a Sunday service in the House of Representatives, as did the

American Harriet Livermore in 1827. Deborah Sampson Gannett, who had disguised herself as a man and fought during the Revolutionary War, went on a speaking tour in 1802 and 1803, describing her exploits as a soldier and performing military maneuvers onstage.[49]

More ordinary women, too, found certain venues where they might speak in public. Graduation exercises at ladies' academies offered a chance for women to speak to an audience of men and women. After graduation some women had the opportunity to address their local militia companies. In times of war women often banded together to sew flags, or standards, for their local troops to carry into battle. From 1798 through the War of 1812, as more units began to drill in anticipation of a possible war with France or Britain, a formal ceremony developed in which the women presented the flags they had made. One woman would speak to the soldiers for the group. In 1807, for example, Miss Sarah Herbert told the Augusta (Georgia) Volunteer Rangers, "Though the female part of the community are but little concerned in the civil or military arrangements of their country, yet we trust that *all our sex* hold in just estimation and respect, those characters, on whose wisdom and prudence they can rely for security." Although tending to be brief and formulaic, these speeches conveyed the women's support to the men who would take up arms in their defense. Even more importantly, these speeches allowed women to express their patriotism in a public fashion—not just symbolically but with their own voices.[50]

The Fourth of July represented one of the most prized days for public orations. Typically at these events a local luminary—a minister, a military officer, or an esteemed member of the community—would offer his reflections on the meaning of independence to the assembled crowd. Certain locales, however, actually featured women as the day's featured speakers. For example, in West Rutland, Vermont, in 1807 Mrs. N. Purdy presented "a very pertinent and impressive oration" mainly to the ladies, though it was noted that "a few gentlemen attend[ed] as spectators." In Mossy Springs, Kentucky, in 1819 Mrs. Meadway gave "an appropriate address," after which the women in attendance passed a series of "spirited and patriotic resolutions" suitable for the occasion.[51]

In 1822 a Vermont town went even further. The citizens of Marlborough, following local tradition, held an election for the position of "Orator of the Day." Significantly, they chose not a male official but rather a "Green Mountain Girl" named Miss Cole for the position. A nearby newspaper, the *Hartford American Mercury*, recorded her speech and reported on the day's events. Cole began by addressing the assembled group of women and men: "*Fathers, Mothers, Friends, and Fellow Citizens.*" Significantly, she seemed to feel no reluctance to address an audience made up of both sexes, identifying herself as a citizen speaking to her "Fellow Citizens." She then turned to the issue at hand: "In the celebration of the birth day of our nation we the representatives of the confederated States of the Union, come among you to join in the general joy." Brandishing a copy of the Declaration of Independence, she proclaimed that the document should be read in order to "recall to the memory of the aged, those principles of political liberty, for which they fought and bled—and that it may impress upon the minds of the rising generation, that abhorrence of royal tyranny, and love of republican liberty, without which the independence achieved by their ancestors can never be maintained." She then reminded the audience of the community's valiant contribution during the war at a local battle that occurred in Bennington, Vermont. In concluding, she urged those in attendance to reaffirm their patriotism: "Rest assured, venerable Fathers and Mothers, that tho' the father of his country, the great Washington, sleeps in his lowly tomb, at the base of Mount Vernon, and only three of those patriots who signed this Declaration of our Independence, yet linger on this side of the grave: yet there is . . . a generation arising who will never surrender, namely, *that Independence* for which their fathers suffered, bled and died."[52]

A local newspaper not only reprinted the speech—noting that it was "composed and spoken by Miss Cole"—but also commented on Cole's achievement. "The ladies usually have been distinguished for powers of graceful and *sometimes energetic* oratory, and rarely wanting in patriotism. . . . They are fast friends of *Union*, and would reciprocate the good old-Revolutionary Toast, '*Join or die.*'" Word of the speech reached Mrs. A. S. Colvin in Washington, D.C., who reported on it favorably in her weekly magazine. "The fact is," she said, "there have of late been so many abortive attempts at oratory by the other sex, that some of the people have determined . . . to be captivated by the charms of an agreeable person." It did not seem to be a problem that the "agreeable person" was female.[53]

In the course of speaking about independence, women also sometimes expressed their own views of women's patriotic rights, roles, and responsibilities. On Independence Day in 1799 a Norwich, Connecticut, woman affirmed her belief in the importance of women's actions for both society and government. In her view, women should exercise their patriotic duties within the confines of their traditional feminine roles. "As mothers, wives, sisters, and daughters," she said, "we may all be important, teach[ing] our little boys, the inestimable value of Freedom, how to blend and harmonize the natural and social rights of man." This role had important implications. Calling on female members of her audience to serve their country, she urged women to "assist our dear country, to be as glorious in maintaining, as it was great in gaining her immortal independence." This ideal of womanhood, which the Norwich orator shared with many other women and men in the early republic, has been termed "republican motherhood." A significant step in recognizing women's political capacity, the notion rescued women from political invisibility, acknowledged their political influence, and established their connection to the polity. At the same time, this notion did not push the boundaries of women's political role beyond the confines of their traditional roles as wife and mother. Instead of acting independently, women would act politically on or through their sons and husbands. Even as women's roles as wives and mothers were politicized, the constraints of those roles were affirmed.[54]

Other women were more bold. A New England "Lady," who later published her remarks under the title *The Female Advocate*, used her public platform to call the nation to task for its treatment of women. Like many other Independence Day orators, this speaker celebrated the patriotic valor of those who fought and died in the American Revolution. Like the Norwich woman, she highlighted the importance of mothers as the first teachers of children and the primary inculcators of patriotic values and ideals. Unlike the Norwich woman, however, she used the occasion to criticize the country for its failure to live up to what she believed were the Revolution's promises to women. Men and women, she insisted, "are designed for mutual improvement in happiness, and for a reciprocation of affections. But this can never be the case, if the one be so much degraded as to act, not like the friend, but the slave of the other." Current notions of freedom, she said, "embrace only half mankind"; they are thus "only *half systems*." Citing the illustrious history of women, she noted that although many women in the past had broken down "the barriers of the tyrant man," men still attempted to keep women in ignorance. She demanded that girls be educated not simply to prepare them to be better wives and mothers but also to take their place alongside men as ministers, in the learned professions, and in government. "Enough, cries my satisfied soul! Let the wise and pious but concede an equality between the sexes; let them reprove the vain, the arrogant and assuming advocates for female exclusion. . . . I aspire to nothing more than the just rank, which God and nature designed, that equality of talents, of genius, of morals, as well as intellectual worth, which, by evident traits, does exist between the sexes; but of which the arrogance of modern self-sufficiency would totally divest us had it the power." This woman demanded nothing less than full equality for men and women.[55]

Her views were no doubt controversial. Nonetheless, her speech was published by two different publishers in two different editions in 1800 and 1808. This fact suggests that her ideas reached an audience that extended well beyond those who heard her speak in person. Those who printed and purchased her work found there a far more vigorous and assertive ideal than that expressed in republican wifehood and motherhood. Instead of suggesting that women should influence the polity indirectly through their influence over their sons and husbands, she called for women's more direct action and participation. For "The Female Advocate" and her supporters, the Revolution not only politicized women's role as wives and mothers but created new opportunities to expand women's social, political, and economic horizons. Independence Day represented not simply a time to celebrate the country's achievements but also an occasion to demand that Americans live up to their revolutionary ideals.

Fears and Fantasies

As political participation spread to the masses, women took an increasingly visible role in the nation's political life. In acknowledgment of this trend, women who had a strong interest in politics acquired their own designation; they were called "female politicians." At this time, the term "politician," did not always or necessarily refer to a person who served in or sought political office. Instead, the phrase referred to individuals who were knowledgeable about contemporary political affairs and ideas. In a letter written in 1755 during the turmoil of the French and Indian War, for example, John Adams told his friend: "Be not surprised that I am turned politician. This whole town is immersed in politics. The interests of nations, and all the *dira* of war, make [it] the subject of every conversation." In the postevolutionary era, people commented on the growing number of women who were "deeply interested in politics." As the author of an article on "Female Politicians" put it, many women now "claimed an equal right with men" to discuss the affairs of state, the machinations of political candidates, and the future of the republic. Whether or not everyone supported this development, the trend was undeniable.[56]

Depending on the context, the phrase "female politician" could be used positively or negatively, as a term of approbation or derision. Like men who were politicians, female politicians had their own political will and judgment. This is precisely what made the notion controversial. Whereas "republican wives" and "republican mothers" expressed their political sentiments indirectly, through their influence over the men in their lives, female politicians voiced their own political opinions, made their own political choices, and expressed their own political preferences. Even if they could not vote, they behaved as if they were independent political beings.

For supporters, the emergence of "female politicians" represented a positive development. "I perceive by your letter," Sen. Jeremiah Mason told his wife, that "you have an inclination to become a politician. As my taste also is inclining that way, I do not dislike being joined by you." Similarly, when Thomas Lee Shippen wrote to his sister about developments in the Confederation Congress in the 1780s, he observed, "You see I cant help wanting you to be a little of a politician and indeed I do most exceedingly and always have reprobated that fashionable notion of excluding from political study or action, all of your sex." Such men shared their political interests with the women in their circle and promoted their views. In New York in the 1790s, the young Margaret Bayard, a member of the Friendly Club, expressed reservations about voicing her political opinions, for fear that her "strong feelings" on the subject were unfeminine. The writer Charles Brockden Brown reassured her and drew out her opinions on issues such as "the leading differences, between the two parties." His encouragement gave Bayard the confidence she needed to pursue her interests and eventually write about political matters.[57]

Women were often proud to claim the mantle of "female politician" and embraced the designation wholeheartedly. An avid newshound, South Carolinian Margaret Manigault declared in 1792, "I am turned a great Politician. I read the papers and talk learnedly about them all." As these women saw it, their political awareness benefited not just themselves but also the country as a whole. During the Quasi-War with France in 1798, an unofficial naval war fought primarily over control of the seas and international trade, the irrepressible Nelly Parke Custis came to her country's aid. She proclaimed herself an "outrageous politician," ready to take up arms in defense of her homeland in the event of a French invasion. Mercy Otis Warren voiced a more judicious view of what it meant to be a female politician. Addressing the great British historian Catharine Macaulay, Warren observed, "I disregard the opinion that women make but indifferent politicians. . . . When the observations are just and honorary to the heart and character, I think it very immaterial whether they flow from female lips in the soft whisper of private friendship or whether thundered in the Senate in the bolder language of the other sex." In Warren's view, when it came to politics the mind had no sex.[58]

Positive attitudes toward female politicians began to make their way into fiction. In her 1797 novel, *The Coquette*, Hannah Webster Foster portrayed a scene in which certain men and women at a social gathering began to discuss the political issues of the day. Although two of the women excused themselves, claiming that they "never meddled with politics," two other women defended their interest in the subject. "We think ourselves interested in the welfare and prosperity of our country," Mrs. Richman declared. "Consequently, [we] claim the right of inquiring into those affairs, which may conduce to, or interfere with the common weal." Not only did women have their own political opinions, she suggested, but they also experienced the effects of government actions on their lives, whether they were single or married, with children or without. "If the community flourish and enjoy health and freedom, shall we not share in the happy effects? If it be oppressed and disturbed, shall we not endure our proportion of the evil? Why then should the love of our country be a masculine passion only? Why should government, which involves the peace and order of the society of which we are a part, be wholly excluded from our observation?"[59]

Although supporters of female politicians did not necessarily believe that women should vote or hold public office, they did advocate a more active and assertive role for women in politics. They saw women's increasing interest in politics as an expression of their growing competence in the wider world, a sign of their political importance, and an affirmation of their connection with the polity. Seeking to promote rather than stifle women's capacities, they viewed women's politicization as an opportunity rather than a threat.

Not surprisingly, many others resisted or rejected this development. For critics, "female politician" was an epithet or term of ridicule. In an 1802 article called "Remarks on Female Politicians," a fictional female character was asked her opinion as to whether "women had not an equal right with men to be politicians." She replied, "When I see a female deeply interested in politics, I tremble for her tranquillity. As the sensibility of women is livelier, and their enthusiasm more ardent than that of men, they are less qualified to decide on the affairs of government." Politics, she suggested, might erode women's traditional feminine virtues: "Political discussion agitates [women's] passions, roughens their manners, and discomposes the garb of female modesty, which should be considered the fairest ornament and brightest charm of a woman." By defeminizing women, politics might also make women more like men. In fact, the author Judith Sargent Murray, who aspired to write about politics, was once warned by her husband that a "female politician" was "an amphibious animal"—an unnatural species that displayed masculine as well as feminine traits.[60]

"Female politicians" posed another kind of challenge as well. Politically informed women might become less dependent on men and less willing to accept their traditional subordinate status. Writing from France in 1785, Thomas Jefferson chided his friend Elizabeth Trist, "Do not you turn politician, too, but write me all the small news; the news about persons and not about states." If women were preoccupied with the "small" world of the home, they would be less likely to involve themselves in the affairs of the larger world of government and politics. Kept in their place, they would not challenge men's monopoly on political power.[61]

Fears about "female politicians" took on an increased sense of urgency in light of the larger public debate over women's rights. Postrevolutionary anxieties about women's political role were not just fantasy; they were based in fact. The Revolution's celebration of equality and natural rights could be construed to imply the necessity of extending formal political rights to women. The experiment in female suffrage in New Jersey showed that traditional limitations on women's political role need not pertain. As one critic sarcastically put it, "The *Rights of Man* have been warmly insisted on by Tom Paine and other democrats, but we [in New Jersey] outstrip them in the science of government, and not only preach the *Rights of Women*, but boldly push it into practice." On the face of it, there was no reason why the experiment had to stop in New Jersey.[62]

The larger fear, of course, was not just for the present. American women and men feared for the future, a future that might involve a wholesale transformation in women's rights, roles, and responsibilities. Female politicians were already pushing the boundaries of women's acceptable forms of political involvement. If women received the vote, it seemed likely that they would soon demand other rights, including the right to hold public office. "As women are now to take a part in the jurisprudence of our state," noted a New Jersey newspaper, "we may shortly expect to see them take the helm—*of government.*" Given the atmosphere of political experimentation that existed in the postrevolutionary era, this proposition, too, was not as far-fetched as it may have seemed in earlier decades.[63]

In fact in 1822 a woman named Elizabeth Bartlett was actually nominated for the position of register of the deeds in Middlesex County, Massachusetts. It is not clear who nominated Bartlett or why they did so. In any case, it is evident that many people took the nomination seriously. In its March 2, 1822, edition, a major Boston newspaper listed Bartlett's name along with five male candidates. The public announcement raised the alarm. A writer calling herself "Susan Thoughtful" wrote to a Boston magazine and ruminated on the consequences if Bartlett were elected. She wondered if Bartlett, who was single, would be eligible to marry while in office. If Bartlett did marry, the author asked, how would she still be able to fulfill her public duties? According to the doctrine of coverture, a married woman was unable to make contracts or sue or be sued in court. A question then arose: Would her husband automatically assume her position as register of deeds?[64]

Perhaps most troubling of all was the notion that a woman might dare to assume the same political role as that of a man. "Susan Thoughtful" noted, "There is now but little difference in the education of boys and girls. . . . As things go on, it seems there is to be but little difference in occupations, rights or duties of men and women." She clearly did not approve of the trend. "If a lady be eligible as a Register of Deeds, is she not also eligible as a Governor, Senator, Representative, Overseer of the poor, or other public office? . . . I have some curiosity to know where we are to stop." In the end the issue was not put to the test. Bartlett herself prevented the matter from coming to a head. On March 6, 1822, shortly after the public announcement, a Boston newspaper published a letter declaring that Bartlett was withdrawing her candidacy. Speaking in the third person, she claimed that the nomination "was made wholly without her knowledge or consent; that she utterly disclaims all pretensions to the office; and that the anxiety and pain it has given her have been abated only by the belief that it originated in motives of kindness." Catastrophe had been averted—this time. Like "Susan Thoughtful," however, many American men and women wondered where their society was headed and "where we are to stop."[65]

Anxieties about women's rights not only produced outright attacks but also generated a rich satirical literature. Ridicule and humor were, of course, traditional means of defusing controversial issues and deflating an individual's or a group's pretensions to power. More than a hundred years before, during the English civil war, authors had begun a tradition of political satire that deployed women as a means of attacking the political opposition. From 1641 to 1656 Henry Neville, for example, published a series of works that depicted women calling together Parliaments composed entirely of women. These assemblies passed laws that legalized gossip, demanded sexually competent husbands, and overturned the gender hierarchy. Published at a time of great upheaval, the works ridiculed not only the aspirations of women but also those of radical reformers who wished to make the English government more representative and inclusive.[66]

Borrowing this tradition, American writers too began to use satire as a means of fantasizing about the potential consequences of giving women political rights. For some people, the object was to express their hopes or wishes that women might realize the promise of equality and natural rights implicit in revolutionary ideology. For most, however, the object was to demonstrate that women were too frivolous, superficial, or ill-prepared to handle such responsibilities. A typical scenario reported the fictional proceedings of an all-female legislature. Significantly, these assemblies dealt only with stereotypically feminine issues, such as marriage, bad language, and fashion. In a piece reprinted numerous times in various magazines and periodicals, a delegation of women met "to consider the ways and means to raise the necessary supplies of husbands throughout the United States." Another article reported that a "House of Ladies" debated the prevalence of cursing, swearing, and bad spelling practices among females. Another urged that the ladies be established "as a body corporate" so that they could "be the sole judges, as to the propriety, or impropriety, of their own dress and fashion. Let them be permitted to enact laws, for their own government, and to exact penalties and punishments of offenders." In yet another variation, an all-female legislature passed resolutions remonstrating against recent trends in men's fashions.[67]

Other pieces explored the supposedly ludicrous results if women did gain a greater voice in government. In 1803 the *Philadelphia Repository and Weekly Register* printed an account, presumably fictional, in which the "respectable Young Ladies of this City" gathered to protest "the false accusations" of "A Misogamist [Misogynist]" against them. As a group, they resolved, "It is the duty of our Sex to support the reputation and sense of our utility to the community." Significantly, however, the piece portrayed the women's collective action as a success. The women defended their names and reputations to the outside world. An 1812 piece, purportedly from the "Female-Citizens of the state of Pennsylvania," expressed women's dissatisfaction in the form of a petition to the legislature. The assembly purportedly was considering a law that limited women's ability to dress in fashionable clothing. Attacking the legislature's efforts "to deprive them of the indefeasible rights of dress," the women protested against the legislature's actions, proclaiming, "that the present Ordinances of Society, have more than sufficiently reduced [women] under the dominion of the other Sex; a fact which they think has been fully demonstrated by the ingenious defender of their rights, Mrs. Wolstonecroft, who had she lived to this period, must have been struck at such an attempt, should it succeed, must ultimately lead to the total prostration of our Rights and Privileges." Although written in jest, the piece made several substantive points. Women were acknowledged to be citizens. They possessed certain rights and privileges. They did not elect members to the legislature or give their consent to laws that directly affected them. Even more important, women were no longer powerless. They now had a vehicle at their disposal—the petition—through which to express their grievances and a new language—the language of rights—with which to express their dissatisfaction.[68]

In effect, satirical works that attempted to undercut women's claim to political rights and privileges sometimes had the opposite effect. Although meant to scorn and ridicule women's potential political aspirations, the pieces revealed deeper concerns and exposed more unsettling realities. Women had no formal voice or representation in the country's existing legislatures. With the brief exception of New Jersey, they did not vote in state or federal elections. Nowhere did they sit in the assembly or hold public office. After reading the pieces, then, other conclusions were possible. Women might well be dissatisfied with a political order that denigrated and excluded them. Their exclusion was unwarranted and unjust. And women now possessed both the means and the opportunity to express their political concerns.

The postrevolutionary era created an atmosphere of ferment about women's rights and receptivity to women's participation in politics. Politics was understood to encompass a capacious realm that involved voters and nonvoters, men and women alike. As white middle-class and elite women became more literate and had greater access to print culture, they became increasingly well informed about political affairs and more vocal in expressing their opinions. As more men entered state and federal government, politicians' wives insisted that their husbands take their wishes into account when deciding whether or not to serve the public. At Fourth of July celebrations and on other public occasions, women were encouraged to participate in patriotic activities and even had the opportunity to speak in public. As women became an increasingly visible force in the nation's political life, highly political women gained their own designation. "Female politicians," as they were called, became a symbol for both the prospects and the perils of women's rights.

While some people welcomed these developments, others regarded them with alarm. With the vantage of hindsight, we know that it would take more than a century for women to obtain the franchise and even longer for them to attain full equality with men. Yet at the time the future was uncertain. In the decades following the American Revolution, the meaning of women's rights was hotly contested. Women were casting ballots in New Jersey. A woman had been nominated for public office in Massachusetts. Although republican wives and mothers were content to influence the polity through their husbands or sons, female politicians asserted more independent political identities. Women were entering politics in ways and on a scale that had not before been possible. For those who paid attention, the direction of change seemed clear. Although women were not yet demanding political rights, it seemed to be only a matter of time before they would do so.

Chapter 3
Patriotism and Partisanship

In 1798 a play called *Politicians; or, A State of Things* featured two female characters, Mrs. Violent and Mrs. Turbulent. Throughout the play both women expressed their political sentiments in the strongest terms. Mrs. Turbulent, a Republican sympathizer, declared that President George Washington was "never equal to the situation he was placed in: vastly have his talents been over-rated." He and his "infamous party," she insisted, "have been the ruin of our country." The Federalist Mrs. Violent, on the other hand, challenged the political opinions of her brother, who "leans toward the democrats." In her view, she told him, Republicans are nothing more than "a wicked, restless, marplotting set." Castigating her female friend, she proclaimed, "Your Jacobin faction are to be charged with all the evils that have beset us, and all the troubles that await our country: you have been abetting the French tyrants from the first to the present moment."[1]

As the play suggests, by the 1790s party politics had swept women as well as men into its fractious vortex. Middle-class and elite white women allied themselves with one party or the other and expressed their partisan views with authority, conviction, and even vehemence. They were "female politicians" with a vengeance. Building on their revolutionary-era experiences, women participated in party functions and rallied behind partisan causes. In their private lives, everything from the hiring of a servant to the choice of a marriage partner might involve political considerations. The emergence of party politics, however, transformed the meaning of women's political involvement. Instead of being patriots, women now acted as partisans. Although men initially welcomed their participation, women deepened the animosity between Federalists and Republicans and intensified the partisan divide. In the noxious political climate of the early republic, the presence of women in politics took on a new, more ominous, and potentially devastating, significance.

The Rise of Party Politics

As we know from Richard Hofstadter and other historians, the framers of the United States Constitution did not anticipate the development of a two-party political system. For the framers, "party" connoted faction, the pursuit of private interests at the expense of the larger public good. Instead, they believed that the country should be governed by a group of wise, virtuous men who would be able to discern the country's best interests. These hopes were quickly dashed. As early as the second Congress, divisions had already begun to emerge on crucial issues such as support for manufacturing, the assumption of state debts, and the establishment of a national bank.[2]

The early Federalists and Democratic Republicans were not political parties in the modern sense. They lacked explicit party platforms, nominating caucuses, permanent staffs, and paid political operatives. Party membership was often in flux; individuals often changed their party affiliation more than once. Nonetheless, a fundamental cleavage had emerged, pitting the supporters of George Washington and Alexander Hamilton against the adherents of Thomas Jefferson and James Madison. By the middle years of the 1790s, these divisions had coalesced into well-defined voting blocs within Congress. Whereas Federalists supported a fiscal-military state that preserved the privileges of the governing elite, Republicans advocated an agrarian republic that emphasized local control and the opening up of political privileges to whole new classes of white men. Aided by the distribution of newspapers and print culture, partisanship soon spread to ordinary people in towns, counties, and regions throughout the country.[3]

The French Revolution represented a key turning point in transforming congressional alliances into popular, mass-based organizations. When the turbulence first began in 1789, most Americans greeted events in France with enthusiasm. French struggles against monarchical oppression resembled the American struggle against British tyranny. The cry of "Liberty, Equality, and Fraternity" seemed to echo the Americans' own revolutionary rhetoric. Yet with the execution of the king and the queen, and the coming of the Terror in the early 1790s, the French Revolution became a divisive symbol of party differences. Rallying behind Jefferson and Madison, one faction, the Democratic Republicans, continued to support the French Revolution, believing that the genius of the French people would eventually allow republican principles to triumph. For Washington, Hamilton, and their supporters, known as Federalists, the French Revolution became a cautionary tale, a nightmare that showed what happened when liberty became licentiousness.

Ordinary citizens took up the cause for or against France. The French Revolution, Thomas Jefferson told James Monroe, had "kindled and brought forward the two parties with an ardour which our own interests merely, could never excite." In cities such as Boston and Philadelphia,

French ideas about liberty and equality led to a leveling in nomenclature in certain circles. Men were to be called "cits"; women were to be addressed as "citesses." Party members leveled vicious slurs at their adversaries. While Federalists maligned their opponents as "atheists," "Jacobins," or "democrats," Jeffersonians decried their adversaries as "monocrats" or "aristocrats." Each side adopted competing symbols, rituals, and civic celebrations. Supporters of France donned red, white, and blue ribbons or cockades, which they wore on their hats, coats, or dresses. French sympathizers hoisted liberty poles, displayed liberty caps, or sang French songs, such as the "Ça Ira." Hundreds of towns sponsored pro-French parades, speeches, and festivities. In imitation of the French Jacobin clubs, some Americans formed Democratic Republican societies that gathered to debate the topical issues of the day. Federalist opponents of the French Revolution had their own alternatives. Anti-French groups ignored Bastille Day and celebrated Washington's birthday instead. In their toasts and public orations, they warned that American "Jacobins" were leading the United States into violence, disorder, and bloodshed. On their clothing they wore golden eagles, black badges in the shape of a rosette reflecting their support of England, or after 1800 a white rose in imitation of French royalists. Partisan newspapers declared their allegiance to either France or Britain.[4]

Although parties soon insinuated themselves into the nation's political life, neither Federalists nor Democratic Republicans welcomed the growth of party politics. Operating in a climate in which the very existence of partisanship was suspect, neither side acknowledged the validity of the other's existence—or even recognized the extent to which their own actions contributed to the creation of a party system. "In *theory*," noted a political tract published in 1812, "Patriotism signifies *the disinterested love of our country, and an earnest desire to promote its best interests. But, in practice,* it too often signifies nothing more than a flaming zeal to promote the ties of the *party to which one belongs,* and an ardent desire to *obtain or to keep an office!*" The emergence of opposing factions shattered the illusion of consensus on a common national good. Patriotism had become partisanship.[5]

As party conflict intensified, both Federalists and Republicans began to vie for women's allegiance. Leaders urged women to demonstrate their support publicly by attending partisan meetings, gatherings, and events. Federalists, for example, welcomed women to commemorations of Washington's birthday and later to ceremonies in honor of his death. The Society of the Cincinnati, a military organization that came to be seen as an "auxiliary arm" of the Federalist Party invited women to attend certain functions. Republicans also solicited women's participation. In order to honor Thomas Jefferson, the women of Cheshire, Massachusetts, made a "Mammoth Cheese" weighing twelve hundred pounds and measuring four feet in diameter, which local men delivered to the White House in 1802. In other localities Republican men invited women to festivities in honor of the French military victory at Valmy or to celebrate the revolutionary "Feast of Reason." By appearing at such activities, women both affirmed their partisan affiliation and expanded the basis of popular political participation.[6]

Party politics even infiltrated the nation's most important patriotic celebration, Independence Day. By the mid-1790s, Federalists and Democratic Republicans throughout the country began to hold separate, competing Fourth of July celebrations. Jeffersonians sponsored raucous public celebrations featuring public readings of the Declaration of Independence. Federalists retreated to private dinners, where they avoided mentioning the Declaration, which contained embarrassing references to "natural rights" and "equality." Women lent their support to these partisan functions. In Caldwell, New Jersey, a Republican stronghold, citizens cheered as "Sixteen young ladies uniformed in white with garlands in their hats" marched in a parade "bearing the Cap of Liberty, enwreathed in laurel, and all fingering *Columbia*, in concert with the German flute." In nearby North Farms the women followed the men "round the Tree of Liberty, accompanied with music, both instrumental and vocal." On the Federalist side, women in New Haven, Connecticut, joined their husbands in singing "Adams and Liberty" or presented flags to local militia groups in an elaborate ceremony. In Deerfield, Connecticut, the women concluded their Fourth of July celebration with a toast: "May each Columbian Sister perceive and pursue the unfallible system of extinguishing Jacobinism." Such scenes occurred repeatedly throughout the country.[7]

Toasts made in public, and later reprinted in newspapers, reveal the intensity with which both parties competed for women's allegiance. Members claimed that the "Fair Sex" preferred their party over the competition. In Carlisle, Pennsylvania, in 1815, for example, the Federalists toasted "The ladies who this day honored *our party* with their presence.—May we ever continue to deserve their favours." Women might solidify their preferences by marrying one of their number. In Patterson, New Jersey, young Republicans hoisted their tankards to "the youthful Fair of Columbia.—May they detest as the worst of evils, the very idea of despotism, and prefer a union with a *Republican Cobbler,* to an *Aristocratic Nobleman.*" Women's participation in party activities was understood as more than passive compliance with men's wishes. Their presence was seen as an affirmative choice.[8]

Through their attire, even women's bodies revealed their partisan affiliations. Federalist women often wore golden eagles or black cockades on their dresses or hats. Imitating their French counterparts, Republican women wore Phrygian caps, also known as liberty caps, an ancient symbol of freedom. It was not uncommon for women to fashion and sew the party symbols worn by men. "With their delicate fingers," one observer remembered, the "fair sex" made "the emblems of the contending parties." Women's fingers, however, were not always so delicate. One congressman claimed that he saw women "meet at the church door and violently pluck the badges from one another's bosoms." The historian Lynn Hunt has described what she calls the "politicization of the everyday" during the French Revolution. So too did ordinary Americans of the early national era, including women, display a personal sense of identification with a larger, national political movement, often responding with a surprising passion and sense of personal conviction.[9]

In fact, the spirit of partisanship drove some women to become avid "female politicians." Like male partisans, they vigorously engaged in party combat. One example was Cornelia Clinton, daughter of Republican governor George Clinton of New York. In 1794 she celebrated recent "good news from France" concerning the French republic and vented her disdain for Federalist "aristocrats," whose actions, she believed undermined the French cause in America. At the other end of the political spectrum, Nellie Parke Custis, stepgranddaughter of George Washington, reacted to news of the Terror by declaring herself "perfectly *federal*" and maligning the French revolutionaries as "democratic murderers." Reflecting disillusionment with France and the rise of Napoleon Bonaparte, the Federalist daughter of Elias Boudinot voiced her contempt for the country's "*democracy*," or "what is called *freedom of the people*." Like men, many female partisans saw party politics as a Manichean battle between good and evil. And like men, they believed that there could be only one victor in the struggle.[10]

The growth of party politics heightened women's growing significance in the political realm. At a time when partisanship itself was regarded as suspect, women conferred a kind of respectability, moral sanction, and legitimacy on party gatherings and events. Because female patriotism was, as Abigail Adams had put it, "the most disinterested of all virtues,"[11] people saw women's allegiance as purer and nobler than men's, untainted by self-interest or the pursuit of personal gain. Through their very presence, women eased men's guilt about the ruptures caused by partisanship and provided a visible symbol of unity, linking the mythical patriotic consensus of the revolutionary era with a factionless era that lay in the (hopefully) not-too-distant future. Their approval transformed the dross of political machination into the gold of elevated principle.

The emergence of party conflict also led the two most preeminent women political authors of the day, Mercy Otis Warren and Judith Sargent Murray, to express their own heightened sense of partisan allegiance. Both women found that the rise of party politics provided new opportunities to express themselves in print. Putting behind some of the timidity of their earlier writing, they grew increasingly confident in their own political judgments. Yet their views reflected the divisiveness of the time. Each woman supported a different political party. Warren was a staunch Republican while Murray was an avowed Federalist.

Warren soon made her anti-administration, pro-Jeffersonian sympathies well-known. In 1788, she wrote a tract, under the pseudonym "A Columbian Patriot," opposing the ratification of the U.S. Constitution. Fearful of a concentration of power and the lack of a bill of rights, she worried that the new government displayed many of the aristocratic tendencies of the rejected British regime. In the 1790s, she became committed to the cause of France, whose "struggles for freedom and the equal rights of man," she said, "ought to [be] cherished by Americans." Unlike most citizens of New England, she also became a strong Jeffersonian, a position that put her in the minority in a Federalist stronghold. In 1805 she published her three-volume *History of the Rise, Progress and Termination of the American Revolution*, which provided a narrative of events from 1760 through 1800 from a decidedly Republican point of view. In no uncertain terms she attacked George Washington's presidency for his "partiality for monarchy" and aristocratic elitism. "It was obvious to every one," she insisted, "that dignified ranks, ostentatious titles, splendid governments, and supernumerary expensive offices, to be supported by the labor of the poor, or the taxation of all the conveniences, were not the objects of the patriot." Warren's politics also turned her against her former friend and mentor, John Adams, whom she now regarded as an aristocratic snob. As Warren saw it, Jefferson's election in 1800 represented a victory for the true revolutionary legacy—a legacy that included "the natural equality of man, their right of adopting their own modes of government, the dignity of the people, and that sovereignty which cannot be ceded either to representatives or to kings."[12]

In terms of both policy and philosophy, Murray felt more comfortable with the Federalists than with the Jeffersonians. Unlike Warren, Murray had supported the ratification of the U.S. Constitution and praised President Washington's efforts to strengthen the union. In 1798 she dedicated her volume, *The Gleaner,* to President John Adams. Mistrustful of the masses, she insisted that liberty depended on nature's "systems, her laws, and her regular chain of subordination." Skeptical of equality, she maintained that tampering with this order might lead to social conflict or even anarchy. "Custom," she claimed, "has judiciously affixed to the various ranks in society its ascertaining marks, and we cannot see her barriers thrown down, or the rushing together of the different classes of mankind, without regret." Whereas Warren's watchwords were "rights" and "equality," Murray's were "Peace, Order, and good Government."[13]

The factionalized nature of party politics in the early republic thus polarized women as well as men. Despite their formal exclusion, Murray and Warren—and many other women as well—felt themselves to be legitimate players in the political drama unfolding before them. Male partisans could not have expressed their sentiments more eloquently—or vociferously.

Political Socialization

In the early national era, women's political allegiances were to some extent formed in much the same way as those of men were. As social scientists have shown, political socialization occurs through a variety of mechanisms, some conscious and others subconscious. Some people deliberately choose their political beliefs and can articulate a coherent philosophical justification for their views. Others absorb their ideas through contact with those around them. The politics of an individual's family is a particularly strong indicator of eventual political allegiance. Personal style, temperament, social class, and upbringing also play a role in determining the choice of one political party over another.[14]

In the first decades of the early republic, the male head of household often exerted an inordinate influence in shaping a family's political allegiance, for the men as well as for the women of the family. Whether because of the father's intellect, his financial resources, or his persuasive abilities, both male and female members often followed his political lead. Recalling his youth in Federalist Massachusetts, Supreme Court justice Joseph Story noted that despite the intense hostility of his neighbors, he had "imbibed the same opinions" as his father and became a Jeffersonian. In a letter to James Madison, a Virginia merchant explained his political origins, declaring that he was "a Republican by Nature[,] Birth[,] and family." Daughters might learn politics in the same way. A Democrat named Lucy Kenney reflected on the influence of her family. "I imbibed the sentiments and principles of my father, whose judgment and principles were as unwavering and unchangeable as the laws of the Medes and Persians. . . . I never breathed any other sentiment than a republican one, nor ever lived in any other atmosphere." More than any other single individual, the family patriarch had the most pronounced influence on family members' political attitudes and loyalties.[15]

Yet fathers and children did not always agree on politics, especially once the children could think for themselves. Sons of eminent politicians such as John Adams and James Bowdoin defected to the opposition and risked their fathers' wrath. Women, too, sometimes repudiated their fathers' beliefs. As an adult Catharine Maria Sedgwick found it difficult to reconcile her personal affection for her Federalist father with his decidedly patronizing attitude toward the masses. She admitted that as a young person she had "entered fully, and with the full faith and ignorance of childhood, into the prejudices of the time." Yet later in life she no longer shared her father's political views. Although he was, she said, "one of the kindest-hearted of men," he routinely referred to "the people" as the "greasy, unwashed multitude," "Jacobins, sans-culottes, [and] miscreants." Distancing herself from his notions, she attributed his prejudices to his "misfortune, and perhaps the inevitable consequence of having been educated [as a] loyal subject of a monarchical government." Much as it pained Sedgwick, her principles forced her to reject her father's political party. No doubt many others—men and women alike—had to make similarly painful choices.[16]

Women's political socialization, however, did differ in important ways from that of men. At times fathers used their control of their daughters' marriage prospects to make certain that their girls married men whose political views accorded with their own. For example, Catharine Maria Sedgwick recalled that her good friend Fanny Atwood nearly lost the man of her dreams because her grandfather insisted that her suitor vote for the Democratic party. As a young man William Henry Harrison, then a Republican, made suit to Hannah Cooper, sister of the novelist James Fenimore Cooper and daughter of Federalist Congressman William Cooper. The elder Cooper nixed the match, and Harrison had to find a mate elsewhere. Politics also doomed one of Joseph Story's early romances. In 1801 the future chief justice fell madly in love with a young woman named Lydia Pierce. Unfortunately, Story's Republicanism clashed with the Federalism of Pierce's male guardian. Desperately trying to win his approval, Story wrote the guardian a long letter in which he denied "that my political opinions are jacobinical" or that he sought "to propagate infidel principles & irreligious doctrines." Resorting to a semantic sleight of hand, he tried to cloak himself in the Federalist mantle, claiming to be a "*federalist* in the noblest sense. I venerate . . . the constitution of my country, as the grand palladium of our rights and liberties." The guardian was not fooled. He rejected Story's pleas, casting the dismayed Republican into months of "sleepless nights," "days of anguish," and "that dreadful languor, which leaves the pruriency of desire without the vivacity of emotion." Although Story eventually recovered and married someone else, the episode left him melancholy for years. Although it is hard to know how often fathers imposed their will in such a heavy-handed fashion, it probably happened enough to be a concern for women—and for their male suitors.[17]

In other cases women themselves chose spouses because of the men's political views. For these women, a man's political affiliation could be as important as his wealth, looks, or personality. The wrong party identity could doom even the most swashbuckling young man's prospects. As a young North Carolina woman confided to her female friend, "Do you know that John is a Monstrous Jacobin. I feel quite provoked with him . . . Besides being morally wrong, it is so unfashionable. . . . I have not heard or seen a Gentleman before the last age that w[ould] dare think of a red cap—or even a french cockade." Another young lady, Sophia May, refused to let romance take precedence over politics. As the daughter of a Federalist congressman from Massachusetts, she was living in Washington, D.C., in April 1812. As rumors of war spread throughout the capital and Federalist opposition mounted, she wrote to her sister that she had taken a stroll with a Republican congressman from North Carolina. As they passed the Capitol, the gentleman reportedly teased May that one day the building would fall down. She took the remark personally. "Soon, then I hope," she replied, "[for] such an event might be the salvation of our country, crashing at one stroke the hydra-headed serpent, which is our deadly bane." Her candor shocked her companion. "He did not like my very patriotic 'hope,'" she told her sister, "although he tried to laugh it off. And swore he would convert me to the true Republican . . . faith before the close of the Session." May, however, refused to be seduced by his blandishments. She insisted that she was "in no danger of infection, not even if 'their tongues drop manna.'"[18]

At least one woman, and likely more, fell in love with a man's politics as much as his person. In 1793 the French government sent a new minister, Edmond-Charles Genêt, to the United States. His task was to persuade officials to abandon neutrality and come to France's aid in its struggle against Britain. In a triumphal procession moving from Charlestown, Massachusetts, to Philadelphia, Genêt became convinced that the American people, if not their government, supported his cause. Although government officials such as Washington, Hamilton, and even Jefferson denounced him, Genêt began a controversial campaign to arm French privateers who would sail from American ports to prey on British ships. In the course of his public activities, Genêt met and at some point began to court Cornelia Clinton, daughter of Republican governor George Clinton of New York. Throughout Genêt's tempestuous visit, Cornelia sent continuing words of support for his cause and admiration for his person. "I hope all those who are in opposition to you," she thundered, "may . . . be confounded." As her affection grew, she described how much he meant to her. "[Your] Democratic principles," she said, "serve but to endear you to me, for notwithstanding your worth I do not think I could have been attached to you had you been any thing but a Republican." When a change in government in France led to Genêt's recall, Genêt, under threat of execution, sought asylum in the United States. Soon thereafter he married the loyal Cornelia. In this case, both politics and love had prevailed.[19]

After marriage a woman's primary loyalty shifted from her father to her husband. It was routinely assumed that the woman's political views would echo those of her husband. "The females," noted a male traveler to western Pennsylvania in 1810, "carry the spirit of party into their coteries, so far as to exclude every female whose husband is of a different political opinion, however amiable, and ornamental to society she may be." Yet the reality was probably more complicated. Even when spouses shared the same politics, there may have been certain instances when the husband followed his wife's lead on political matters rather than vice versa. In the case of strong and opinionated women such as Mercy Otis Warren and Judith Sargent Murray, this was certainly the case. In each of these households husband and wife shared the same political philosophy. In both cases, however, the husband seems at some point to have yielded precedence on political matters to the wife. Judith Sargent's first husband, John Stevens, was a bankrupt ne'er-do-well who died in 1787, leaving her with a string of debts. During their brief marriage he seems to have had little time for, or inclination toward, politics. Her second husband, John Murray, was a founding father of the Universalist religion in Massachusetts, an endeavor that consumed his complete attention. After he suffered a stroke in 1801, Murray handled the family finances and worked to publicize his religious ideas. Through it all, Murray continued to publish her own books, plays, and articles, which reflected her Federalist sentiments. Her political views, not his, were the ones that mattered.[20]

In the case of the Warrens, the wife's political acumen soon superseded that of her husband. During the American Revolution, James Warren had been active in state and local politics, but he retired in 1780 from public life. During the debate over the U.S. Constitution, both spouses published critiques of the proposed government. While James's tract had little impact outside Boston, Mercy's treatise, published under the pseudonym "A Columbian Patriot," was reprinted in newspapers throughout the country. His influence diminished while hers increased. In 1790 she published her *Collected Poems and Plays* to great acclaim. Even after both partners became disillusioned with politics and alienated from government, political leaders such as Elbridge Gerry continued to seek out her opinion on contemporary political events. In 1805 Mercy

Warren issued her majestic, three-volume history of the American Revolution. Her work not only recounted the story of independence but also assessed the state of the nation through the presidencies of Washington and Adams. Although Mercy may have remained deferential to her husband in private, her public reputation surpassed his. In this case, the woman, not the man, took the political lead.[21]

While few other women at the time were as prominent as Warren and Murray, it is likely that at least some women did assert political opinions independent of those of the men in their household. Mothers disagreed with sons. Hiram Hardwood of Bennington, Vermont, reported in his journal that "a warm debate took place" between a male visitor, his mother, and himself over an upcoming election in 1828. While his mother supported one candidate for the state legislature, he and the other man supported another. His mother did not back down. Women also felt free to disagree with their husbands. Reporting that their minister had denounced the War of 1812 in a sermon, Mary Jackson Lee told her husband, who was away in India on business, that she objected to the minister's virulent language as well as his Federalist views. As for her husband, Lee told him in no uncertain terms, "You may agree with which you please, . . . [but] I think your real sentiment will be with me tho' you may not honestly declare it." Other women engaged in more surreptitious maneuvers. In 1803 a friend teased Thomas Dwight, a Federalist congressman from Massachusetts, about his wife's Jeffersonian sympathies, saying, "I suppose [your wife] is impatient for the coming of the day [that you leave for Washington], when she can go on with the work of making democrats of her boys without any interference from you." Mary Palmer Tyler recorded another kind of female insubordination. Tyler reported that when her mother, a staunch "Whig" (that is, revolutionary-era Whig; a republican), visited her home, bitter disputes erupted between the mother and Tyler's husband, a Federalist judge. Although Mary Tyler stayed out of the fray, her mother obviously felt no need to defer to the man of the house. As for the judge, he routinely scheduled business trips to coincide with her visits.[22]

As party politics grew in strength in the early republic, members of the same family tended to share the same partisan affiliation. This shared identity strengthened familial bonds and tightened family cohesion. Party politics, however, could also tear a family apart. Women, in particular, were supposed to defer to men's political judgment. In practice, it did not always work that way. Young ladies sometimes wanted to marry men whose politics differed from that of their families. Wives sometimes knew more about politics than their husbands. Women sometimes challenged their husbands', sons', or fathers' political views. The more women participated in party politics and identified themselves as partisans, the more difficult it became to shield the home from the larger political controversies wracking the nation.

Female Partisans in Action

The emergence of party politics profoundly changed the nation's political culture and, with it, the meaning of women's political participation. National crises deepened women's partisan commitments and divided women as much as men. One of the first flash points was the public battle over the Jay Treaty. In 1795 John Jay negotiated a treaty with Britain that was supposed to resolve certain outstanding issues with the former mother country, especially regarding trade. Yet Republicans found the treaty abhorrent. Besides objecting to undue secrecy surrounding the negotiations, they believed that Jay had not, among other things, received sufficient concessions for American shipping in the West Indies nor guaranteed the safety of American neutrality on the high seas. Jeffersonians throughout the country rose up to prevent the treaty's ratification. Burning Ambassador Jay in effigy became a favorite form of protest. Women took sides in the controversy. Commenting on events in Philadelphia, Federalist Elizabeth Drinker noted with surprise that the "mob" had been orderly. Participants had paraded "quietly up one street and down another, without making any noise, with the Cartwheels muffled, then went back to Kensington where they burnt the effigy after midnight." Obviously relieved, she remarked, "Tis well was no worse." Federalist Judith Sargent Murray expressed her support for the treaty. Reading about congressional opposition plunged her into the "depth of misery," reflecting her sense of "impending darkness . . . [on] the political horizon." Only after the treaty narrowly won approval in the Senate did she confidently assert that "every well disposed American must felicitate himself that the eventful scale hath preponderated in favour of Order and good government." Because many Americans were not prepared to "felicitate" themselves to the Federalist order, the partisan battles raged on.[23]

The coming of the Quasi-War with France in 1798 prompted both parties to mobilize its female backers. In response, Federalist women voiced their views on the necessity of an official declaration of war. Rumors of a possible French invasion sent Nelly Custis into a partisan frenzy. "I am becoming an outrageous politician," she told her friend, "determined even to lend a hand to extirpate [the French] Demons, if . . . their unparell'd thirst of conquest could make them attempt an invasion of our peaceable happy land." In order to prepare the country for armed conflict, many Federalist women stitched flags or banners, which they presented to local militia units in elaborate public ceremonies. Republican women, on the other hand, defended France and rejected the Federalist drumbeat for war. "These are no doubt vexatious and perplexing times to the Statesmen and Patriot," wrote Catherine Few, wife of a former congressman, to her sister, the wife of Albert Gallatin. She continued, "Good heavens—how dreadful is the sound of War—Why should the policy of a few interested individuals be permitted to lure on the vengeance of that tremendous Republic?" Ironically, it was Federalist John Adams whose patience in negotiating with the French saved the country from war. Yet Adams himself paid a price when he lost favor in his own party and was defeated in the next presidential election by Thomas Jefferson.[24]

Jefferson's election in 1800 signaled a momentous turning point in politics, one which Jefferson himself immodestly termed "the Revolution of 1800." Before his inauguration, however, fears of armed violence, or even a coup d'état, preceded him. For the first time in history, members of the party holding the presidency would voluntarily transfer power into the hands of their avowed adversaries. Although women grasped the significance of what they witnessed, they, like many men, interpreted the events through their own partisan lenses. Chronicling Jefferson's inauguration ceremony, Republican sympathizer Margaret Bayard Smith noted, "I have this morning witnessed one of the most interesting scenes, a free people can ever witness. The changes of administration, which in every government and in every age have most generally been epochs of confusion, villany, and bloodshed, in this our happy country taken place without any species of distraction, or disorder." Mercy Otis Warren, like her husband, viewed Jefferson's election as the victory of true republican principles over aristocracy and corruption. To the Warrens, Jefferson's inauguration represented "the Triumph of Virtue over the most malignant & virulent & slandering Party that perhaps ever existed."[25]

Federalist women, on the other hand, anticipated Jefferson's presidency with apprehension and dread. Some feared for the country's economic future. "Do not thick clouds hover over the United States?" asked Judith Sargent Murray. "Will not the new President make regulations which will affect the remotest dependencies of the general government? . . . Will not the energies of Commerce be paralised? In one word, will not many of the horrors of a revolution, usher in the approaching Century?" Others feared the prospect of violence and bloodshed. Visiting New York City on inauguration day, Harriet Trumbull reported sourly that the day was one of "great rejoicings" for the Republicans. "There were," she noted, "so many disorderly creatures in the streets" that she and her sister could not return to their home and had to stay overnight with a family friend. Rebecca Woolsey Hillhouse took some dim comfort in the fact that the day passed without a major incident. Now that Jefferson was president, she told her husband, it was unlikely that his supporters would be "takin up arms or cuting off heads [as] they have threatened." With the example of France's Reign of Terror fresh in people's minds, the fear of violence may not have been far-fetched.[26]

Foreign policy issues provoked particularly intense responses among women. A state of near war had raged for years on the high seas. In 1807 a particularly troubling incident caused Congress, at Jefferson's behest, to pass the Embargo Law, which put an absolute ban on the export of American goods. As they had during the revolutionary era, Republicans urged Americans to put themselves on a war footing by returning to simple values, forgoing imported luxuries, and becoming economically self-sufficient. By mid-1808, however, the sanctions appeared to be hurting the United States more than Europe. The value of exports plummeted. Goods rotted aboard ships. Harbor life came to a standstill. Internal trade ground to a halt. Federalist New Englanders opposed the policy and agitated for repeal. In Boston harbor all the boats sat tied up at dock, flags at half-mast, with black ribbons of protest flapping in the wind. Not even a pleasure boat could leave.[27]

As men had learned during the Revolution, the support of women for a political boycott could make or break their cause. However, this time the men were bitterly divided. In the propaganda battle Federalist men did little to solicit women's support. Attempting to build popular opposition to the embargo, they sought to convince women to oppose the policy. One antiembargo broadside, for example, featured a woodcut showing a satanic figure, complete with devil's tail, trying to tempt a shapely woman into violating the ban on imported goods. (See Figure 7.) In practice, Federalist women could often do little more than express their dissatisfaction in private. Rosalie Stier Calvert of Maryland lamented the embargo's negative effects on her community: "This embargo is ruining a vast number of people. If it continues for some time yet, the consequences will be incalculable." Her next remark revealed the depths of her Federalist sentiment: "[The Embargo] is going to be the means of effecting a total revolution in popular opinion and of destroying the Democratic party." Some women did more than just talk. In the fall of 1808 a group of women in Augusta, Maine, reportedly marched en masse to the local jail and "liberated several of the prisoners, confined there for breaches of the embargo laws." Federalist women, like Federalist men, used whatever means they had at their disposal to exhibit their opposition to the policy.[28]

On the other side, Republican leaders realized that in order for the embargo to succeed, they needed to enlist women's support. As during

Figure 7. "THE EMBARGO," A New Song—Tune "Yankee Doodle" (1808). The woodcut at the top of this broadside, published during Jefferson's embargo, visually depicts the way in which political parties tried to win women over to their side during times of political controversy. In this image, a satanic figure attempts to lure a woman into violating the ban on importing goods from foreign countries. (Courtesy, American Antiquarian Society.)

the Revolution, they utilized a variety of popular mechanisms to reach out to women, including print media, orations, and personal persuasion. Making the connection between past and present explicit, the men of Orangeburg, South Carolina, urged local women to "emulate the Fair of '76 in domestic manufactures, and in sentiments and deeds of patriotism." Working together, they said, men and women would be able to replicate their earlier collaboration. "Our women," opined the *Richmond Enquirer*, "should all learn to spin, card, weave, dye, and manufacture, in the various modes for flax, hemp, cotton and wool. We may not have open markets abroad for years, and our planters will want the aid of our manufactures to keep up the price of their produce, and to furnish supplies." In many places, Republican women did rally behind the cause. Women in the South appeared in homespun at Independence Day festivities in July 1808. Richmond women mobilized themselves into a volunteer corps to show their support for the troops. Some women made preparations for war. "The Ladies of Norfolk," reported various newspapers, displaying "a patriotism which does them much honour," made cartridges for men's guns. Some even risked their neighbors' wrath. Living in Federalist Massachusetts, Republican Sarah Connell Ayer stood by her Jeffersonian principles and condemned those who opposed the embargo. "Can it be the steady people of Newbury Port, formerly so remarkable for their correct habits, who thus rise up in base sedition against their country?" she asked. People who "ridiculed" the government, she said, "deserve not the title of Americans."[29]

For a variety of reasons, however, the embargo failed to achieve its purpose. American shipping remained exposed to attacks from both the French and the British. Britain, in particular, harassed American commercial ships, confiscating cargo and impressing Americans into the British navy. British troops, stationed illegally on the frontier, were also suspected of instigating Indian attacks on American settlements. By 1812 James Madison and the Republican Party had prepared for a war that Federalists bitterly opposed. Even women and young girls felt the repercussions. "The political animosity existing between the two parties," recalled Julia Hieronymus Tevis, "was bitter beyond expression. . . . It was not an unusual thing to see the girls of our school in battle array on the green common . . . fighting like furies." Sophia May, the daughter of a Federalist congressman living in Washington, described the atmosphere in the nation's capital. "The approach of War which is nearing with rapid strides," she told her sister, "makes us shake. No longer do our homes seem secure to us." Whether Republican or Federalist, women would all feel the effects of a war—especially one fought on American soil.[30]

The War of 1812

The coming of the War of 1812 tested the political convictions of women from both parties. They knew that even though they would not be called to take up arms, war could transform their lives. At best, if their husbands or sons were called to the field of battle, women would bear the burden of caring for farms, families, and businesses on their own. At worst, it meant that their loved ones might be killed or maimed in action. Neither option seemed particularly appealing.

Republican leaders tried to assuage women's fears and cultivate their sense of commitment to the common good. They appealed to women to imitate their predecessors in the American Revolution. Solomon Aiken recalled that during the Revolution it was "the fire of *female patriotism*" that had stimulated men to go off to war. Unwilling to "submit to the degradation of becoming mothers of a progeny of slaves," the women had told their husbands, "Go! Go, under the protection of Heaven, and save our country." Attempting to flatter feminine vanity, Ebenezer French observed, "Our women all know and value the blessings of INDEPENDENCE; value our fathers, who fought for it, and value the sons, who will strive to preserve it." Anthony Haswell beseeched the "matrons" of Bennington, Vermont, to teach their daughters how to inspire military zeal in men, as they had during the Revolution. A woman's opposition might deter a man from enlisting; her vocal support might convince him to join the cause. "Urge then your husbands, your brothers, your sons, and your lovers, to those scenes where danger calls, and glory invites," insisted another speaker. "Bid them rally around the standard of liberty, planted by the hands, and watered by the blood of your fathers." Leaders were not averse to a touch of hyperbole. "Remember," declared Elias Glover, "that no heart can resist the voice of patriotism, when urged by the lips of beauty and innocence."[31]

By reaching out to a female audience, men acknowledged women's continuing political role and influence. The war effort would be successful, they suggested, only if both women and men rallied behind the nation in its time of need. In a poem written in New York and addressed to "the Patriotic Ladies of our Metropolis," one author stressed women's contributions:

> Ye Fair of our city! To you we appeal,
> Whose hearts are not wrapt in a casement of steel;
> Ye who weep o'er the soldier and share in his woe,
> Whose tears for your fond-one in sympathy flow.
>
> .   .   .   .
>
> To the forts on the heights of rough Brooklyn repair,
> And with us the joys of our misery share,

How gladly we'd see you! we'd shout and declare,
"The Hero alone is deserving the fair!"[32]

The function of women was thus twofold: to encourage men to go off to war and to reward them upon their return. In both cases women would provide the secret weapon that would help make victory over the British possible.

The actions of Republican women during the War of 1812 did, in fact, resemble those of their revolutionary predecessors. In Charleston they made shirts; in New York they made socks; in New London they made bedding. Women, however, did not simply do men's bidding. They also undertook activities on their own initiative. Just as Esther DeBerdt Reed led a campaign in Philadelphia during the Revolution to collect money for the Continental Army, so the "ladies" of Frankfort, Kentucky, took it upon themselves in 1812 to take around a "subscription paper" soliciting funds for the troops. A newspaper reported that although "we have not understood what amount was subscribed," a "number of liberal donations [were] received." In October 1814 thirteen New York City women founded the Stocking Society at the home of Mrs. General Lewis. Its purpose was to collect money and donations of wool for "Socks, Mockasins, Mittens, and Cloth Hoods" for American soldiers and the state militia. The printed subscription lists contained the women's call to action: "We whose names are underwritten, having long enjoyed the blessings of peace and national prosperity, and participating also in the calamities of war with which the Almighty has been pleased in infinite wisdom to visit the United States—are desirous, as far as possible of alleviating the sufferings to which our Fathers, Husbands, Brothers, and Friends are exposed in defence of their country." Their creed reflected a sense of mutual participation and shared experience in the fate of the nation. Although the broadside referred to "their"—meaning men's—country, the society's private correspondence spoke of "the future of *our* Country" (emphasis added). A group of women in upstate New York undertook a similar initiative to collect stockings for the troops. As during the Revolution, women were patriotic in a manner befitting their sex.[33]

The Republican press portrayed their women as exemplars of unselfish patriotism who put the national cause above their personal reservations and fears. In 1812 *Niles' Weekly Register* printed the story of Mary Pruitt, wife of John Pruitt of Abbeville District and the mother of two daughters and fourteen (!) sons. When a recruiter came through their community seeking enlistments, two sons decided to volunteer. Although the father hesitated to give his approval, he sent them to ask their mother's opinion. The mother immediately gave them her blessing, saying, "Be virtuous, faithful and honest, and my fears are at an end." The newspapers praised her conduct and admonished readers, "Let those who think lightly of female virtue and patriotism read this and blush for shame." Women's patriotism would provide an inspiration to men.[34]

As the war's reality hit home, women personally experienced its costs. Writing to her friend in Ohio, Mrs. Waldo of Salem, Massachusetts, reported the sad news that a mutual friend had been wounded while serving on the frigate *Constitution* and lost a limb in battle. "Naval victories, and naval feasts," she observed, "are pleasant enough to those who only hear of one, and partake of the other, but are dearly purchased by the actors themselves." Recounting the British invasion of New Orleans, Mary Eliza Williams Chotard, then a teenager, recalled her fears of British depredations as well as bloody slave uprisings. "We all had pieces of gold concealed about our persons in case we should have to run," she observed, but "we asked each other, in what direction could we run? The river was in front and not a boat, the negroes were above and . . . the swamp was back and impenetrable." As the war dragged on, even Republican women had to decide whether they wanted to continue to make the sacrifices required. Writing in her diary in 1813, Hannah Apthorp Bulfinch sadly noted, "War with Great Britain leaves us an unhappy, divided people, many taking part with the mother country, many turning their hearts against her as the cause of all our ills."[35]

Unlike their Republican counterparts, Federalist women did not feel the need to be patriotic do-gooders. They expressed their opposition to the war as much by what they refused to do as in what they said. During the War of 1812 they did not make homespun or darn socks or collect money for the troops. Recalling the summer of 1812, Harriet Livermore, daughter of a Federalist congressman, remembered the period as a "melancholy season. . . . I abhorred the measures adopted by our rulers to secure sailors' rights, and avenge maritime affronts and injuries." Livermore's precise formulation—a war to protect "sailors' rights" and to vindicate "maritime" interests—reflects both her political sophistication as well as her intense partisanship.[36]

Yet even women who opposed the war knew that they too might be asked to sacrifice their husbands or sons for the war effort. Federalist politicians and ministers deliberately fanned the flames of women's resistance to the war. During a sermon Sally Ripley's minister condemned "everyone who contributed the smallest degree of their influence to aid the unjust and unrighteous cause." Ripley voiced her own dissent in her diary. "There are calamities of a private nature and affect only individuals, but we are likewise called to suffer public misfortunes," she wrote. "*War*, with all its horrors, is dislocating our country and ravaging our towns." When the men of her Massachusetts town were drafted in 1814, Ripley reacted with dismay: "Public worship was this forenoon suspended and instead was heard the beating of drums. . . . Many young men are thus called at short warning to leave their homes and families and quiet lives, for the din of war, the bustle of a camp and perhaps the battles' rage." The war had come home, endangering her friends and neighbors. Now she could only pray for a good outcome: "May Jehovah be the God of our Armies and go with our troops whether to the field or to peace."[37]

Partisanship even tinged women's reactions to peace. According to Republican Julia Cabell Rives, in Richmond, the announcement of peace provoked a "universal rejoicing" expressed in "the thunders of innocent artillery, fire-works and illuminations [that] testified to the happiness and contentment of the inhabitants of our cities." However, Sally Ripley sounded a more cautionary note: "Many precious lives have been lost and much treasure wasted while the nation has won nothing but disgrace." Far from fostering unity, the war exacerbated divisions among women as well as men.[38]

Although it has sometimes been called the "Second War for American Independence," the War of 1812 differed profoundly from the American Revolution. The roles, attitudes, and behavior of women during the later conflict demonstrate just how much women's relationship to politics changed within a few short decades. Although many individual women and men had initially opposed independence, the experience of the war itself converted many skeptics or neutrals to the American cause. Many of those who were most bitterly opposed often took decisive action and left the country altogether. By the war's end, a clear majority of Americans favored the cause. No strong internal opposition remained. The winners, the patriots, could then define the collective memory of the American Revolution without facing strong competing myths. Selective in the remembrances, they stressed unity and minimized dissent. They gave women a central role in this myth. As symbols of unity, harmony, and consensus, women came to symbolize what was best about the American people at war: their selflessness, courage, and willingness to sacrifice for the public good. Without them, so the story went, the patriots may not have succeeded against their tyrannical British foes.

It was not possible to construct such a myth about the War of 1812. In contrast to the American Revolution, the later war wrenched the country in two, deepening the cleavage between parties. Although Republican women behaved much as their revolutionary foremothers had, Federalist women did not. They sat out the war or privately opposed it. They found their own ways to resist or dissent. Moreover, an end to war did not mean the end of internal conflict. New Englanders, whose delegates sponsored the Hartford Convention, harbored secessionist impulses. Some Americans doubted whether they wanted to stay within the union's embrace. A legacy of bitterness and suspicion persisted. Thus even after the war ended, there was not—and would not be for many years—a final victory for either Federalists or Republicans. The two factions unhappily coexisted, each claiming to be the true heirs of the American Revolution.

Thinking "with" Women

Despite the animosity between them, Federalists and Republicans shared more in common than either side realized. Members of both parties wished to preserve the existing gender hierarchy in which men were dominant and women subordinate. Neither wished to relinquish their hold on political authority to women. Outside of New Jersey, neither side advocated the cause of female suffrage. This consensus on gender issues revealed itself in the very language that partisans used to discredit and attack one another.

Members of both parties used verbal images of women to disseminate their views and convert people to their side. Newspapers at the time did not pretend to be objective but were, instead, openly partisan. Print functioned as a weapon. In what historian Joanne Freeman has called "political combat,"[39] each side attempted to undermine and malign the opposition. Malicious gossip often substituted for truth. Rumor was employed as much as fact. Anything was fair game, including an opponent's alleged sexual indiscretions, perceived character flaws, or suspected financial improprieties. In these verbal exchanges, partisans used female images and symbols to score points against their adversaries. Although women were not the primary objects of men's attacks, they nonetheless suffered in the process.

The depiction of females, both visually and through words, has a long history. Woman was a symbol, a labile construct capable of being manipulated and appropriated in many ways. Woman could symbolize Eve, the temptress, but she could also be Mary, the chaste mother of God. She could be used as a symbol of vice and excess or the representative of innocence and simplicity. During the American Revolution printers often produced images of America as a bare-breasted woman with a Native American appearance, evoking both the ferocity and the militancy of the American cause. Over time the iconography shifted. The new nation was represented in the female form of the goddess Columbia, in an attempt to link the country with the classical heritage of ancient Greece or Rome.

One of the most common visual images at that time was of "Miss Liberty." The country appeared as a young woman bearing an American flag and, at imes, holding a liberty cap on a pole. (See Figure 8.) Appearing in books, newspapers, magazines, paintings, embroidered textiles, and ceramic objects, this depiction capitalized on the malleability of the female form to create a new icon for representing the depth and vitality of Americans' commitment to freedom. The fact that women themselves did not enjoy the full range of liberties accorded to white males did not deter people from deploying the image for their own purposes.[40] (See Figure 9.)

Women also appeared as symbols in the words that men used in addressing other men. In his discussion of the ancient world in *The Body and Society*, Peter Brown has shown how historians can use anthropological theories to interpret the meaning of feminine imagery from distant times and places. When fifth-century Catholic theologians wrote about certain issues plaguing the early Church, they often employed feminine symbols and metaphors in their writing. These images allowed men to express their ambivalence on certain key points, "to verbalize their own nagging concern with the stance that the Church should take to the world," without being specific in their criticisms. It is important, Brown stresses, not to read these references literally, as evidence of women's actual role or position in society, but as a reflection of male thought processes. According to Brown, "Ancient men tended to regard women as creatures less clearly defined and less securely bounded by the structures that held men in place in society." By appearing to talk about women, men could avoid direct confrontation with other men, especially on controversial or disturbing subjects.[41]

In the early republic, Federalist and Democratic Republican men also used women to "think with." In the heat of verbal combat, members of both parties found that women were a useful tool through which they could attack the opposition and advance their own cause. The particular use that partisans made of women differed according to context. When partisans invoked real women, as opposed to mythical goddesses or symbolic abstractions, they often diverged in their portrayal of the women. In fact, a woman who was a heroine to the Federalists was often a villainess to the Republicans. This was especially true with regard to depictions of women in the French Revolution. Women had played a significant role in events in France. Elite French women had hosted salons, nurtured revolutionary thinkers, and written incendiary political tracts. Through their participation in food riots, the storming of the Bastille, and the march on Versailles, ordinary women had helped bring down the monarchy. As the French Revolution began, Frenchwomen met in debating societies and demanded changes in the laws that oppressed them or kept them in a subordinate legal status.[42]

American partisans, however, were often less interested in the wom-

Figure 8. *Miss Liberty* (c. 1810–20). This image portrays the goddess Liberty as a young woman attired in a style of dress fashionable in the early nineteenth century. In her right hand she carries a palm branch, representing peace, and in her left hand, a liberty pole with a cap and an American flag with sixteen visible stars. (Abby Aldrich Rockefeller Folk Art Museum, The Colonial Williamsburg Foundation, Williamsburg, Virginia. Gift of Abby Aldrich Rockefeller.)

Figure 9. *Columbia Teaching John Bull his new Lesson,* by William Charles (1813). Print on wove paper, etching with watercolor. This print reflects the multiple ways in which images of women could be deployed. Produced to generate support for the War of 1812, the image portrays the United States as Columbia, or Liberty, holding a staff with a liberty cap, browbeating France (represented by Napoleon) and Britain (represented by the symbol of John Bull). (The Library of Congress.)

en's contributions to the French Revolution per se than in how the women's actions confirmed or undermined their own domestic political agenda. Women received very different treatment depending on which party discussed them. Publications that supported the Republicans celebrated women who promoted the ideals of liberty, equality, and fraternity that they both shared. For example, the French noblewoman Madame Genlis was praised because she "always inculcated" the proper revolutionary ideals in her children, family, and friends. These ideals included "that birth was accidental, hereditary distinction transitory, and that the only things which a good man can deem certain, are his knowledge and his virtues." Federalists, of course, had a different point of view. For them, Genlis represented a threat to the existing social order, a woman whose actions contributed to the Revolution's turmoil. Each side also portrayed the fate of Marie Antoinette, the French queen who was executed along with her husband and family, in disparate terms. Republicans, though they objected to the bloodshed, sympathized with the principle behind the event. In contrast, Federalists mourned the loss of the royal family and bemoaned the fate of the "beautiful" Marie Antoinette who simply performed the role allotted to her. One Federalist publication described in excruciating detail how the queen was "dragged from [her] solitary cell to answer before the revolutionary tribunal. . . . Surrounded with barbarians, wretches rejoice[d] in her calamity and insult[ed] her sorrow. With what affecting propriety might this unfortunate Queen adopt the pathetic complaint of Job?" Without proper safeguards, it was suggested, these democratic excesses might afflict the United States as well.[43]

In other cases, too, real women came to embody significantly different notions to each of the two political parties. During the late 1790s the husband of Deborah Logan, Dr. George Logan, made his way to France and attempted to negotiate directly with French officials in an effort to avoid war. Both the Philadelphia man and his wife soon became fodder for the press. Republicans celebrated George Logan for his initiative and principled support of the public good. Federalists, on the other hand, criticized the fact that a private citizen was meddling in high-level diplomatic affairs and, not incidentally, undermining the Federalist case for war. During the many months while her husband was away, Deborah Logan faced intense scrutiny from the press. When Vice President Thomas Jefferson offered her his support, Federalists immediately circulated rumors of an illicit sexual liaison between the two. "It is said that JEFFERSON went to his friend Doctor Logan's farm and spent three days there, soon after the Doctor's departure for France. *Query:* What did he do there? Was it to arrange the Doctor's *valuable manuscripts?*" Other Federalist publications jumped on the rumors and embellished their salacious content, recognizing in Deborah a vulnerable target for their partisan hostilities. In response, Republican papers rose to her defense. They compared Deborah favorably with the heroines of the French Revolution, especially Madame Roland, who suffered execution during the Terror, in part because of her husband's political activities. The same woman, then, received vastly different treatment at the hands of the competing parties.[44]

One particular woman attracted more attention, and generated more scorn, than any other: Mary Wollstonecraft. Depending on their differing partisan agendas, each party had different reasons for reviling her. Republicans tended to object to Wollstonecraft's personal vice or immorality, lambasting her for her illicit love affairs and for her flouting of contemporary standards of respectability. For Federalists, however, Wollstonecraft's immorality merely confirmed the deeper and more troubling aspects of her ideas. Her sin was not only to challenge the gender status quo but to assault the existing social and political order.

Two years after publishing *A Vindication of the Rights of Woman,* and in response to Edmund Burke's denunciation of the French Revolution, Wollstonecraft traveled to France to witness the event herself. She then published a book that portrayed events there in a favorable light. For Wollstonecraft, France represented a symbol of hope, a place that proved that western Europe might well be able to throw off the dead hand of the past and claim a democratic legacy for itself. Her views were shared by a circle of political radicals with whom she associated in England, including the philosopher William Godwin, whose anti-author-itarianism verged on anarchy, and the writer Thomas Paine, who authored the notorious *Rights of Man* and *The Age of Reason.*

Wollstonecraft's views did not sit well with conservatives on either side of the Atlantic. A 108-line poem satirically called "'The Enlightened Eighteenth Century': or, 'The Age of Reason,'" published numerous times in the United States and in Britain, attacked Wollstonecraft as much for her political radicalism as for her support of women's rights. Portraying her and her colleagues as seditious, the author equated their views with treason:

Though logical Godwin new morals may preach,
That ends sanctify means—though he artfully teach,
The world still call, a robber, a knave
And his lecherous Mary of passion the slave.
In this virtuous age though traitors abound,
And Barlows and Paines are scattered around,
Still treason retains both its vice and its name,
And is punished with halters, with scorn, and with shame.

Thus although Wollstonecraft was deemed "lecherous," she shared in the same "vice and shame" as her male cohorts. Still, because she was a woman, she gained special infamy. Her ideas not only threatened the social order that legitimated Federalist rule; they also, according to a Federalist newspaper, "directly or indirectly attack the institutions and maxims of all well-regulated society." Federalists saw Wollstonecraft as a true revolutionary whose incendiary ideas must be thwarted.[45]

Whatever the discrepancies in the ways Federalists and Republicans portrayed actual women, they shared a great deal in common when it came to using women as symbols and metaphors. Unlike real women who had a contemporary political resonance, feminine imagery had a more abstract quality. In these cases the differences between the parties disappeared. Both Republicans and Federalists drew on the same set of

assumptions about gender relations and the same conventional stereotypes about women. These images often reinforced the most negative or
traditional perceptions about women's rights, roles, and responsibilities.

A common belief in female inferiority or foolishness provided a convenient means for political partisans to satirize the opposition. A Republican magazine ridiculed the Jay Treaty of 1795 by asking, "Is it not
probable that we should have obtained better terms in a certain treaty,
had not some WIDOW been appointed to negociate it, instead of an
extraordinary MALE minister?" The absurdity of the proposition seemed
self-evident: even a woman could have produced a better treaty than the
actual negotiator, John Jay, had. Other authors used the silliness of wom-
en's fashions to score political points. A Federalist periodical, *Port Folio*,
published a letter purportedly from a woman calling herself "Sacah-
rissa," who blamed the twin evils of the day, Jacobinism and revolution,
for changes in women's dress: "What, comparing great things to small,
can be more like to the casting off a hoop, than a national revolution?"
As she saw it, both situations created a shift "from a state of dignified
decency to wanton nakedness," the result of "a silly seeking after
change." In conclusion, she suggested that if women reformed their
manner of dressing, "then may we expect stability in governments, as
well as in female conduct." Republicans, it seemed, were nothing more
than frivolous women who changed governments as casually as women
changed fashions. In another article called "Gun Boat," Federalists
taunted the Jeffersonian policy that drastically reduced the size of the
American navy and delegated responsibility for maritime defense to a
small contingent of gunboats patrolling the shore. The piece pointed
out three supposed similarities between women's bonnets and Jefferson's strategy: both cost more than they were worth; both could navigate
only "shoal waters"; and both were "calculated to make a mere shew of
defence . . . while in fact they invite aggression." Once again, negative
female stereotypes provided the means of attacking political adversaries.
Although the primary point was to criticize the opposition, the pieces
denigrated and patronized women in the process.[46]

Each party also invoked conventional notions of feminine helplessness and masculine power to buttress its position on a particular issue.
During the debate over the embargo of 1807–8, a Federalist broadside
opposed the boycott by highlighting women's supposed disaffection
with Jefferson's policy:

> Thus Tommy destroys,
>   A part of our joys;
> Yet we'll not let the beautiful Fair go;
>   They all will contrive

> To keep commerce alive,
> There's nothing they hate like Embargo.[47]

As women's valiant protectors ("we'll not let the beautiful Fair go"), Federalist men claimed to have won the support of women who "hate[d]" the embargo and kept "commerce alive" by rejecting the nefarious policy. Republicans, however, also used female imagery to validate their claims. Disparaging the opposition's contentions, their broadside maintained,

> Thus Tommy destroys intriguers' chief joys;
>   But to ruin will not let the Fair go;
> For he will secure, our damsels so pure,
>   By keeping off rogues with EMBARGO.[48]

Whereas Federalist "intriguers" would allow "rogues" to prey on American women, Republicans would protect their purity through enforcement of the ban. They were the true guardians of American womanhood. In an effort to garner support, both parties reverted to conventional images of women as hapless damsels in distress in order to provoke sympathy for their causes.

Authors also drew on notions of female helplessness to urge men to come to the aid of their country. As war with England approached in 1812, Republicans tried to generate prowar sentiment by issuing a broadside, sung to the tune of "The World Turn'd Upside Down," that proclaimed:

> Look on our *wives* and *infants*, who piously *implore*,
> To be preserv'd from blood hounds, who now infest our shores,
> Let not those helpless *innocents* become the lawless prey,
> Of *English Wolves*, and *Indian Dogs* who *distress America* today.[49]

In this view, women and infants were categorized together as "helpless innocents." Only if men rallied to the cause and asserted their masculine prowess might the "lawless prey" who "now infest our shores" be defeated. Masculine martial ardor would protect Americans in distress.

Women, however, were not always portrayed as helpless victims. When it was convenient, members of both parties portrayed images of masculinized women in order to shame or intimidate the opposition. Drawing on fears of gender inversion, authors used the prospect of women in arms as a way of goading men to war. In 1791 Quakers and Republicans in Congress resisted Federalist proposals to increase defense appropriations and organize state militias. A fictitious letter to the editor in the

Philadelphia General Advertiser reported a conversation among several women about the matter. Disparaging the country's supposedly timid male population, one woman made a startling proposition. "Let us boldly declare," said Maria, "that we will never marry a man who cannot, in case of need, protect us and our children." Another woman made a similar threat. "I anticipate the glorious day," Thalestris declared, "when American ladies shall be Commanders, Presidents of Congress, Ambassadors, Governors, Secretaries of State, Professors, Judges, [and] Preachers." In other words, if the men did not act, then women would usurp their roles. The prospect of women in arms would shame men into defending their country.[50]

A few days later the *General Advertiser* published a related article, "The humble Address of ten thousand Federal Maids." Disappointed by men's failure to defend their country, these women ostensibly petitioned Congress for the power to act in their stead. "If our young men will not learn how to defend their liberty and property, . . . —then order us into the field," the petition said. "We shrink indeed from violence; some of us cannot without pain kill a chicken: But alas! The sword is yet in this civilized era, the ultima ratio. . . . This land of liberty must be defended against foreign and domestic foes."[51] A similar strategy was employed during the War of 1812. If men's "valor be slack," then women would take over men's role and do the job themselves:

> We'll the breeches assume, upon my honor tis true,
> So determine maids, widows, and wives,
> First we'll march, beat the foe, then march back
>   and beat you,
> Aye, and wear 'em the rest of our lives.[52]

The message was clear: any man who refused to take up arms would be considered a cuckold and a coward.

Both Republicans and Federalists assumed without question that in defending their country, men defended their masculinity. The literary critic Dana Nelson has called this idea "national manhood," a collective notion that defined manliness "in national terms, as national power." Originating in the period after the American Revolution, this construct "promised redress for men's various anxieties in a nostalgically configured fantasy of powerful manhood, revivified and certified through its attachment to national strength, unity, and economic expansion."[53] By extension, then, the failure to take up arms emasculated a man and stripped him of his superior place in the gender hierarchy. Yet appeals to national manhood had a downside for women. They depended for their power on the belief that no one could possibly want women to take up arms. Even if it were true, this assumption reinforced conventional gender roles and undercut women's potential claim to equality. In the heat of partisan battle, women's strength became a liability.

Both parties also used sexual imagery to characterize themselves or the opposition. Federalists portrayed the opposition as a threat to the sexual purity of American women. Inveighing against the immoral and antireligious Republicans, James Hopkins maintained that their "lawless passion and unbridled licentiousness" would affront "our sisters, our wives, and daughters." A Federalist magazine in South Carolina described one of its goals as preserving women from the "pursuits of the atheists, and jacobin-spoilers of the present day," whose presence ushered in all kinds of violations. Republicans, they said, were "incessantly labouring, by every artifice, and with the most unblushing audacity, to turn [women] over, as poor, wretched forlorn victims,—to shame, and remorse, and anguish, and tribulation, and barren sorrow, and irretrievable destitution." The implication was clear: if Republicans would defile and defame women, Federalists would rescue them. But a further implication was also apparent: women needed to be rescued.[54]

Yet the obverse was also argued. If women appeared as sexual innocents, they could also be cast as the opposite: licentious whores. Each party maligned the other by using images of women's lewdness and sexual promiscuity. An 1807 Federalist tract called *The Echo*, for example, featured in its opening pages a caricature labeled "Infant Liberty nursed by Mother Mob." (See Figure 10.) The picture shows a grotesque mother figure, whose breasts bear the words "whiskey" and "rum," suckling a young infant, with a barrel of spirits poised nearby. A winged figure is setting fire to law books. In the background is a reference to the French Revolution, a mob tearing down the Bastille. Obviously, the image implied that the Republicans gained their much-vaunted popularity by bribing the voters and plying them with liquor. Liberty was nothing more than a function of licentious behavior, leading to rioting and anarchy. The accompanying poem reinforced the sexual innuendo. It coyly mentioned rumors of

Congress-men, and Congress-Women too,
Their private bargains, and their party leagues,
Their public brothels, and their sly intrigues,
Their assignations, and their tricks at play,
Their debts of honour, paid in honour's way.
For neither station, title, rank, nor place,
Should screen a public robber from disgrace;
But round his steps let injur'd Justice bawl,
And on his head a nation's curses fall.[55]

Figure 10. *Infant Liberty nursed by Mother Mob*, drawn by Elkaneh Tisdale, engraved by William S. Leney (1807–8). This image, drawn by a Federalist supporter, satirizes the Democratic Republican Party by using female imagery. A grotesque mother figure feeds her infant with whiskey and rum; a winged figure burns statute books; and a mob in the background tears down the Bastille in France. (The Library of Congress.)

Republicans gave as good as they got. They too employed misogynistic images for their own purposes. In a satirical poem called *The Genius of Federalism*, published in 1813, Henry Bliss portrayed the New England states as a group of "loving federal sisters" who have "lately grown insane," maintaining their faith in federalism "Against the light of common sense." Bliss employed an array of negative stereotypes about women in order to mount his critique:

> Behold, her Ladyship CONNECTICUT,
> Stript naked to her under-petticoat,
>   A thin and slazy kind of frieze,
> Which in those seasons shew'd her knees,
> And which so humble she could get on,
> Through homage due to mother Britain![56]

By linking Federalists with women's nakedness, underwear, and lack of modesty, Republicans cast Federalists as the whores of Great Britain.

Like a certain kind of woman, Federalists should be nothing more than the objects of derision and contempt.

Whatever the disagreements between Republicans and Federalists on matters of policy, ideology, and governance, members of both parties drew on a common store of assumptions about women and gender roles. In their political propaganda, partisans appealed to other men using a gendered imagery that magnified the power of their message and gave invectives more bite. Women were portrayed as masculinized threats who might usurp men's power or place. At the same time women were depicted as helpless victims or pawns who seemed incapable of political thought, much less political action. Misogynistic beliefs transcended the partisan divide. All men, it was presumed, would be susceptible to the cries of a helpless female. No man would allow a woman to shame or blame him. Even if a man were uncertain about his politics, he knew how he felt about tramps and whores. Contradictory as those images might be, they all reinforced the same conventional, negative stereotypes about women at the time.

Stereotypical depictions of female helplessness, sluttishness, passivity, or inferiority served to undermine some of the American Revolution's transformative potential for women. Partisan rhetoric demeaned women and diminished their stature. In a discussion of twentieth-century Iran, the historian Joanna De Groot notes that differences between men's political positions can be less significant for women than the language within which they are expressed. A discourse can "simultaneously entwin[e] gender at the core of political language and marginaliz[e] the expression of women's autonomous interests."[57] The verbal combat between Federalists and Republicans did just that. Gendered imagery advanced men's interests, not those of women. Although women were not the primary targets, they nonetheless suffered from collateral damage.

Although the emergence of the Federalist and Democratic-Republican Parties was unexpected and unwelcome, the development seemed to offer women new opportunities to involve themselves in politics. Building on revolutionary-era patterns, women made homespun, boycotted goods, and attended public gatherings in support of their chosen political causes. As "female politicians," they asserted their political opinions and made choices of everything from servants to spouses based on their party affiliations. Male partisans courted women's political support and welcomed their attention to party causes and events.

The bitterness of party conflict complicated the scenario. After Jefferson's election in 1800 and through the War of 1812, both parties remained in place, clinging to their positions and locked in mortal combat. This divisiveness raised troubling questions about the wisdom of women's politicization. Women's political activities exacerbated and intensified the existing tensions between men. In an era in which the very existence of parties was suspect, women's approval had conferred moral sanction on men's activities. Now women were as complicitous as men in supporting factionalism. Although women had once been seen as trump cards, proving the superiority of one side over the other, now they were Jokers, laughing reminders that neither side could claim absolute moral or political authority.

Chapter 4

Women and the "War of Politics"

As she reflected back on her life, Catharine Maria Sedgwick recalled the trials and tribulations of growing up as the daughter of a Federalist congressman. She remembered the 1790s as a time when party feelings divided towns, dissolved friendships, and pitted neighbor against neighbor. At home she witnessed the battle firsthand. Partisan antagonisms wrenched her Massachusetts community in two. Her father, whom she believed to be "one of the kindest-hearted of men," was also a vehement partisan. True to his Federalist sentiments, he contemptuously referred to "the people" as the "greasy, unwashed multitude" or the "miscreants."[1] From her window she could see the town horse, Clover, "converted into a political instrument." As he trudged up a big hill each day he became "a walking gazette," carrying a placard with Federalist slogans. Strolling back down to the valley, he returned with the "militant missives" of the Democratic Republicans covering his "ragged and grizzled sides."[2]

From the vantage point of 1835, however, what seemed most remarkable to Sedgwick was the degree to which women had participated in the melee. Women had been full and active participants in the party battles. At church, Federalist women proudly displayed symbols of their party affiliation, wearing golden eagles on their dresses or bonnets. Partisanship influenced personal friendships and private passions. Sedgwick's friend Fanny Atwood nearly failed to marry the love of her life—not because of his personal failings or lack of economic prospects but because he happened to belong to the "wrong" political party. While her family was staunchly Federalist, he was a Democratic Republican. Sedgwick marveled at the depth of these hostilities, especially among women. "I now look," she said, "almost unbelieving of my own recollections, at the general diffusion of political prejudices of those times. No age nor sex was exempt from them." Women, men, and unsuspecting horses were all enlisted in the battle between parties.[3]

After Jefferson's election in 1800, it was clear that party conflict would not end anytime soon. The rise of party politics not only undermined the country's political unity but destroyed its social cohesion as well.

Hostilities were so deep that passion replaced rationality in public and private discourse. People stopped speaking to friends and neighbors. Communities divided in two. Even families split apart. "Soon the most intimate ties of relationship were sundered. The political contagion operated like the contagion of the plague in Athens. The father forsook the son and the son forsook the father." Instead of being a refuge from the outside world, the home became another arena for tumultuous disputation and partisan wrangling.[4]

In this environment women's continuing involvement in politics intensified social tensions and deepened the split between Federalists and Republicans. Although male politicians continued to invite women to support their causes, the prescriptive literature of the day began to convey a different message. A new discourse arose urging women to withdraw from party politics. Using their roles as wife and mother, they could act as peacemakers and mediators between warring factions of men. Deploying their feminine traits strategically, they could instill a spirit of political toleration and openness to debate in their husbands and children. Instead of acting as partisans, they would become impartial patriots. As early as the Panic of 1819, the message seemed to be having an impact.

Parties and the Spirit of Violence

American men and women feared political parties not only because of their effect on government but also because of their influence on society. Parties destroyed sociability—the sense of comity, civility, and cooperation that made union possible. Unlike European nations whose inhabitants shared a long history and common traditions, the United States was a new nation, a heterogeneous society whose government was far off and at a distance. Differing economic interests, religious differences, and regional loyalties all threatened to tear the nation apart. The country's success depended not only on a commitment to shared political principles but also on a spirit of mutual affection and cooperation that would overcome these differences. Party conflict eroded the fragile bonds linking families into communities, communities into states, and states into a nation.

The existence of political parties affected social relations as well as political affairs. "Every social feeling, every generous emotion, every noble sentiment," noted one commentator, "is usually sacrificed on the altar of *Party Spirit*." The spirit of parties, observed another, is "the spirit of violence." Party spirit did, in fact, produce an atmosphere of violence in early American political life, permeating every aspect of people's daily lives. It was not unusual, for example, for taverns, shops, and churches in New England to cater to either Federalists or Republicans—but not to both. In Hingham, Massachusetts, Federalists and Republicans sailed on different ferries to Boston. Some individuals preferred to sleep overnight on the dock rather than share the voyage with their political adversaries. People affiliated with others who shared their political beliefs. The membership of the Society of the Cincinnati, composed of former Revolutionary War officers, and the Washington Benevolent Society both became Federalist strongholds, while the Tammany Society and various artisan and mechanic groups allied themselves with the Republicans.[5]

Not only did members of different parties avoid one another, but they often cut their existing ties with individuals who held opposing views. In Federalist-dominated Philadelphia, noted Deborah Logan, "Friendships were dissolved, tradesmen dismissed, and custom withdrawn from the Republican party." Thomas Jefferson observed with concern, "Men who had been intimate all their lives cross the streets to avoid meeting, and turn their heads another way, lest they should be obliged to touch their hats." Recalling his boyhood in Salem, Massachusetts, where his family belonged to the minority Republican Party, future Supreme Court justice Joseph Story remarked, "The lines of distinction were drawn with even personal animosity, and there was almost no social intercourse between those who differed in politics." As one Georgia woman sadly concluded, "The rage of party & the storm of politics . . . are unfriendly both to Religion and Friendship."[6]

Women's involvement further complicated matters by bringing party conflict into that most sacred refuge, the home. Looking back from a later time, one commentator recalled that partisanship had "infected all classes of society and so mingled the bitter waters of strife with the closest relations of civil and domestic life, that some of its aspersions stained, for a moment, the pure candor, even of the gentle sex." If women were active partisans, the home became a battleground. "I have heard, and seen families divided and torn asunder by female interference in politics," noted an article reprinted several times in popular periodicals. "Husbands have forsaken their homes; parents and children have clashed, and wounded one another." Minister Solomon Aiken of New Hampshire warned of the dire consequences: "The father is against the son, the son against the father, and the mother against the daughter, and the daughter against the mother." No place seemed safe from the deleterious effects of party spirit.[7]

At its most extreme, partisanship produced actual physical altercations. Violence erupted in Congress, at local elections, and in the streets. Politicians settled their disputes through violence rather than with words. In 1794 during a heated congressional election in Virginia, it was said that one candidate, the Federalist Capt. Francis Preston, intimidated his opponent's supporters. He marched seventy federal troops to the polling place and threatened to harm anyone who did not vote for him. Not surprisingly, Preston won the election—though by a smaller margin than he might have expected. When Preston's opponent contested the election, one of the congressional investigators excused Preston on the grounds that such incidents were not unusual. The committee member reported that at another member's election a riot had occurred. "[S]till worse," he said, "this riot was in a church; [and] was raised by a magistrate who with his own hand dragged one of the opposite party out of the church."[8]

Violence erupted even in the halls of Congress. In an infamous case occurring in 1798, Republican Matthew Lyon responded to an insult from Federalist congressman Roger Griswold by spitting on him. After the House failed to expel Lyon, Griswold returned to the Capitol several days later brandishing a stout club. When Lyon grabbed a pair of fire tongs to defend himself, the two men fell into a pitched battle, bludgeoning each other on the House floor until they were wedged apart. In this atmosphere the Madisonian belief in governing by consensus seemed not only a distant ideal but also a nearly unattainable pipe dream.[9] (See Figure 11.)

The situation was no better outside the capital. Party differences could erupt into violence at any moment. In Philadelphia, Deborah Logan, wife of a politically active doctor, reported, "Many gentlemen went armed that they might be ready to resent any personal transgression." On a Boston street in 1806, Republican Charles Austin physically assaulted a Federalist lawyer whom he believed had slandered his father. Austin himself was then shot dead. In 1808 James Pettigru of South Carolina silently bore the taunts of a political adversary. When he was called "a damned Federal," he could restrain himself no longer. He lashed out and decked his opponent. In Georgia, Catherine Few, wife of former congressman William Few, reported that she as well as her husband felt in constant physical danger from their political enemies. Her husband, she reported, "never left me [in the house] without weapons of defence, owing to a political quarrel with a person of this State." In this context, the Burr-Hamilton duel of 1804, in which Aaron Burr mortally wounded Alexander Hamilton, represented but one example of a more extensive pattern of physical violence that plagued political relations between Federalists and Republicans in the early national period. Yet by resorting to violence, lawmakers endangered the very rule of law itself.[10]

The social crisis was a political crisis as well. Newspapers, magazines, and public orators lamented the disastrous effects of party spirit on both

Figure 11. *Congressional Pugilists* (1798). This etching illustrates a fight that occurred in 1798 on the floor of the House of Representatives between Matthew Lyon of Vermont and Roger Griswold of Connecticut. Griswold insulted Lyon, suggesting that he was a coward, and Lyon spit in Griswold's face. Several days later Griswold attempted to beat Lyon with a club; Lyon responded by using fireplace tongs as a weapon. The episode is an extreme example of the partisan violence that recurred throughout the 1790s. (The Library of Congress.)

society and government. "Party animosity," observed one commentator, "swallows every social feeling. Neighbour looks at neighbour as an enemy . . . and each man regards his friend with a jealous eye." Lest the reader suspect exaggeration, the writer added, "Every man now conversant with society will bear witness that the above representation is *literally true.*" The breakdown in social trust made political cooperation nearly impossible. "By its defoliating waves," said another commentator, "social intercourse has been driven from our houses—friends have been estranged—families divided— . . . [and] our government threatened with ruin." No longer did a spirit of amity overcome differences. According to a Virginia newspaper, the country's atmosphere seemed like nothing so much as a domestic "war of politics."[11]

The decay of sociability threatened to rend the union apart. Mutual suspicions undermined the trust necessary for government to function. During the embargo of 1807–8, Rosalie Stier Calvert of Maryland reported, "People talk openly of dissolving the union of states, as we fear, they continue with the present political system, that time is not far away." Each party claimed that the other's policies arose not out of mistakes or misunderstanding, but out of evil and seditious intentions. "Between these two great parties," maintained another observer, "there exists an asperity, which . . . will inevitably terminate in a civil war." As the War of 1812 approached, southerners felt increasingly defiant, while New Englanders felt increasingly betrayed by the rest of the country. As one newspaper warned, "[There is] no union among our citizens, except in the belief of this one solemn truth, that our disunion will soon put an end to our liberties." During the war itself, the Hartford Convention of 1814, with its purported plans of New England secession, seemed to confirm people's worst fears. Only Andrew Jackson's victory at New Orleans and the coming of peace alleviated the immediate threat. The damage, however, had been done. Party conflict had undermined the delicate bonds uniting the country into a single nation. Americans not only lost confidence in their rulers but, according to a Connecticut newspaper, had also lost "all confidence in each other." If "*social society* is destroyed," warned the paper, "we are undone." Fragmentation seemed imminent.[12]

Political Religion

One reason that partisanship was so divisive was that neither side recognized the legitimacy of the other's existence. Each party considered itself to be the rightful heir of the American Revolution and the sole possessor of the true method of governance. In fact, many partisans viewed their party allegiance in the same terms as they did their religious beliefs. Just as established religions once claimed to have a monopoly on religious truth, so too did each party believe it had a monopoly on political truth. As in the battle over religion, both parties saw themselves as the defenders of the one true faith. "Truth," as John Taylor put it in his 1794 work *Definition of Parties*, "is a thing, not of divisibility into conflicting parts, but of unity. Hence both sides cannot be right."[13]

American men and women routinely used religious images and metaphors in discussing politics. People talked about their "political creed," with each party advancing certain well-defined, unquestioned doctrines. Those who switched parties were called "converts" by their new comrades and were derided as "apostates" by their former colleagues. Children were indoctrinated using "catechisms," such as Elhanan Winchester's

Plain Political Catechism intended for the Use of Schools, in the United States of America, or Hezekiah Packard's *Political Catechism, Designed to Lead Children into the Knowledge of Society and to train them to the Duties of Citizens.* Recalling her childhood upbringing, Catharine Maria Sedgwick commented that she had "been bred, according to the strictest sect of my political religion, a federalist." Thomas Jefferson, who was usually cagey about his personal religious convictions, was much more open about his politics; he believed that his views represented "the true faith." Similarly, a Pennsylvanian maintained that his political principles were as "sacred" as his religious beliefs: "Are we not, each of us, federalist, just as we are a christian, or a man of morality, from the thorough conviction of the truth and rectitude of the fundamental elements of our faith?"[14]

As long as party differences were cast in semireligious terms as disputes over truth, disagreements were never simply a matter of differing opinions. They were, instead, a contest for the nation's "political salvation." As Minister Solomon Aiken saw it, "There is a rooted enmity between modern Federalism and Republicanism. They are totally opposite in principle." It was as dangerous for people of differing political views to "mingle," he claimed, as it was "for the Jews with the Heathen." Party members embraced their views with a religious zeal. "In matters of conscience, and on questions of principle, there are not half-way measures. There are but a right and a wrong. . . . There can be no communication where the touch is pollution." As long as dissent was considered a kind of political heresy, then, party conflict was tantamount to holy war.[15]

As in a war of religion, each party claimed that the other's policies arose not out of mistakes or misunderstanding but out of evil and seditious intent. In a 1798 sermon the Reverend Holloway Hunt accused the Democratic Republicans of having fallen under the influence of the atheistical and murdering French. These "deluded Americans," he said, had become "traitors to [their] country." Unless freed of this scourge, the whole country would "fall by party faction." Republicans portrayed their opponents in similarly apocalyptic terms. Writing in 1808, "Aristides" warned the citizens of Maryland, "Federalism is leading you blindfolded to the edge of a precipice; it is lulling you to sleep with the soporific potions of delusion." Pointing to the Federalists' attacks on civil liberties, he declaimed, "Citizens tear the bandage from your eyes; awake from your slumbers, or to you it will be the sleep of death." Under such terms, compromise and reconciliation seemed not only unlikely but also nearly impossible.[16]

Jefferson's election in 1800 inaugurated a new phase of partisan warfare. In his first inaugural address, the third president made an ostensible gesture of conciliation, famously stating, "Every difference of opinion is not a difference of principle. We have called by different names brethren of the same principle. We are all republicans; we are all federalists." However, as various historians have noted, Jefferson did not intend to suggest that Federalist views were as valid as those of his own party. Although conceding that both parties shared a common commitment to the "same principle" of a republican form of government, Jefferson continued to believe that in time Federalists would come around to his vision, merge into his party, and disappear from the nation's political life. His was a vision of total victory, not of accommodation.[17]

The pernicious effects of party conflict lingered beyond the War of 1812 and into the so-called "Era of Good Feelings." After Jefferson's election, although the Federalists entered into a long period of decline, the party did not disappear for many years. As late as 1819 a Pennsylvanian noted that "party spirit" still remained "the dark cloud on our political horizon." In that same year a report from Baltimore noted that the "rancour" of party spirit marred the city's annual Fourth of July festivities, "so that the day which ought to be commemorated with all the cordial and benevolent feelings, is too often sacrificed to party spite and resentment." In 1820 Massachusetts citizens gave a toast to "party spirit," noting, "Though its extinction can never be expected—May it never rage so as to disturb domestic happiness, or endanger our national existence." In many localities conflict between Federalists and Republicans continued unabated into the 1820s. With their legitimacy suspect, political parties continued to be seen as necessary evils, not as positive goods. Only in the 1830s, according to historians, would a more salutary conception emerge. In the interim, however, members of both parties would have to find a way to coexist without destroying their families, their communities, or their country in the process.[18]

What was needed was a change in the terms of the debate. Instead of casting politics as a semireligious debate about truth, it would be preferable to see the subject as a dispute among reasonable people who disagreed. What might be called a "liberal" view of party conflict began to emerge. It is important to understand the meaning of "liberal" as used in this context. In the late eighteenth and early nineteenth centuries, "liberal" did not stand in opposition to "conservative" or refer to a progressive stance on the political issues of the day. Rather, "liberal" had a meaning closer to its Latin root of *libertas*, or "free." "Liberality" implied a lack of prejudice, an open-minded willingness to consider the views of others, a mindset, as one Virginian put it, free "from vulgar prejudices and unmanly bigotry." Enlightenment thinkers applied the notion of liberality to a wide range of areas, including government, religion, and trade. A commitment to liberality, in this sense, was often considered the hallmark of an educated mind.[19]

A liberal approach to party politics, then, referred to an openness toward and toleration of opposing political viewpoints. The 1798 play *Politicians; or, A State of Things* criticized the corrosive effects of party sentiment on American society. One of the main characters, aptly named "Conciliate," articulated his solution in these terms. He urged men and women to be "as liberal in politics as religion." The key to this liberality, as other commentators made clear, was to restore a sense of civility to public discourse. Although individuals might disagree about politics, even vehemently, they should treat each other with mutual respect. The purpose of political discussion, emphasized one author, should be "to get information, not to make converts to our opinions of men and things." People should be able to air their views freely, without fear of physical or verbal intimidation. Addressing his fellow congressmen, William Gaston of North Carolina urged politicians to "uphold your measures by the force of argument, not of denunciation. Stigmatize not opposition to your notions with offensive epithets. These prove nothing but your anger or your weakness." Mason Locke Weems, known more for his mythical treatment of George Washington's life than for his views on party conflict, expressed similar concerns. Encouraging "Honest Adamites and Jeffersonians" in Virginia to find common ground, he insisted that partisans should "honor all men, yes, even those who differ from us in political sentiments. They may love their country as dearly as we do, and may with equal sincerity, be aiming at her best interests, tho' they do not approve of the same means." The stakes were high. According to the author of a treatise pleading for reconciliation between parties, the recognition that there were "faults on both sides, Federal and Democratic," would lead to "mutual forgiveness and harmony" and "save our common country from ruin." A more congenial social and political atmosphere would result.[20]

American liberality in religion helped make the case for liberality in politics. If people accepted political differences as a matter of opinion rather than a dispute over fundamental truth, then reason would replace passion in public debate. Just as religious toleration had led to peaceful coexistence among competing religious sects, so, too, would political toleration allow greater cooperation between parties. Coming on the heels of the divisive War of 1812, James Monroe's presidency was often portrayed as an example of this new liberal sentiment in action. In 1817, soon after assuming office, Monroe undertook an extensive journey across the country, visiting states up and down the eastern seaboard as well as in the interior. Consciously imitating Washington's earlier visitations, Monroe meant his expedition to heal the partisan wounds left by the war and reaffirm the country's essential unity. In a book describing the trip, the author Samuel Putnam Waldo acknowledged Monroe's success and in the process articulated a more expansive

understanding of party conflict. Acknowledging the continuing existence of opposing political ideas, he noted that the disappearance of
such diversity was unlikely anytime soon. "An entire union of sentiment,
upon *political* subjects," he commented, "is not to be expected among a
people who think for themselves, read for themselves, and act for themselves." Americans knew too much and were too independent to think
exactly alike on political matters. As a result, people would, at least for
the foreseeable future, continue to form divergent political parties.[21]

Yet the existence of parties, Waldo insisted, need not necessarily be
a source of constant upheaval and division. Waldo quoted (somewhat
imprecisely) the words of the Virginia Statute of Religious Liberty. Written by Thomas Jefferson and passed by the Virginia legislature in 1786
with the assistance of James Madison, the document provided not just
for religious toleration but also for complete freedom of conscience, for
nonbelievers and believers alike. This statute characterized religious
belief as an opinion, subject to debate and contestation, rather than as
an absolute truth, which had to be taken on faith and could not be questioned. While there might be only one truth, there could be many different opinions. Waldo foresaw the same shift occurring in politics: "That
erroneous opinions" in politics "*may* be adopted is without a question;
but '*errors of opinion will never become dangerous, as long as reason is left free
to combat them.*'" Significantly, Waldo did not assume, as many Americans
would within a few decades, that all parties had equally valid points of
view. Rather, he suggested that if partisans expressed their political opinions freely and subjected them to scrutiny and debate, then erroneous
ideas (presumably those of Federalists) would be discredited and the
correct notions (presumably those of Republicans) would prevail. All
political opinions were not equal. In the meantime, however, both sides
would treat each other with respect, dignity, and toleration.[22]

The liberal view of party politics echoed the most progressive attitudes
toward religious freedom of the time and projected those ideas onto the
political realm. This ideal offered a reasonable hope for rescuing American society from the ravages of party conflict and restoring civility to
public life. If American women and men expressed the same attitudes
toward political differences as they did toward religious diversity, then
competing political factions would be able to coexist without tearing the
country apart. Republicans and Federalists might disagree with one
another without coming to blows. Politics could stop being a matter of
faith and start becoming a matter of public policy.

Female Influence

As the contours of the liberal approach to party conflict took shape,
indications suggested that men may not be the best individuals to dis-

seminate the new ideal. Male political leaders had lost the faculty for calm and rational deliberation. Party "passions and prejudices," remarked one observer, "have so increased in magnitude that their influence seems to bid defiance to the dominion of reason. Cool and passionate disquisitions have given place to the asperity and malignity of party zeal." These "*over-heated* politicians," another commentator noted, had "by the strength of their attachment to their party" revealed "the weakness, if not total demolition of their intellects." Caught up in the "irascible delirium" and "the insane intoxication of party spirit," said another, men had forgotten about everything, even including their own "self-interest, to say nothing of public welfare." Nothing could compare in importance "with the sharp conflict, and electioneering squabble, excited by the all absorbing question: which of the two political parties should be uppermost?" Men seemed too involved, too distracted, and too passionate to dampen the flames of party conflict and division.[23]

Women, on the other hand, might be better positioned than men to inculcate the new liberal attitude toward party politics. As Enlightenment thinkers made clear, women, despite their lack of formal political power, could exert a significant influence over society and politics. As many commentators remarked, women had a demonstrable impact on what people said, thought, and did. They affected the spirit of public discourse and the tenor of social relations. They instilled moral values and inspired virtuous behavior in their husbands and children. Their actions propelled society from a state of rudeness to civility. In fact, women's very lack of formal political power might make them the ideal purveyors of the new liberal ideal. Unlike men, they would not be as personally invested in the outcome of the political contests of the day.

By the first decades of the nineteenth century, the notion of women's influence had become a staple in the prescriptive literature of the day, especially in literary periodicals and ladies' magazines. Women were, according to one New Yorker, "beings of the highest consequence, and on them depends the healthiness or the contagion of social intercourse." Articles on "female influence" typically made expansive, even extravagant, claims about women's power. "Even in the most polished nations," declared one periodical, "female influence is the grand mover which actuates the political and the social body." Although it was a notoriously hard variable to measure, female influence, it was said, "has been infinitely greater than appears in historical records. Wars and revolutions, religious sects and spiritual leaders, often traced their origins to women." Like the water that fish swim in, women's influence was omnipresent but transparent, invisible to the naked eye.[24]

A key aspect of women's influence was its indirect nature. "We feel, but we cannot describe the powers by which [women] subdue, captivate, and command," commented the *Lady's Weekly Miscellany*. "They are too subtle to be clothed in words, and pass directly to the heart, too rapid even for observation. They operate like spells, or charms, and raise the most unaccountable, as well as the most delightful sympathies, which the human frame can feel." Married women, in particular, were said to have enormous influence over their husbands and children. "Nineteen times in twenty," said one author, "while [the husband] thinks he is pursuing an independent course, and assumes all the credit of his success, the suggestions or persuasions of his companion are influencing his opinions and controlling his conduct." Although women exerted their influence indirectly, they nonetheless were thought to shape their families' ideas, values, and behavior.[25]

Despite contemporaries' claims about the scope and importance of women's influence, modern historians have been more skeptical. They have doubted the efficacy of this influence or seen it as a pale substitute for real political power, which continued to be monopolized by men.[26] While contemporary claims cannot be taken at face value, they need to be taken seriously. Even today political scientists treat influence as an important variable in political relations. As the political scientist Robert Dahl has noted, influence can be used by weaker parties to "raise the cost of control, overcome domination on certain matters important to them, acquire some measure of political autonomy, and by virtue of their bargaining position, even create a system of mutual controls in which subjects influence the ruler in important respects, even though the ruler remains the dominant (though no longer totally dominant) actor in the system."[27] To assess the full significance of women's influence, then, it is useful to compare notions of female influence on politics with contemporary conceptions of male influence.

Before the mid-eighteenth century, when the term "influence" was used in relation to men, it often referred to the covert exercise of political power. As inheritors of the Real Whig tradition from Britain, Americans of the colonial era understood "influence" to mean corruption—the informal, private, and suspect means by which the Crown manipulated Parliament to do its bidding. While good government was open, transparent, and aboveboard, bad government occurred behind closed doors, in an opaque realm beyond public scrutiny and control. Over the course of the eighteenth century, colonists often invoked the language of influence in attacking the chief executives of their colonies. In particular, leaders often accused their royal governors of using illicit influence to bribe legislators or gain unwarranted control over their assemblies. By the 1760s colonists saw the hand of influence in their increasingly testy relations with Britain. They thought that the mother country's harsh and ill-conceived policies must be the result of "ministerial influence," the secret plotting of the king's ministers, done without his knowledge or approval. Only when it was apparent that the king himself was implicated did Americans see the need to revolt against the mother country.[28]

After the Revolution, popular suspicion about the illicit effects of male influence on politics persisted. Members of each political party accused the other of susceptibility to influence, especially when exercised by foreign nations. "The management of foreign relations," commented Republican James Madison, was particularly "susceptible of abuse . . . because they can be concealed or disclosed, or disclosed in such parts & at such times as will best suit particular views; and because the body of the people are less capable of judging . . . than of any other." Federalists believed that France posed the greatest threat, while Republicans pointed to Britain. Each party, however, continually inveighed against the ill effects of "foreign influence" on the country's moral fiber, patriotic vigor, and sense of autonomy.[29]

An incident occurring during Thomas Jefferson's presidency demonstrates the continuing hostility toward the exercise of male influence in politics. As U.S. diplomats sought to acquire West Florida from Spain in 1806, John Randolph of Roanoke and the so-called "Tertium Quids" accused Jefferson, a member of their own party, of sending secret messages to Congress and failing to reveal his true motives in the negotiations. Randolph objected, insisting that these tactics opened the door to "backstairs influence—of men who bring messages to this House, which, although they do not appear on the journals, govern its decisions." Emphatically rejecting that "invisible, irresponsible influence" which "pervades and decides everything," Randolph and his allies became a separate faction within the Republican Party itself. As they saw it, their party must remain committed to government conducted in an open and public manner, free from hidden motives and the threat of corruption. Jefferson and his allies obviously disagreed, or at least believed that practical exigencies forced them to act differently. Nonetheless, the notion of male political influence continued to carry negative connotations well into the nineteenth century.[30]

Attitudes toward women's influence on politics were more complicated. Some observers did portray women's influence in a hostile light. With respect to women, however, the fear was not simply that they would exercise their power in secret but that they would use their distinctive feminine charms, especially their sexual power, to subvert the political process. The French philosopher Montesquieu, for example, warned western European nations to avoid the treachery of oriental despotisms, where women in harems traded sexual favors with their masters in return for political concessions for their sons or relatives. In Britain some political radicals, including Catharine Macaulay, feared that elite women's illicit use of sexual influence could corrupt the government, including ministers, members of Parliament, or even the king. If the wives or mistresses of those in power used their sexual wiles for their own purposes, they might thwart the popular will and undermine the public good. During the 1780s Thomas Jefferson feared that French-women exerted too much influence on the politics of their nation. "The manners of the nation," he said, "allow them to visit, alone, all persons in office, to sollicit the affairs of the husband, family, or friends." Uncontrolled by legislation, they could use their powers over men for their own purposes. The "omnipotence of [their] influence," he feared, would hamper attempts at political reform. Jefferson was not alone in this belief. Suspicion toward Frenchwomen persisted for decades throughout popular discourse; they perennially represented the nega-tive form of female influence.[31]

In contrast, a more positive conception of female influence emerged, primarily by way of the Scottish Enlightenment's stadial theory of his-tory. American men and women adopted these ideas in ways appropriate for their own country. Women, it was said, not only had an influence on society but influenced the polity as well. Addressing the "lovely daugh-ters of Columbia" in 1795, a male commencement speaker at Columbia College urged the women in his audience to "assiduously employ [your] influence over men, promoting their happiness and the best interests of society. . . . The solidity and stability of the liberties of your country rest with you; since Liberty is never sure, 'till Virtue reigns triumphant." Their role was said to be particularly important under a republican form of government, where the people governed themselves. "In republics especially," proclaimed the *Rural Repository,* "virtue in the people is the one thing needful. It is the grand pillar, which alone can support us; and when that falls, the constitution falls with it. . . . The benefits, which females, are capable of bestowing on society, are beyond conception." By giving society its "tone," the educator Emma Willard said, women could ensure that "our latest posterity [might] enjoy the same happy government, with which we are blessed." The stakes were high, for "republics have failed when [women] calmly suffered that influence, to become enlisted in favour of luxuries and follies wholly incompatible with the existence of freedom." In their own way, then, women could be as crucial to the republic's success as men.[32]

Drawing on this more salutary ideal, American thinkers took the idea of female influence in a new direction. Women were asked to use their influence not simply to affect men's manners or morals but also for explicitly political purposes. Women might be able to ease the tensions between male partisans and instill the new liberal attitude toward party politics in their husbands and children. Donald Fraser's pamphlet *Party-Spirit Exposed*, published in 1799, represented an early articulation of this notion. "With a view of blunting (in some degree) the baneful edge of Party-Spirit in this country," he urged both Federalist and Republican men to be more open-minded toward the political opposition. If a man practiced greater tolerance in politics, then he, "whatever party he is of, cannot fail of being a good member of society, and a lover of his native, or adopted country." Fraser's advice, however, did not stop there. Appended to the pamphlet was a section addressed specifically "to the Ladies." Commenting on women's ability to influence their husbands and children, Fraser suggested that women might help quell the "baneful" effects of party conflict. "[Women] have it in their power," he said, to inculcate "respect, sobriety, and decency in the youth, and pointedly to with-hold their smiles and civilities from all who transgress these in the smallest degrees. This is a method of proceeding that will most certainly be victorious." By rewarding certain behaviors and sanctioning others, women could turn society away from party strife and toward mutuality, harmony, and unity. "What a noble fund of self-estimation would our fair partners acquire to themselves," he exclaimed, "if, by reforming the manners of the rising generation, they should be the means of restoring peace to the world."[33]

Other commentators explained in more detail how women might do this. The "stubbornness of party zeal," one woman writer noted, was "deaf to argument" but could be overcome if women used the "eloquence of tears" to "quell the opposition." Female indirection was said to magnify rather than lessen women's power. Rather than convince men through reason or logic, they should manipulate them with the power of their beauty, the "magic" of their smiles, the "threats" of their tears, or the virtue of their moral example. Acting as her "husband's faithful friend and privy counsellor," a wife could take advantage of his "childlike moods," when "his feelings and affections are melted and softened into unusual plasticity," and turn his ambition, self-interest, and doubt "onto the path of virtue." Women's feminine sensibilities would counteract men's irrationality and dampen the heat of their immoderate partisan passions.[34]

Using their femininity in this strategic fashion would allow women to act as peacemakers and mediators among men. If the subject of party politics arose at home, women should turn the discussion toward other, less controversial subjects. "When the harmony of [her husband's soul] is disturbed by political discord," insisted one author, "she should be its regulator, and by her gentleness, attune it again to love and domestic delight. . . . It is her duty to tranquillize his passions, and to turn the impetuous current of his feelings into a more orderly channel." Even when a wife agreed with her husband's opinion, she should refrain from expressing her own political views. If she allowed "her bosom . . . to swell with the turbulent spirit of party," then she would "agitate rather than soothe her husband." Women should be domestic pacifiers. As a Roxbury, Connecticut, orator told the "Columbian Fair," "By the persuasive mildness of your conversation, and the sovereign influence of your example, soothe party discord to friendship and unity. Remember, no heart can resist the voice of patriotism, when urged by the lips of beauty and innocence." Instead of encouraging men's partisan sentiments, women should neutralize their feelings and turn them in another direction.[35] (See Figure 12.)

Women's actions would make the home a refuge from politics. Their "benevolent affections" would "heal the dissentions of individuals and of society" and make men more yielding toward their political adversaries. "Woman's kindness of heart," insisted the *Ladies' Magazine*, would restrain "political and polemical disputation . . . within the limits of decency and propriety: local contentions [could] be charmed away, and men [might] be softened down into beings altogether better fitted for the great purposes of life." Their assistance would ease partisanship's corrosive effects on society. "Were commotions to arise from the feuds of faction, or the rancour of party spirit, that would threaten to embroil the state in civil discord . . . [women] would be enabled . . . to unite the contentious, to heal the disaffected, and restore tranquility and peace to their country," declared another periodical. Women's actions would ameliorate the nation's most serious political tensions.[36]

Women would also play a key role in inculcating a liberal attitude toward party conflict. Acting in their roles as wives and mothers, they would encourage in their husbands and children toleration and respect for opposing political views. In a speech to the Harrisonburg Ladies' Academy, Daniel Bryan expounded on this notion. "As man becomes more enlightened," he told the young women in his audience, "the violence of party malignity, which is the offspring of prejudice, jealousy, avaricious competition, and conflicting pride, abates as *liberality* increases." Women, he insisted, would be the ones to encourage and nurture these views. "It is," he continued, "in the power of the well-educated and refined mother, to inspire the infant son with noble and expanded sentiments, to implant in his bosom correct views of an original diversity of the human mind, and convince him of the consequent impossibility for all men to think alike on subjects involving a complexity of interests." If the new generation understood politics as a debate over subjective opinions, not as a battle over a monolithic truth, the country might be able to withstand the strains of party conflict and find grounds

Figure 12. *Election at the State House* (c. 1815), by John Lewis Krimmel. Pencil and watercolor (detail). This illustration is a small section of a larger image depicting an election scene in Philadelphia in the War of 1812 era. It vividly depicts women's role as peacemaker and mediator between men. A woman holding a baby physically intervenes between two combative male partisans, presumably a Federalist and a Jeffersonian, who have come to blows over the election contest. For the full image, see Figure 13. (The Historical Society of Pennsylvania.)

for reconciliation and compromise. Open to a wider range of political ideas, they would be, as another observer put it, "men of moderation."[37]

In order to achieve these goals, women would have to withdraw from politics and rise above the disputatious fray. "By guiding the inquiries, enriching the minds and forming the childish and youthful habits," noted one male speaker, women could shape the "future Citizens, future Legislators, Magistrates, Judges and Generals." If, however, women chose to continue to participate in party politics and "assume a part in political disputes," he warned, they would meet with resistance, rejection, and ridicule. Others agreed with this course of action. An article called "Daughters of Freedom," originally written for the *Scioto (Ohio) Gazette* and republished in 1809 in a Vincennes, Indiana, newspaper, praised the virtues of female nonpartisanship. The writer, who called herself "Laura," admitted that her husband was a Federalist but said the she eschewed party labels. Addressing women "without distinction of party," she spoke to her audience "in the unbiassed language of a sister patriot." Party labels, she insisted, were productive of nothing but conflict: "Fed. and Rep. and Demo. ingrate to woman's ear, [and] cause dissention. Names how odious! Fie, Fie!" Although some people urged women to withdraw from all political activities, in Laura's view, to be nonpartisan was not the same as being nonpolitical. At a time of international conflict, the country needed women. Like their female forebears during the Revolution, women of the republic should abjure fashion and frivolity, take to the spindle and loom, and most importantly, teach their children to love their country. Although not well suited for "the arduous duties of the cabinet and legislative bodies, and the honors and exploits of the field," women, she said, did have a duty to be informed about political matters. They had "a part assigned behind the scene," especially as "the nation, [was] assailed by feuds within and *potent* foes without." Most importantly, women should raise their children free from the taint of party labels and conflicts. "Let it then be woman's part," Laura said, "to . . . disarm Fed[eralist] and Rep[ublican] and Demo[crat] and reconcil[e] man to man . . . and save the land from pending woe." Their efforts might even extinguish the flame of partisanship altogether: "A race of heroes then may rise, not Fed[eralist] and Rep[ublican] and Demo[crat]. . . . Let men be brothers, women sisters; all Fredonians." Female nonpartisanship might mitigate the parties' most injurious effects.[38]

By rising above the partisan fray, women would be in a better position to promote the nation's aspirations toward unity and harmony. During the tumultuous years of Jefferson's embargo, Sally Hastings wrote a poem inveighing against the divisive effects of party politics. Addressing the country's male leaders, she proclaimed, "Then do not meanly, for

your private gains / Dissolve the Union, which our peace maintains."
Turning to her larger audience, she insisted that they shield themselves
from the influence of party warfare: "Let no Party-zeal / E'er interrupt
the Happiness you feel!" Significantly, Hastings portrayed women as
those who maintained the "peace" while men, through the pursuit of
their own "private gains," threatened the country's stability. Another
poem, published in 1814 in a Saint Louis newspaper, pointed out the
advantages of female nonpartisanship over men's divisive factionalism:

> Among the men what dire divisions rise,
> For *union* one—and one *no* union cries;
> Shame on the sex which such disput[e] began,
> Ladies are all for UNION, *to a man.*

In this capacity women could reclaim the mantle of impartial patriot. If
politics were indeed a domestic "war of politics," then women should
play the role of noncombatants.[39]

Among her many supporters, Dolley Madison was often portrayed as
the ideal of impartial patriotism. Although her husband, James Madison,
was a founder, along with Thomas Jefferson, of the Democratic Republican
Party, his wife somehow created an atmosphere of openness toward
those who held divergent political views. First as the wife of the secretary
of state and then as first lady, she was known for her welcoming manner
and gracious hospitality, which brought members of all political persuasions together in the same room. Margaret Bayard Smith, a Washington
writer and hostess, celebrated Madison's role in mediating party conflict, saying that Dolley's "uniform good nature, kindness of disposition,
frank, gay, [and] cordial manners . . . softened the asperity of party feeling, disarmed prejudice, [and] conciliated general good will." The
effect, Smith said, was that "*Party* was lost in *social spirit.*" Another author
saw a comparison between the contributions of Jefferson and those of
Dolley Madison. Quoting Jefferson's famous inaugural address, he
observed, "A politician of the present day, exclaimed on a memorable
occasion, 'we are all federalists, we are all republicans.' In her intercourse with society, Mrs. Madison reduced this liberal sentiment to practice. . . . At a time when the restless spirit of party covered every path
with thorns, this lady held the branch of reconciliation." For Madison,
a difference of opinion did not constitute a difference of principle—or
at least, so it was said.[40]

Ironically, as Catherine Allgor has shown, Madison functioned as an
effective political operative in her own right, securing patronage for
family and friends, pursuing her own political agenda, and promoting
her husband's career at every turn. As a skilled tactician, however, Madi-

son's politicking remained beneath the surface, exercised in a distinctly feminine manner and obvious only to the most astute observers. To most Americans, Dolley Madison had "reduced" the "liberal sentiment" of nonpartisanship "to practice." In effect, she succeeded in translating the liberal spirit of religious toleration into the political realm. Just as the disestablishment of church from state enabled dissenting religious groups to coexist peacefully, so the separation of women from politics would allow competing male factions to indulge in their internecine battles without tearing society to pieces.[41]

At a time when the notion of men's political influence continued to have negative connotations, and when many European nations considered women's political influence as insidious or corrupting, American women and men often held a more positive outlook. Women were seen as vital players in the new republican order, crucial contributors to the country's social stability and political cohesion. By using their influence to serve the larger good, they could alleviate the social and political tensions wracking the country. By acting as mediators and peacemakers between warring male partisans, they would prevent the nation from veering into civil war. By inculcating a liberal view of party politics, women might change the country's whole attitude toward party conflict. Future generations might seek to cooperate with members of the opposing party rather than desire to eliminate them. Politics would then become a contest of opinions, not a debate about ultimate truth. Women's efforts were potentially of immense significance.

Women, however, would pay a price for this contribution. In order to rescue the country, women were asked to withdraw from party politics and electoral affairs. They were to renounce their partisan affiliations and relinquish their independent political identities. Instead of acting as their own political agents, they were to exercise their political role indirectly, primarily by means of influencing their husbands and children. They would, in a sense, give up some of the political possibilities that the American Revolution had created for them. Although women still might act like good republican wives and mothers, there would be less room for "female politicians."

Over time, attitudes toward women's indirect political influence became absorbed into the discourse of separate spheres, as articulated in the prescriptive literature of the day. According to its proponents, men and women occupied separate but equal roles in society. Although both sexes contributed to the common good, the tasks and duties of each sex differed. Men would govern the public realm, which included business, religion, politics, and government. Women would prevail in the domestic sphere, where they would oversee the household, raise the children, and regulate the family's moral and spiritual life. The men's world was tumultuous, corrupt, and corrupting. In contrast, the domestic realm was to be a safe haven, a refuge from the immorality and disorder existing beyond the household walls. Men's and women's roles would complement one another rather than overlap or conflict. Separate spheres ideology, it should be emphasized, was a normative ideal rather than a descriptive construct, a discussion of what society should be rather than what it actually was. Nonetheless, by the mid-nineteenth century the notion had become the dominant framework for understanding gender roles in the United States and was enormously influential in shaping popular perceptions about the way men and women should behave.[42]

Historians have usually portrayed separate spheres as a tool used to *prevent* women from entering politics. It may in fact have represented something more. Although typically associated with increased urbanization and changing labor patterns, the concept of gendered spheres had a political dimension as well. The notion gained prominence at the very same time that women were participating in politics in ways and on a scale that had never before occurred. This was no coincidence. Along with the discourse on women's rights, women's political activities challenged the male monopoly on political power. Although some male politicians continued for a time to invite women's participation in political causes and functions, others began to discourage their attendance. Political leaders began to shift their attention away from the population at large, which included women and other nonvoters, in order to focus exclusively on those who cast ballots: white male electors.

Separate spheres ideology, then, may actually have been a reaction *against* women's more extensive involvement in politics, a convenient way to explain and justify excluding women from party politics and electoral activities. If women had already ventured outside the home, invading the male realm of politics, it was all the more necessary to convince them to leave. The shift was evident in popular discussions about women and politics. In contrast to an earlier climate of openness to new possibilities, women who participated in political activities became increasingly subject to virulent attacks. In a typical article published in 1830, a New York newspaper disparaged women's desire to discuss political issues, both in public and in private. Women who discussed the subject at home, it was said, violated their appropriate feminine roles and disrupted the peace and harmony that should prevail in the domestic realm. "The eternal wrangling of discordant opinions about men and offices, and the petty details of elections and caucuses may impair the harmony of one's social circle, interfere with the domestic arrangements of one's family, and drive from its intercourse all sensible company." Women who spoke out in public created even bigger problems and attracted even greater abuse. "When a lady . . . steps forward as a public declaimer, and actually enlists in the party warfare waged by the press, it is difficult to restrain the expression of pity, if not contempt, which the spectacle must excite in every well informed mind. . . . A more disgusting object cannot well be conceived than a blustering woman, with a stentorian voice, clamouring for the success of an alderman and offering bets upon the number of votes which may be calculated upon for a favorable constable." Instead of depicting women's interest in and involvement with politics as a contribution to the polity, their actions came to be seen as a betrayal of women's true feminine role. "There can be no excuse," the article insisted, "for a female deserting her allotted privacy and volunteering to encounter gladiators in the political arena. She has all to lose—nothing to gain." The term "female politician" began to lose its positive connotations and become strictly a term of opprobium. "Female politicians," it was said, should be shunned as "evil."[43]

The Panic of 1819

It is important to remember, of course, that prescriptions against women's involvement in politics were just that: prescriptions. Women did not disappear from politics merely because they were told to do so. Yet a sea change had begun. The new discourse about womanhood began to undermine what the American Revolution had opened up: norms sanctioning women's active involvement in party and electoral politics. In contrast to the revolutionary rhetoric that had welcomed them, women now faced a constant barrage of rhetoric urging them to renounce their partisan loyalties and eschew political involvement. The Panic of 1819 offers a case in point. Women's curiously muted, even apathetic, response to the panic suggests that the prescriptive rhetoric was indeed having an impact.

The Panic of 1819 represented the first big economic downturn faced by the United States as an industrializing nation. During the War of 1812 American industries, especially the textile industry, had expanded to satisfy consumer demands. After the war a flood of foreign imports entered the country. Many fledgling American industries could not compete. American citizens went heavily into debt to finance their foreign purchases. A simultaneous boom in land speculation led to an overextension of credit. When the newly chartered Second Bank of the United States demanded that state banks redeem notes in specie, state banks began calling in their loans, leading to a sickening wave of property foreclosures and bankruptcies. Creditors could not pay their debts. Farmers lost their land. Factories closed. Laborers lost their jobs. Economic distress was widespread, and the national government appeared to be ill-equipped to deal with the consequences.[44]

Ordinary citizens rallied to alleviate the crisis. As in previous crises, the call went out to reaffirm the traditional values of simplicity, frugality, and virtue. Local organizations formed in an effort to address the country's economic problems at the grassroots level. Matthew Carey of Philadelphia, for example, encouraged the founding of Societies for the Promotion of Industry throughout the New England and mid-Atlantic states. Dedicated to nurturing American industries, these groups urged Congress to pass tariffs and other laws that would cripple foreign competition and restore American prosperity. Other citizens responded by taking a different kind of action. They identified a source of blame closer to home: their own spendthrift habits. A Cincinnati organization dedicated itself to "the improvement of agriculture, and the encouragement of domestic economy." The members, all male, promised to "observe a rigid economy in every branch of our expenditures." As a symbol of their commitment, they resolved to adopt "habits of industry, economy, and frugality" and vowed that their families would buy only practical items made in the United States. Only through these practices, they said, could the country succeed in "keeping our money at home, and our people employed."[45]

Women were expected to do their part. In 1819 the writer Washington Irving published a short story, "The Wife," in a Pennsylvania newspaper. The story provided a model for the way in which women should respond to their husbands' financial setbacks during the current crisis. In Irving's story, the panic forces a young man to go bankrupt, and he loses all his worldly possessions. Fearful of the consequences, he is reluctant to tell his wife. Finally, with a great deal of trepidation, the man confesses. To his great relief, the woman accepts the bad news calmly and with understanding; she does not blame him or rebuke him. Immediately beginning preparations for their new life together, she agrees to move from their large, comfortable home in the city to a much smaller abode in the country. "Oh," she says "brightly," "we shall be so snug!" The lesson was clear: women should submit to the current situation and do whatever men needed or asked of them.[46]

As in previous crises, male politicians publicly solicited women's support for their efforts. At Fourth of July celebrations, speakers appealed to women's patriotism. In Harrisburg, Pennsylvania, for example, the men toasted "The Fair daughters of Columbia—May they show the world by their example, that the sons of America are clothed by their industry." In Fredericksburg, Virginia, locals celebrated "The fair patriots who persist in our infant Manufactures." Women, it was said, could be decisive in ending the downturn. Their frugality and virtue, insisted the *Ladies' Literary Cabinet,* would be "of the greatest consequence" to the nation. Another commentator was even more emphatic. Women, he said, can "do more for the reformation of manners, than all our politicians can do, if they possessed the power of Bounaparte in his proudest day." Such pleas would seem hard to ignore.[47]

Men, however, also blamed women for bringing about the crisis. Articles appeared that unfavorably compared women of the present day to their revolutionary-era predecessors. Magazines and newspapers attacked women's preference for purchasing goods from abroad rather than making them at home. A fictional dialogue in the *Connecticut Courant* featured a Mr. Coulter, who berated his wife about her "imaginary wants" and frivolous spending. Whereas his wife desired "Turkey carpets and gilt looking glasses," her grandmother and mother had been "industrious, prudent and economical—they thought it was an honor to them to be good spinners and weavers and good dairy women—they took an honest pride in shewing their bundles of yarn, their cloth and their cheeses." His conclusion: that the present "hard times" were primarily due to "a want of moderation in our present mode of living." Others voiced similar complaints about women. "Our ladies, generally," noted a male author, "are not sufficiently industrious." They needed to turn their gaze homeward, recommit themselves to frugality and virtue, and return the country to its former prosperity. Another commentator proposed a different kind of solution, appropriate in an industrializing economy: "Our wealthy females, instead of preferring, without examination, everything that is imported from abroad, [should] encourage domestic industry among their indigent countrywomen." If elite women no longer wished to produce goods themselves, they should find lower-class women to do the job.[48]

One of the most elaborate appeals to women appeared in the form of a letter, published in a Philadelphia newspaper on June 11, 1819. Signed by the "spirits" of the Founding Fathers (many of whom were already deceased), the letter called on women to gather in Philadelphia on July 4, 1819, for the purpose of organizing "a society for the promotion of economy, encouragement of general industry, and support of the country in its present perils and afflictions." Both flattering and patronizing, the article appealed to women's patriotism as well as their vanity. "Fame, durable fame, rarely falls to the lot of females," said the letter, "but here is a time for the ladies of Philadelphia to seize and appropriate it." The women were to meet at a specific time and place: "10 o'clock A.M. in the room of the State House, where the American Independence was declared." The notice seemed to be an effort to mobilize women behind efforts to end the panic in the manner used in previous national crises. Publications in New York state and elsewhere in Pennsylvania, including

Pittsburgh, disseminated word of the proposed gathering beyond the Philadelphia region.[49]

A few days later the same Philadelphia newspaper that had printed the original announcement, *Poulson's American Daily Advertiser*, published an encouraging response. Announcing her readiness to come to the country's aid, "A Lady" first demanded assurances that the announcement was not in jest. Then she urged other women to rally behind the call and gather in Philadelphia on Independence Day to enact the proposals. "Come forward ye *Lucretias* of the age," she declared, "and prove your attachment to domestic happiness and virtue, by steadfastly opposing by concert and combination, the ruinous habits, resulting from our love of ostentatious show and finery." Another woman, writing to a different Philadelphia newspaper, was also enthusiastic about the initiative. Pointing out the desirability of collective action, she noted, "Few of us have the fortitude, individually and alone, to oppose fashionable vices . . . but in a society we should have the countenance and support of one another." Once again women seemed poised to rescue the country in its time of distress.[50]

Independence Day in 1819 came and went, however, with no evidence that the Philadelphia gathering ever took place. Philadelphia papers made no subsequent mention of women founding any societies for the promotion of industry and economy. The only organized response seems to have come from tiny Mossy Springs, Kentucky, where, as the *Ladies' Visiter* reported, the women gathered on July 4 and formed a patriotic association dedicated to "renounc[ing] all foreign ornaments and luxuries [and] to preferr[ing] in every case, articles of our own to those of foreign manufacture." The editor used the event as an opportunity to reiterate the call for collective action. He urged other "FAIR readers" to "imitate this distinguished example of devotion to the interests of their country, and that of their own households." There is no sign that women in other parts of the country did so. An article in a Philadelphia paper sounded a desperate note: "Let [women] be no longer allured by the Gewgaws of the old world, the possession of which renders them, neither more beautiful, nor more virtuous. Let them in all their selections of dress, choose only American! . . . It is believed they will not refuse!" In terms of their collective response, however, American women turned a deaf ear to the men's pleas.[51]

Several factors may have contributed to the weakness of women's response to the Panic of 1819. Unlike previous crises, this event did not involve the possibility of foreign invasion or war. It was more strictly an internal domestic issue. Perhaps even more important, the structure of the country's economy had changed significantly since the time of the American Revolution. Whereas women's contributions had been crucial in a preindustrial, barter and credit economy, their position seemed less central in an industrializing cash nexus. With the establishment of banks, more paper currency flowed. Throughout the country money was replacing credit and barter as the means of exchange. Women were producing fewer items at home and purchasing more items from outside the household. Factories now often produced goods such as shoes and textiles. Whereas the country had only four textile factories in 1807, it had over fifty-eight by 1815, many of which employed female workers. By this time, according to the historian Jeanne Boydston, women who made homespun did so more as a symbolic gesture than as a practical way to satisfy the country's needs. By the Panic of 1819 it was less important that women make things at home than that they stop buying goods from abroad. They may have seen their actions as having a less direct effect on the outcome. More detached from the crisis, women may have felt less able to contribute to a solution.[52]

Women's failure to act during the Panic of 1819 also represents something more: an important shift in the forms of women's political engagement. Unlike the outpouring of patriotic sentiment that occurred during the American Revolution, the Quasi-War with France, the embargo, and the War of 1812, women apparently went about their own business during the Panic of 1819. Even with substantial changes in the economy, women could have found ways of expressing their concern. If they had desired to do so, they might have written manifestos acknowledging the crisis, signed agreements to abjure the purchase of foreign goods, or made symbolic offerings of homespun simply to show their solidarity with other Americans. By and large, however, the country was left to right itself without women's public assistance or support.

The Turn toward Social Reform

Women's lack of interest in the panic does not seem coincidental. As many historians have observed, the early decades of the nineteenth century witnessed the founding of a tremendous number of organizations dedicated to the cause of social reform. As early as the 1790s, well-off and elite "ladies" began to establish charitable organizations or benevolent societies throughout the country. These groups flourished in all parts of the country—in the South as well as in the North, in rural areas as well as in urban enclaves. One of the earliest "Ladies' Societies" in New York, founded in 1797, sheltered widows during the city's cold winters and enabled their children to go to school. The Boston Female Asylum, founded in 1800, established an orphanage for young girls. Other groups collected money to buy Bibles and distribute them to the poor; provided relief to the poor; funded missionaries who would proselytize to non-Christians in foreign lands; visited female prisoners; or aided sick people by providing bedding, clothing, and food. In 1802 over two hundred women in Savannah, Georgia, formed the Female Asylum, an organization dedicated to rescuing orphaned or fatherless girls and putting them on the path to a useful life. In 1803 women in Fredericksburg, Virginia, established a boarding school for poor white girls; Norfolk, Richmond, and Petersburg soon followed suit. By 1830 New York City had eighteen societies and Boston had seventeen such organizations.[53]

At least some observers attributed women's lack of attention in the crisis of 1819 to their increasing participation in benevolent societies and charitable organizations. Although some men supported women's efforts on behalf of the poor and disadvantaged, they wanted women to turn their attention to the crisis at hand. Warning that Americans were about to fall back into the economic clutches of the British, "Domesticus" encouraged women to take the lead in boycotting foreign goods, as they had during the American Revolution. "What have [women] not brought about by their various combinations for the promotion of the principles of humanity and religion? And without relaxing their efforts in the cause of the *latter*," he suggested, "may we not expect them to countenance a plan, that will in a great measure do away with the necessity of Societies and contributions for the support of the *former*?" If the country were on a sound economic footing, in other words, women would not have so many people in need of their assistance. Another male critic argued that while women were out helping others, the country was facing economic ruin. He claimed that women's charitable activities not only "encourage[d] pauperism instead of industry" by supporting the indigent but also made the women "ambitious of the honor of being members in these multiplied associations; civil, ecclesiastical, and mechanical societies." He urged women to turn their attentions back to the domestic realm, "where, after all, true happiness is only to be found." In fact, in the face of increasingly strident injunctions against "female politicians," women may have decided that it was more convenient to eschew men's causes and focus on their own. In social reform organizations they found other alternatives for contributing to the public good.[54]

Charitable societies and benevolent organizations gave women new opportunities to participate in public activities outside the home. Providing social services at a time when the government had little role in this arena, groups often had to deal with government offices or officials. Although some societies had male advisory boards, many were founded by women, run by women, and made up entirely of women members. They wrote their own constitutions, established bylaws, and held elections for female officers. Women kept the organizations running. They raised money, solicited donations, petitioned for incorporation, or secured property for their organization's use. These experiences gave women new areas of expertise and a sense of personal autonomy outside the home.[55]

In their role as social reformers, women had the opportunity to meet other women and, at times, to play a leadership role in the organizations. Because they built the organizations from the ground up, they could often see that their activities had useful and immediate results. In 1803, for example, a group of 117 women formed the Newark Female Charitable Society in order to provide assistance to the city's poor families at a time when the government did not do so. In contrast to male politics, with men running the operation and setting priorities, women in this organization held the reins of power. The women, mostly from Newark's wealthier families, quickly wrote a constitution for their group and elected a board of officers made up entirely of women. They divided the city into six districts and chose a manager to supervise operations in each district. After raising money, the managers would visit needy families in their districts and decide what kind of help to provide. The society often supplied food, clothing, and firewood for heat. At the same time that the New Jersey legislature was stripping women of the vote and their participation in male politics was increasingly under attack, these women had found a different venue for expressing their commitment to the larger public good. Through their own actions and efforts, they would continue to have an impact on society and government.[56]

After 1830 the nature of women's social reform activities began to change. Women increasingly began to join organizations whose purposes were broader in scope and more ambitious in aim than those of the benevolent societies had been. Desiring nothing less than the perfection of American society, the groups sought to eradicate what they deemed fundamental social evils, such as slavery, prostitution, and the consumption of alcohol. Alcohol, they said, contributed to a degeneration of morals and the deterioration of family life. Prostitution, they suggested, led to the degradation of men as well as women. Slavery, they insisted, not only curtailed economic growth but also corrupted the morals of slaves and slaveholders alike. Growing rapidly, these mass movements appealed to men as well as women and drew in people from a wide variety of social and economic backgrounds.

In pursuit of their goals, these organizations employed a variety of techniques. Some reformers believed that the political system was so corrupt that they refused to work within it. Employing what was called "moral suasion," they tried to change public opinion through speeches, publications, and dialogue. Once people saw the justness of their cause, they believed, popular revulsion would bring evil practices and institutions to an end. Other reformers, however, rejected moral suasion as "balderdash." Fighting slavery, ending the sale of hard liquor, or abolishing prostitution, they said, required quicker and more immediate action. This would occur only by working through the existing government. These reformers urged legislators to pass laws that would achieve the changes they desired. They lobbied officials and worked to elect candidates who supported their causes. Reaching out to the larger public, they instituted economic boycotts and undertook massive petitioning campaigns designed to influence both state and national legislatures.[57]

Yet many social reformers, especially women, maintained that politics represented only a means, not an end in itself. Their goal remained the moral improvement of society. Female reformers, moreover, insisted that social reform represented an extension of their feminine role, not a challenge to it. If as wives and mothers women were supposed to foster virtue, refine manners, and relieve distress, these groups allowed them to do those things—on an even broader scale. Commenting on the "real benefit" derived from female societies, the *Ladies' Literary Museum* applauded women who "unit[ed] in harmonious bands, to protect the orphan, and provide for the needy and helpless, or [who were] actively employed in instilling . . . into the youthful minds of their adopted children, fit lessons of religion and morality." Although they may have been working in or through the political system, these women did not see their actions as political in intent or focus.[58]

In fact, both before and after 1830 female reformers consistently disassociated themselves from political parties and distanced themselves from the tawdry world of male politics. They took care to differentiate their activities from those of male partisans. In a tract issued in 1806, a Boston antislavery society maintained that the group took "peculiar solicitude to avoid distinguishing themselves as a party in any public contest." They wanted to assist their country rather than contribute to the atmosphere of divisiveness. Other groups insisted that they had no desire for political power nor any intention of challenging male authority. "Let us beware of exerting our power politically," warned Sarah Josepha Hale to the readers of her *Ladies' Magazine.* "The influence of woman, to be beneficial, must depend mainly on the respect inspired by her moral excellence, not on the political address or energy she may display." Women claimed that their nonpolitical status gave them a moral authority that men lacked. As Maria Weston Chapman's antislavery society declared in 1842, "Deprived though we are of the elective franchise, we yet might spend our strength in partizanship, did we believe it in the least calculated to promote our object; did we not feel that our aim ought to be higher and nobler." Claiming the mantle of impartial patriot allowed female reformers to rise above the partisan fray. Although women might have had a political impact, they consistently removed themselves from any association with male politics.[59]

This was true even for individual women. Lydia Maria Child was one of the most visible and active female reformers of the antebellum period. Throughout her long career Child championed Indians, women's rights, the antislavery movement, and many other causes. Not only was she a tireless activist, but she also authored numerous articles, short stories, and novels on a variety of subjects. Her 1833 work, *The Appeal in Favor of That Class of Americans Called Africans*, was highly influential in bringing the abolitionist case to a wider public. Child nonetheless firmly denied the political nature of her activities. She viewed politicized women with distaste, or even disdain. In her 1835 work, *The History of the Condition of Women, in Various Ages and Nations*, she maintained, "The women of the United States have no direct influence in politics, and here, as in England, it is deemed rather unfeminine to take an earnest interest in public affairs." Child, like other female reformers, reaffirmed the social and moral, rather than political, aims of her activities.[60]

Other reformers went to even greater lengths to distance themselves from party and electoral politics. Throughout her life Catharine Beecher, the sister of Harriet Beecher Stowe, chronicled the American domestic economy and authored numerous works on moral, educational, and religious subjects. Although a supporter of female education, she firmly believed in the separation of masculine and feminine spheres. In 1829 she took on a new challenge. As president, Andrew Jackson proposed to move Indian tribes from their homelands in the East and resettle them on reservations west of the Mississippi River. Appalled at the human cost, Beecher mounted the first national petition campaign by women in American history. In her manifesto "Circular Addressed to Benevolent Ladies of the U. States" she spelled out the reasons why removal was wrong and why women should care. Drawing on her extensive contacts, she urged women throughout the country to hold public meetings to discuss the issue, after which they would circulate antiremoval petitions among women friends and neighbors. The petitions would then be submitted to Congress. Over the next two years more than fifteen hundred women in six states signed such petitions.[61]

Significantly, however, Beecher claimed that the petition drive represented a moral and religious, not a political effort. She denied that women should be involved in party politics. "Women," she wrote, "are protected from the binding influence of party spirit, and the asperities of political violence. They have nothing to do with any struggle for power, nor any right to dictate the decisions of those that rule over them." Just a few years later, Beecher repudiated her earlier activism. In 1837 she attacked the Grimké sisters for their support of an antislavery petition drive. In fact, Beecher denied women's right to petition Congress at all. "In this country," she declared, "petitions to Congress, in reference to the official duties of legislators seem, IN ALL CASES, to fall entirely without the sphere of female duty." In her much-reprinted tract *Treatise on Domestic Economy*, first published in 1841, she confirmed her rejection of women's involvement in politics. "In this Country," she maintained, "it is decided, that, in the domestic relation, woman takes a subordination station, and that, in civil and political concerns, her interests be intrusted to the other sex, without her taking any part in voting, or making and administering the laws." Significantly, her phrase "it is decided" hints at the previous decades' controversies over women's rights. From her perspective, however, the matter now appeared to be decided and was no longer subject to debate. Women did not belong in either party or electoral politics.[62]

In an atmosphere that was hostile or resistant to women's actions, female reformers were able to achieve many successes, both large and small. Benevolent societies and charitable organizations aided stricken widows and orphans, spread the Gospel, and provided education for those who otherwise might not have had the opportunity. Women who participated in abolitionist societies, the temperance movement, and antiprostitution movements brought these issues to local, state, and national attention. Their efforts helped secure, among other things, the passage of temperance laws, antiprostitution statutes, and the ending of the slave trade in Washington, D.C.

Rejection of male politics was thus both a rhetorical strategy and a deliberate tactic. Operating within the realm of what Mary Kelley has called "civil society," women found a place for themselves that included "any and all publics except those dedicated to the organized politics of political parties and elections."[63] Defining social reform as an alternative to male politics provided women with the ability to continue to contribute to the public good without intruding on masculine turf or violating traditional feminine roles and expectations. By portraying politics as a tawdry realm populated by corrupt men, women shielded themselves from the criticism that they were meddling in masculine affairs. Turning a liability into a strength, they used their lack of formal political power as a way of claiming moral superiority. Their goals were "higher and nobler" than those of men. Rather than seek the country's political salvation, they would pursue its moral reformation instead.

Yet the reformers' rejection of politics contained an inherent tension. Despite their protestations to the contrary, female reformers engaged in what modern observers would characterize as political behavior. In lobbying for the passage of laws, circulating petitions, and trying to influence male politicians, they used political means to obtain their ends. Although women emphasized that their goals were social or moral rather than political in nature, the line between the two was not as clear-cut or obvious as they believed. Today we would consider the women's actions as politics by another means.

Women's rejection of politics, however, cannot be simply ignored or dismissed. Self-perception is a key part of self-definition. Self-definition, in turn, has crucial consequences for the way people understand their present possibilities and future prospects. Certain self-perceptions open up new possibilities; others can limit or restrict what appears to be the appropriate scope of individual or collective action. In the decades immediately following the American Revolution, some women actively embraced politics and claimed a political role for themselves. In contrast, female reformers of the antebellum era who denied the political nature of their activities foreclosed certain possibilities. While their denials gave them room to maneuver in a hostile political climate, they made it harder for women who sought more formal and direct means of political participation to receive a hearing. In effect, they weakened women's ability to claim that participation in politics was not just a privilege but a right.

During the first decades of the new nation's existence, conflicts between Federalists and Republicans grew so intense that they undermined both the country's social relations and its fragile political bonds. Party warfare damaged families, split communities, and repeatedly brought the country to the brink of civil war. In an effort to repair these bonds, a new prescriptive discourse emerged that urged women to withdraw from party politics and relinquish their partisan identities. Criticisms of women who were interested in electoral politics mounted. Attacks on women's independent forms of political participation, especially "female politicians," grew in number and intensity. At the same time, women were told that they still had a political role to play. Much like the republican mothers of the revolutionary era, they were to exercise their influence on politics indirectly, by means of their husbands and children, not primarily through their own agency. In an effort to alleviate partisan strife, they could act as peacemakers and mediators between warring male partisans. In their homes, they could foster domestic peace. They could also instill a new liberal attitude toward party conflict among family members. Women would be nonpartisan patriots.

These injunctions, combined with the rise of separate spheres ideology, seem to have had an impact. During the Panic of 1819, women were conspicuous in their absence. Whereas women had played key roles in rescuing the nation from earlier national crises, such as the Quasi-War with France, Jefferson's embargo, and the War of 1812, they did not appear on the public scene in response to the Panic. The country was left to right itself without their apparent aid or support.

In fact, women found new ways to express their commitment to the common good. In the early decades of the nineteenth century, they began to turn their attention to activities outside the realm of party and electoral politics. Substantial numbers of middle-class and elite white women joined charitable organizations, benevolent societies, and social reform organizations. Although the goals of these organizations changed over time, one thing did not. Women reformers consistently denied the political nature of their activities. By denying that they engaged in "politics," women influenced government and society without interfering in party politics or electoral affairs. Yet the strategy had a downside: it reinforced a gendered division of labor. Men would take care of politics and government while women would take care of the home and society. What began as a useful tactic soon became a constricting barrier that would justify women's exclusion from politics and government.

Chapter 5

A Democracy—For Whom?

In July 1829 Sarah Josepha Hale's *Ladies' Magazine* published "Political Parties," a fictional story that revealed just how much had changed regarding attitudes toward women and politics since the time of the American Revolution. The story tells the tale of one Miss Pope, an elderly woman who looks back over her life and recounts her youthful follies to her two young nieces. In 1798, she tells them, she was engaged to a dashing young man named George Kendall. This, she reminds her nieces, was during the Quasi-War with France, a time "when party spirit raged so bitterly" and Thomas Jefferson gained many new supporters. Kendall soon set off for college. To Miss Pope's dismay, he returned a changed man; he had become a Jeffersonian Republican. Recalling her reaction, she reports, "Strange as it may seem to you, strange indeed as it now seems to me, I did then believe that if the democratic party succeeded in electing their candidate, our liberty, laws and religion would all be sacrificed." Horrified, she tried to change his mind. He resisted. She was appalled, telling her nieces, "I made the sentiments of my party the standard of rectitude, and had George committed a murder, I should hardly have been more shocked than when he declared himself a republican." At one point Kendall accompanied Pope to her home, where he encountered her father, a died-in-the-wool Federalist. A heated argument ensued, ending when Mr. Pope banished the young man from his house forever. Miss Pope, however, believed that love would triumph over politics. She fully expected that Kendall would recant his erroneous views. He did not. He moved away and never came back, leaving his opinionated lady friend to live and die "an old maid." Lest anyone miss the point, the woman warns her nieces, "I have told you this story that you may be warned against indulging the rancor of party feelings. I do not say ladies should abstain from all political reading or conversation. . . . But their influence should be exerted to allay, not to excite party animosities: their concern should be for their whole country, not for a party."[1]

During the period from the American Revolution until Andrew Jackson's election in 1828, the political landscape changed dramatically.

Typically, this period is understood as a time of democratization, of increasing political opportunities and openness in the political system. Yet while political changes since the American Revolution had continued to create new possibilities for white men, there was a closing down of certain opportunities for white women. Some of these changes were deliberate; others were incidental by-products of larger structural or institutional changes in politics, culture, or society. Nonetheless, they all tended to produce the same unfortunate results: the marginalization of women in electoral politics and the more explicit exclusion of women from government.

The Limits of Universal Suffrage

At the same time that the "rights of woman" were gaining popularity, Americans were also debating the scope and meaning of men's rights. Contemporaries understood this debate as part of a larger reconsideration of the rights question throughout the transatlantic world. This question had particular salience in the early republic, where both the Federalist and Democratic-Republican Parties claimed to be the true heirs and rightful protectors of the American revolutionary legacy. Struggling to establish their role in the new nation, each party also defined its own distinct understanding of the meaning of that legacy.

Federalists viewed the Revolution primarily as a political struggle, fought in order to reject British rule and preserve the colonists' traditional rights and liberties. After the war had ended, the contest was, in their minds, also over. Traditional elites should rule. Order, hierarchy, and deference should be restored. Horrified at events in France, they feared that their own country could easily disintegrate into licentiousness or anarchy. Although committed to representative government, they did not want to expand the popular basis of government. Voting should remain the privilege of the propertied classes. Their ideal was, as Federalist Samuel Stone put it, "*a speaking* aristocracy *in the face of a silent* democracy."[2]

In contrast, Republicans, following their leader Thomas Jefferson, regarded themselves as true "friends of the people." They believed that the War for Independence represented the first step in a larger struggle to transform the social order. The French revolutionaries' call to liberty, equality, and fraternity resonated with their own revolutionary ideals. In subsequent years they would seek to fulfill this vision by wrenching power from the hands of traditional elites and broadening political participation to include all social classes. In particular, Republicans viewed the persistence of property qualifications for voting as an archaic hangover from the country's monarchical past. Suffrage should be considered a fundamental right rather than a privilege of property.[3]

In the mid-1790s Republicans began a campaign to push for changes in the franchise throughout the country. This was necessary because although many states had lowered their property requirements for voting, only two states had come close to realizing the principle of universal manhood suffrage: Pennsylvania, whose 1776 constitution allowed all men who paid taxes to vote; and Vermont, which when entering the union in 1791 had abolished all property and wealth qualifications for voting. In the years since independence, the problem of disfranchisement had grown. The number of propertyless men, including artisans, wage laborers, and mechanics, especially in cities, was increasing. Waves of foreign immigrants increased the ranks of nonvoters. Once enfranchised, both groups would likely support the more egalitarian Democratic Republicans rather than the Federalists who were portrayed as aristocratic and elitist. Jeffersonians thus found both practical and ideological reasons to support an expansion of the franchise.[4]

Because the U.S. Constitution had left the question of voting qualifications up to each state, Republicans had to wage their campaign for eliminating property qualifications state by state. During the period from 1789 to 1830, many of the original thirteen states revised their first constitutions; eleven new states wrote constitutions in order to be admitted to the union. In each state Republican supporters of universal suffrage faced off with their opponents, who opposed the expansion of the franchise. Republicans thought that they would seize the moral high ground by framing the question in terms of natural rights. If all men were equal, their argument went, then all men should be entitled to vote. The ownership of land, they said, did not necessarily give individuals the requisite reason, judgment, or virtue to vote. Those who did not own property had as much stake in society and commitment to the country's welfare as those who did own property. Voting should be considered a right rather than a privilege. As a 1792 pamphlet put it, "The rights of suffrage are to a free people, what the rights of conscience are to individuals; and neither can be infringed or attacked, without violating the laws of nature and the inherent privileges of man."[5]

Nonetheless, both sides soon realized that despite their restrictiveness, property qualifications possessed a certain enviable concreteness, clarity, and simplicity. A person either owned enough land to vote or he did not. In contrast, treating suffrage as a natural right opened up all sorts of troubling questions. If all human beings possessed these rights, then why should only certain groups and not others be allowed to vote? Indeed, women themselves began to point out the similarities between their own qualifications for voting and those of the non-property-owning men who Republicans believed should be allowed to vote. In a letter to the *Richmond Enquirer*, published while the Virginia state constitutional convention was meeting in 1829, an author calling herself "A Virginia Freewoman" protested the convention's failure to attend to the question of women's rights. "Why is it," she asked, "that the pretensions of almost every other class of society have been duly weighed," but "*one half of the Society*" continued to be "cut off, at one throw from all share in the administration of government." This, she believed, was not just. "Are we [women] not as free as the Lords of Creation? Are we not as much affected by the laws which are passed as the Lords of the Creation themselves? What just reasons can be given for this unjust exclusion?" Federalists and other political conservatives had no trouble refuting this reasoning. They rejected outright the claim that the franchise was a natural right. Instead, they continued to see suffrage as a privilege that should be confined to propertied males. As a result, they saw no need to extend the franchise to women. "The Rights of Man had already been tried with considerable success among the refuse of male society," noted one sarcastic author. "The Rights of Woman was sure of finding an audience equally numerous and select among [the] female sex." As conservatives saw it, neither unpropertied males nor women had a valid claim to suffrage.[6]

Republicans, however, did not seek to extend the franchise to all people but only to white males and, in a few states, free black males. Opponents of universal suffrage quickly seized on the logical contradictions in the Republicans' argument with regard to women. In state after state they hammered away at the inconsistencies in their adversaries' position—not because they wished to enfranchise women but because they wanted to undermine the case for broadening male suffrage. At the Massachusetts state convention in 1820, for example, Josiah Quincy pointed out, "[It is said that] 'every man, whose life and liberty is made liable to the laws, ought therefore to have a voice, in the choice of his legislators.' Grant this argument to be just. Is it not equally applicable to women and to minors? Are they not liable to the laws? Ought they not then to have a voice in the voice? The denial of this right to them shows that the principle [of universal manhood suffrage] is not just." If voting were considered a natural right, on par with the ownership of private property, then, as a Rhode Island report observed, suffrage "ought to be common to all, without distinction of age, sex or color." Politicians in other states agreed. At the New York constitutional convention in 1821, Colonel Samuel Young noted, "In New-Jersey, females were formerly allowed to vote; and on that principle, you must admit negresses as well as negroes to participate in the right of suffrage. Minors, too, and aliens must not be excluded, but the 'era of good feelings' commenced in earnest."

When they were honest, opponents of universal suffrage admitted that they did not actually advocate enfranchising blacks and women. As Judge Abel Upshur of Virginia acknowledged in 1829 at the Virginia convention, "I use the argument only to shew what consequences this demand [for universal suffrage], founded on a supposed law of nature, must inevitably conduct us." The important point remained: the more that voting was defined as a right of persons, not of property, the more tenuous were the grounds for not including women.[7]

In response, Republicans had two choices: they could choose to be consistent and extend the principles of equality and natural rights to include other dispossessed groups, such as free blacks and women; or they could simply affirm the exclusions and basically admit that their commitment to universal principles was not truly universal. In almost every state they chose the latter course. Although a New York delegate admitted in 1821 that women comprised "the better half" of the population, enfranchising women would be neither "prudent, wise [nor] convenient." Republicans remained supremely confident in the gender status quo. Presenting their case to the Virginia convention in 1829, the nonfreeholders of Richmond maintained, "For obvious reasons, by almost universal consent, women and children, aliens and slaves, are excluded. It were useless to discuss the propriety of a rule that scarcely admits of a diversity of opinion." Because they believed (correctly) that the opposition shared their unwillingness to enfranchise women, they could reject their adversaries' arguments with disdain rather than with a reasoned response. At the Virginia constitutional convention of 1829–30, Philip Doddridge tartly asserted, "It will not do to test any rule by extreme cases. I presume it cannot be necessary for me to assign a reason for the exceptions. In this [my opponent] and myself would doubtless agree." Thus, when legislators writing new state constitutions considered the issue of women's rights, they usually did so as a way of discrediting the movement for universal male suffrage. When pressed, Republicans refused to go out on a limb for the sake of consistency in their principles. They depended on the belief that their opposition would not push the matter further. The representatives' shared commitment to the existing gender hierarchy meant that both sides used female suffrage more as a rhetorical ploy than as a genuine opportunity for reform.[8]

Outside the convention, however, there were others who wished to pursue the issue. In their view, it seemed unjust that women, who might be as intelligent, virtuous, or committed to the government as men, could not vote. Expanding the franchise to include men who may not have been as educated or well informed as many women highlighted the inequity of women's exclusion. A poem called "Petition to the Convention in Behalf of the Ladies," published in a popular magazine and directed to the statesmen meeting in the convention in Albany, New York, pointed out the tenuous basis for women's continuing exclusion:

> That ev'ry one must have a vote,
> Who does not wear a petticoat,
>   Is generally admitted;
> But why should women be denied
> And have their tongues completely tied,
>   For party broils well fitted.[9]

Once the property qualifier was dropped, men—even disreputable men who had "forfeit[ed] all pretentions / To decency and common sense"—enjoyed "the birthright of election." At the same time, women, though they might be as "pure as Eden's queen," could "never to election come." Women, it was clear, were not excluded because they lacked sufficient property, education, or virtue but simply because they were women.

The letter from "A Virginia Freewoman" published while the Virginia constitutional convention was meeting in 1829 expressed an even stronger sense of injustice over this development. Noting that she had followed the convention debates in the local newspapers, "Freewoman" expressed her "astonishment and indignation" that no one had come forward "to vindicate 'the Rights of women.'" Because men without property were being enfranchised, the fact that few women owned property (and would not be able to do so until the widespread passage of married women's property laws in the 1840s) no longer constituted a sufficient justification. Taking into account the existence of coverture, "Freewoman" acknowledged that even if married women could not exercise the franchise, it was only fair that single women be enfranchised. She ended her letter with a demand and a plea:

We call upon the Convention, then, in the name of Justice and of Truth, to listen to our Claims, and secure our rights. This is the day of Reform. While so many others are recovering their long-lost Rights, why should we alone be excluded from the benefits of the Convention—We call upon that wise and honourable body, to listen to the just language of our complaint—and admit us to a participation of their power.[10]

Although now construed as a "natural right," voting had essentially become a different kind of privilege—a privilege of those who had happened to be born male. Like unfranchised men, "Virginia Freewoman" too wanted to enjoy her "day of Reform."

This discussion of women's rights continued to percolate just below the surface of American political life. As the historian Lori Ginzberg has shown, two years before the women of Seneca Falls organized their convention, six women from Jefferson County, New York, actually presented a petition to their state constitutional convention in which they voiced their demand for female suffrage. Drawing on the power of their revolutionary heritage, they declared that "the present government of this state has widely departed from the true democratic principles upon which all just governments must be based by denying to the female portion of community the right of suffrage." Bypassing the language of deference or submission, these women then insisted instead on addressing the delegates as equals, asking the convention to "confer upon them [the women] no new right but only to declare and enforce those which they originally inherited, but which have ungenerously been withheld from them, rights, which they as citizens of the state of New York may reasonably and rightfully claim." Thus even before the Seneca Falls Convention of 1848, other women scattered throughout the United States had begun to promote the cause of woman suffrage.[11]

Republicans had been overwhelmingly successful. By 1830 they had expanded the franchise to include almost all adult white males throughout the country. Most of the original states had abolished their property qualifications for voting. Most new states entering the union placed no property restrictions on their voters. Even Virginia, South Carolina, and Tennessee, which continued to retain certain property qualifiers, offered alternative methods for individuals to meet the requirement without actually owning land. Yet the gains for white males came at the expense of other dispossessed groups, specifically women and free blacks. Virtually every state constitution written after 1790, including revised constitutions from the original states and constitutions from new states just entering the union, included race and gender exclusions. Whereas before the language had been gender-neutral, now the language restricted voting to "males," or more specifically to "free white males" or "white male citizens." Even in those few states without an explicit gender qualifier, there was a more conscious awareness of women's exclusion. As a Massachusetts author put it in 1820, "Only free male citizens legally possess an elective franchise. This explanation was not precisely warranted by the words of the Constitution, but was undoubtedly just and reasonable." In the process of expanding the franchise, suffrage had become an explicitly male prerogative.[12]

In effect, the debate over universal suffrage inadvertently opened up a much broader issue: the question of inclusions and exclusions from the polity. Broadening the franchise to include all white men transformed the basic rationale for distinguishing between voters and nonvoters. As long as property qualifications had existed, suffrage could be understood primarily as a privilege of wealth, not necessarily related to the individual's race or gender. Because most suffrage provisions prior to 1790 did not mention the voter's sex, women's exclusion tended to be incidental and customary rather than overt and explicit. This kind of exclusion—what one might call a sin of omission—allowed certain experiments, such as women voting in New Jersey, to occur. However, once women were legally and explicitly excluded from the franchise, such experiments were no longer possible. Gender and race became the fundamental lines of demarcation, separating those who could vote from those who could not.

The debate exposed an assumption that had long been implicit in American society: the sexual basis of the social contract. Some modern political theorists, such as Carole Pateman, Joan Landes, and others, have argued that the social contract on which liberal polities, such as the United States, rest is by its very nature a "fraternal contract," essentially "masculinist" in character. The exclusion of women, they say, is not an incidental feature of such governments but part of their fundamental makeup, traceable back to John Locke's original formulation. "Structural sexism," they claim, has made these nations extremely resistant to altering the status quo for women. Indeed, some theorists maintain that liberal polities may find the full incorporation of women structurally impossible.[13]

Yet the demise of property qualifications for white males suggests that the problem is not in the theory of liberalism per se but in the contingent circumstances in which liberal nation-states emerged. In the eighteenth and nineteenth centuries, liberal principles were applied not to all people but rather only to white males. At the time it was what the historian Hilda Smith has called a "false universal."[14] Yet the debate did not end there. The triumph of universal white male suffrage in effect validated the idea of universal rights as the primary standard for judging political participation. Henceforth, any exclusions from this standard, or deviations from this norm, could not simply be assumed; they had to be justified and explained. Having been exposed as limited, liberal principles became transparent and subject to debate, contestation, and open discussion. The real debate had just begun.

The Marginalization of Women in Party Politics

In addition to facing new legal exclusions from the franchise, women also began to face new structural barriers to participating in politics. Although Americans had subscribed to a belief in the rule of law, different norms governed the popular expression of political sentiment at different times. Before the Revolution, Anglo-Americans had regarded

politics out of doors and in the streets as an important and valid means
of political participation. Although colonists could not elect members
to Parliament, they could hang stamp-tax collectors in effigy, dump tea
into Boston harbor, or ostracize those who violated boycotts against British goods. After the Revolution, a celebratory political culture that
included parades, processions, and patriotic gatherings helped build
party spirit as well as unite Americans into a single nation. Americans
gathered together at Fourth of July celebrations and on other occasions
to remember their common origins and to reflect on their commitment
to shared political ideals. This expansive understanding of politics made
it possible for both voters and nonvoters—women as well as men—to
have a place in the political system.

In the first decades of the new republic, politics continued to exist out
of doors as leaders of both parties, seeking a kind of legitimacy through
numbers, sponsored a variety of activities. After Jefferson's election in
1800, however, Federalists as well as Republicans realized the importance of systematizing party operations in an effort to recruit supporters
who could make the most difference in electing their candidates. The
older, deferential tradition of "standing for office" went into decline.
Instead of running simply on the basis of reputation, candidates would
have to gain their parties' nominations, publicize their views on particular issues, and meet with voters in order to gain popular support. Newspapers became important campaign tools. Members of both parties
resorted to aggressive tactics that spread rumors or disseminated false
information about political opponents. Parties themselves became more
highly organized, developing regular procedures for nominating candidates, bringing out the vote, and rewarding loyalty through patronage.
Even Federalists, who had initially loathed such techniques, began to
adopt electioneering tactics that would make their message more
appealing to a mass electorate.[15]

Party competition stimulated increased voter interest and participation in the electoral process. In the early national era, about one-fourth
to one-third of all eligible voters cast ballots in state and federal elections. In highly contested elections, when two divergent candidates ran
for office, turnout was much higher. In fact, Jefferson's election in 1800
ushered in a period of tremendous increases in voter participation. In
the election of 1800 itself, as many as 90 percent of all eligible electors
voted in some places. During Jefferson's embargo as many as 70 percent
voted. Combined with the expansion of the franchise, these changes
meant that citizenship was increasingly defined in terms of voting rights
and that voting rights came to be understood as the most important privilege of citizenship. In 1789 David Ramsay noted, "Citizenship confers a
right of voting at elections and many other privileges not enjoyed by

those who are no more than inhabitants." By 1828 Noah Webster's dictionary defined "citizen" as a "person native or naturalized who has the privilege of exercising the elective franchise or qualifications which enable him to vote for rulers." Whereas voting in the colonial era had been one of many vehicles through which individuals could express their political sentiments, by the Jacksonian period the franchise came to be seen as the primary, if not exclusive, means of expressing the popular will and the highest form of citizenship.[16]

As more men could vote, the focus of politics shifted from out of doors and in the streets to the internal activities of each particular party. Especially after 1800 both Republicans and Federalists increasingly directed their primary attention toward actual or potential voters. Fraternal organizations proved to be fruitful recruiting grounds for party members. Federalists dominated the Washington Benevolent Society and the Society of the Cincinnati, while Republicans prevailed in the Tammany Society and various artisan and mechanics guilds. Militia organizations often maintained party affiliation. Men joined particular groups based on their desire to associate with like-minded men. At times the parties also used military-style forms of organization to draw voters to the polls and mobilize support for their candidates. On election days party leaders might order members to gather in formation, parade together down the streets to the polling place, and preside as a "committee of vigilance" over the day's activities. In Philadelphia in 1808, for example, Federalists and Republicans, in their own distinctive uniforms, marched on election day to a local polling place and stood in formation, opposing each other. Members carried guns, though supposedly participants were told to bring only blank cartridges. Despite reports that an atmosphere of "menace" had prevailed, the sides did not actually come to blows. At a time in which election riots were not uncommon, this was no mean achievement. Nonetheless, such activities reflected important changes in the nature of partisan political participation. Military-style activities obviously had no place for women, except perhaps in the ceremonial presentation of flags or banners to the troops. All-male rituals increasingly replaced mixed-sex functions.[17]

The more these activities became central to the recruitment and retention of party members, the less important women became to party leaders. As party operations became more formalized and regularized, each party devised procedures for involving ordinary men at the grassroots level. Men organized activities to support their candidates, rallied other party members to get out the vote, and held festivities to celebrate their parties' victories. In Bennington, Vermont, for example, a middling farmer named Hiram Harwood described in his journal his enthusiastic participation during the second decade of the nineteenth century in local Republican Party activities. At some point before an election he and other male party members would canvass neighborhoods trying to get a sense of the electors' choices. Armed with this information, the town's leading Republicans, consisting solely of men, gathered together in a caucus, called the "Grand Committee of Vigilance," to calculate their prospects for victory and work out an electoral strategy. Afterward they would ask sympathetic male partisans, such as Harwood, to write out "tickets" listing the party's candidates. In fact, Harwood was so dedicated to the cause that in 1815 he spent the morning after his wedding compiling a voter list. On election day he and other male partisans stood near the polling place, wearing hats or badges bearing their party affiliations, and handed out tickets to their potential supporters. In this kind of political system, there was less need for women to participate in party activities and less desire to invite them to do so.[18]

The gradual disappearance of the Federalist Party and the triumph of the Republicans also contributed to a less receptive environment for women's political participation. In localities where Republicans faced no opposition, party members had less need to court women's approval for their activities. Partisans had all the supporters they needed among white males. Moreover, Republicans as a group had always been less sympathetic than Federalists to women's involvement in politics. They took their cue from their leader, Thomas Jefferson. Even before becoming president, Jefferson had probably thought more about educational matters than any other member of the founding generation had. Yet he never turned his attention to the education of women. Except for his daughters, he admitted, "a plan of female education has never been a subject of systematic contemplation with me." For his daughters, he essentially wanted training in ornamental areas, such as dancing, drawing, and music. He abhorred their reading of novels and urged them to learn French, the language of refinement and gentility. Jefferson dismissed the possibility that his daughters would play a role in educating their sons. Only if the "fathers be lost, or incapable, or inattentive," he said, should a mother become involved in the process.[19]

More generally, he scorned women's interest in politics. Commenting on the tumult leading up to the French Revolution, he remarked, "Gay and thoughtless Paris is now become a furnace of Politics. All the world is run politically mad. Men, women, children talk of nothing else." Obviously disapproving, he hoped that was not the case in America: "Our good ladies, I trust, have been too wise to wrinkle their foreheads with politics. They are contented to soothe and calm the minds of their husbands returning ruffled from political debate. They have the good sense to value domestic happiness above all other, and the art to cultivate it beyond all others." As president, he abruptly dismissed a woman's request for a position as postmistress. This was not, he said, an "innovation for which the public is prepared, nor am I." Contrary to Jefferson's suggestion, however, this was no innovation. At least a few other women had previously served as postmistresses, usually after their husbands had died in office. Mary Katherine Goddard, for example, served as postmistress in Baltimore for over a decade, from 1775 to 1789. When she was dismissed in 1789, numerous citizens petitioned President George Washington—unsuccessfully, as it turned out—for her reinstatement. Jefferson, however, simply could not tolerate the notion that women might hold political power of any sort.[20]

The attitudes of rank-and-file members also varied by party. Federalists tended to depict women as active patriots who vigorously embraced their political role. In a typical remark, Keating Lewis Simon celebrated women's contributions during the Revolution, saying, "To the fair of our country, we are as much indebted for that glorious achievement, as to the generous souls, who endured the toils of the camp, and withstood the shocks of battle. Warmed by the same honorable feelings, [women] maintained, throughout, the same devotion to the cause. Their patriotism became the more noble, as it was of a kind entirely suited to their sex." Although women's sacrifices may have been different than men's, they were essentially equal in significance. In contrast, Republican rhetoric, while acknowledging women's contributions, often portrayed women merely as men's ancillaries or adjuncts. They were passive patriots who acted at men's behest, not of their own accord. Discussing women's participation in the American Revolution, Richard Dinsmore told the Tammany Society of New York, "In times demanding the exercise of public virtue, . . . the fair daughters of America, contested the palm of patriotism with, and emulated the decisive patriotism of their husbands and brothers." The suggestion was that women imitated men's more "decisive" patriotism rather than acted on their own volition. Women's patriotism was subordinate to or derivative of men's greater contributions. Similarly, in a kind of backhanded compliment, Reverend Solomon Aiken recalled women's "patriotic concurrence" during the Revolution. "Our heroines, in their place," he said, "were not a whit behind our foremost heroes." Aiken's formulation aptly captures the passivity inherent in the Republicans' trope. Women "concurred" in their husbands' patriotism rather than exercised their own independent judgment. Although "heroines," they still should be kept "in their place."[21]

Over time, the disappearance of Federalists from the political scene and the triumph of the Republican Party further eroded women's presence in electoral politics. A corollary to the Republicans' portrayal of women as passive patriots was a heightened emphasis on the quintessentially male character of the political realm. Instead of portraying liberty and freedom as benefits open to all Americans, they focused on the masculine nature of those prerogatives. An 1808 poem, written in the era of Jefferson's embargo, not only appealed primarily to men but also depicted men as the country's primary political actors:

Prepare! Columbia's sons, prepare!
    We'll die before we'll yield our right.
For he who gave us life, gave thee,
    Our country's pride—sweet *liberty*.
Father above, in thee we trust—
    A band of *brothers* look to thee;
We own thy *power*, but know thee just,
    And trust that nature made us free,
Yes, He who gave us life, gave thee,
    Our country's pride—*our liberty*.

In contrast to the earlier political space populated by women and men alike, Jeffersonian politics emphasized the importance of male bonding. Although an 1815 song, celebrating Andrew Jackson's victory in New Orleans, depicted the country as "our mother," it was men who had saved the nation from annihilation:

Then let each son and brother,
Stand firm by one another,
    And sing the song of joy.

"Columbia's sons," not her daughters, apparently had the first, and exclusive, claim on patriotism. Republicans reveled in their masculinity. As a Vermont orator put it, the American "band of brothers" was "More bound to liberty/ Than husband is to wife." A homosocial construct, the Republican vision of the polity left little place for women.[22]

Ironically, the Republicans' inability to think creatively or expansively about women may have been a result of the radicalism of their vision for white males. Federalists could afford to be gracious to women because they knew who their women were: maids and matrons of the respectable classes. Even rabble-rousers such as Nelly Parke Custis or the widows of New Jersey who voted could be counted on to behave in a manner befitting those who possessed a substantial amount of wealth and property.[23] In seeking to open up voting and office holding to people of all social classes, however, Republicans attacked deference and challenged the existing social hierarchy. In reaching out to people of various social classes, they opened up the possibility of including those who might be unpropertied, disorderly, or disreputable. Their agenda was so controversial, Republicans believed, that to include women as well as men might well doom the entire project. Democratization for white men, then, would proceed at the expense of all women.

A gap persisted, however, between the rhetoric and the reality of the Republicans' program. Despite an ostensible commitment to universal rights, Republicans did not seek to destroy social hierarchy altogether; rather, they aimed to replace one hierarchy with another. In rejecting birth and wealth as the bases of political privilege, they devised a social order in which supposed biological differences, as defined by gender and race, determined relative status. Subordination would be for those for whom, as the historian Pauline Maier puts it, "dependency seemed right and natural." As Dr. Samuel Johnson noted in a different but comparable context, "Your *levellers* . . . wish to *level down* as far as themselves, but they cannot bear levelling *up* to themselves; they would all *have some people* under them; why not then have some people above them?" All white males could be leveled up because women, children, blacks, and Indians were to be leveled down.[24]

The growing exclusion of women from party and electoral politics corresponded with the growing acceptance of a two-party political system. The shift is vividly illustrated in two paintings of election scenes from two different eras in early America. During the waning days of the first party system, the artist John Lewis Krimmel decided to memorialize an election day in Philadelphia. His image is among the few contemporaneous visual portrayals of elections in early America that are known to exist. Painted in the aftermath of the War of 1812, the image suggests both the continuing intensity of partisan animosity and the capaciousness of the political realm. The painting portrays the election as a raucous, carnivalesque affair in which the citizens of Philadelphia mingle on an urban street, with American flags waving overhead, engaged in a wide variety of activities: talking, drinking, arguing, and even fighting. Significantly, a wide diversity of individuals are present. Well-off gentlemen wearing fine clothes and top hats dominate the scene, but others, including children, members of the lower classes, African Americans, and women, appear.

The depiction of women is particularly significant. On the left side is a white woman holding a baby. She is positioned between two men who are presumably of opposing political parties and are apparently engaged in a fistfight. As the prescriptive literature of the day suggested, this woman was acting as a peacemaker and mediator between the warring partisans, not just figuratively but literally. (See Figure 12.) Another well-dressed white woman, apparently horrified by the looming brawl, strolls

Figure 13. *Election at the State House* (c. 1815), by John Lewis Krimmel. Pencil and watercolor. This image of a Philadelphia election in 1815 reveals the inclusive nature of party and electoral politics in the early part of the century. Although wealthy white men who were potential voters predominate, the scene also includes lower-class men, African Americans, white women, and children, none of whom could vote. Krimmel's image highlights the importance of politics that took place in the streets, outside of the State House, rather than what took place inside, the actual casting of ballots. (The Historical Society of Pennsylvania.)

down the street arm in arm with a male companion. Nearby, an African American woman in a cloak, crouching down close to the ground, apparently is stealing an apple. What is most striking, however, is what Krimmel does not show. Although he called it an "Election Scene," he did not portray the actual act of voting anywhere in the painting. The casting of ballots apparently occurred offstage, inside the Philadelphia State House on the right. The implication seems to be that what happened in the streets on election day was as important as what happened at the ballot box—perhaps even more so. Krimmel portrayed an inclusive kind of politics that reflected the participation of nonvoters, including women, in the political process.[25] (See Figure 13.)

In the 1840s and 1850s the painter George Caleb Bingham produced a very different series of election scenes. In particular, his painting *The County Election* from 1851–52 represents a striking contrast to Krimmel's earlier portrayal. Bingham portrayed a local election in rural Missouri during the heyday of the second party system, the Whigs and the Democrats. Like Krimmel, Bingham included a diverse array of activities and participants in his election scene. Children play, dogs prowl. Men of business discuss weighty matters while farmers chat. Other men take advantage of a flowing supply of liquor, and some apparently indulge to excess.

The visual focus of the painting is on the right, slightly off-center and above ground level. A man, presumably an election official, stands framed by the columns of a porch. He is raising his hand, ready to administer the elector's oath. A voter (whose shirt is painted a vivid red) mounts several steps and places his hand on a Bible in order to take the oath. At his left, a politician hands out party tickets. Behind him, other voters stand in line. These details stand in sharp contrast to Krimmel's image. Bingham did not include either black people or women in the scene. All those present are white males. Even more important, unlike Krimmel, Bingham makes the act of casting the ballot the picture's central feature. Voting has moved from offstage to become the visual focus. Although not all individuals in the scene display intense interest in the electoral process, Bingham clearly highlighted voting as the defining act of citizenship. Both in the image and in reality, the result was the virtual erasure of women from the electoral scene.[26] (See Figure 14.)

Despite the general tendency toward exclusion, women did make one other brief, but significant, appearance in electoral politics during the Antebellum era. As the historian Elizabeth Varon has shown, the emergence of the Whig Party created a new space for women's political participation in the late 1840s and early 1850s. In certain parts of the country, women rallied to support Henry Clay and William Henry Harrison in their bids for president. Like their predecessors, Whig women attended public rallies, wrote pamphlets, and collected money for their candidates. Male leaders welcomed their support. Nonetheless, as the Whig Party declined, so did the women's participation. Neither the Democratic nor the Republican party offered the kind of sustenance to women that the Whigs or, in an earlier day, the Federalists had provided.[27]

The triumph of universal male suffrage and the growing acceptance of a permanent two-party political system meant that the structure of politics itself was less hospitable to women. Party politics increasingly focused on those who determined the outcome at the ballot box: white male electors. Once virtually all white men could vote, voting became

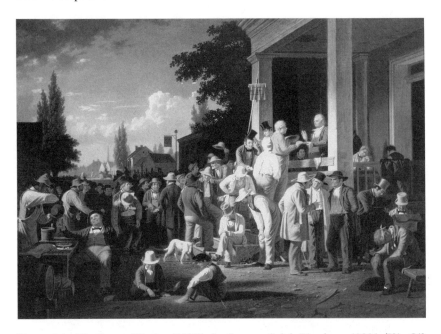

Figure 14. *The County Election* (1852), by George Caleb Bingham (1811–79). Oil on canvas. This image shows an election scene in rural Missouri during the era of the second party system, the Whigs and the Democrats. Although men of various ages and social classes appear, they are all white males. At the right, the painting's focal point centers on a man who administers an oath to an elector about to cast his ballot. By this time voting had become the defining feature of citizenship. (Saint Louis Art Museum. Gift of Bank of America.)

the sine qua non of political participation and the defining feature of full citizenship. Party leaders saw less need to court women and had less desire to seek women's participation in their functions. Individual partisans participated in activities and rituals that built bonds with other male party members rather than reaching out to the larger community. Whereas a politics conducted out of doors and in the streets had been able to incorporate women and free blacks, a politics centered on the ballot box did not.

The Turn to Biological Essentialism

Despite women's growing marginalization in electoral politics, American women and men faced even deeper questions about the basis of women's exclusion from government. Before the American Revolution, women's exclusion had been more assumed than explicit, taken for granted as a matter of custom and habit rather than as the result of a deliberate decision. By the late eighteenth century, however, a combination of factors—Enlightenment ideas about women's equality, Wollstonecraft's assertion of women's natural rights, women voting in New Jersey, and women's increasing, albeit informal, involvement in politics—had challenged these assumptions. Subsequent political developments expanding male suffrage had the effect of highlighting the excluded status of women. Once voting emerged as the quintessential privilege of membership in a liberal polity, these issues came to a head. Although many American men and women had been prepared to entertain the notion that women had rights and were in some respects equal to men, there was insufficient support for enfranchising women or granting them formal political rights. They thus faced a dilemma: how could a nation committed to equality and natural rights reconcile those principles with a desire to exclude women from government?

Even during the War for Independence, some men and women had begun to consider these questions. Reservations about women's ability often focused on women's domestic obligations and maternal duties. *The Essex Result*, a pamphlet written in 1778 in Massachusetts, claimed that women were not prevented from voting because of "a deficiency in their mental powers" but rather because "their retired mode of life, and various domestic duties prevent that promiscuous intercourse with the world, which is necessary to qualify them for electors." In effect, women's household chores would prevent them from becoming well informed and fully participatory in politics. John Adams made a similar argument. Although women possessed "as good judgments, and as independent minds, as those men who are wholly destitute of property," their "domestic cares," especially "the necessary nurture of their children," rendered them "unfit for practice and experience in the great businesses of life . . . and the arduous cares of state." The circumstances of a woman's daily life, then, would preclude women from taking their place as electors alongside men.[28]

The weaknesses of these arguments soon became apparent. As the case for women's intellectual equality with men gained acceptance, women could not simply be dismissed because they lacked the intellectual capacity to understand political issues. As women acquired greater literacy and education, they could not be rejected primarily because they lacked knowledge of the affairs of state. As women became informally involved in politics, it was clear they had an interest in the issues. The ubiquitous histories of women published in England and America throughout the eighteenth century, including William Alexander's popular *History of Women*, showed that women were as capable as men of exercising political authority. In fact, Americans' own recent experience demonstrated that women were willing and able political actors. During the Revolution, women had often put aside their domestic chores and demonstrated their support for independence through a variety of public activities. John Adams had actually encouraged women such as Mercy Otis Warren to use her "masculine genius" to write poems and plays attacking British tyranny. In New Jersey numerous women had overcome their feminine modesty and cast ballots in various state and federal elections. Although women's "retired mode of life," "domestic duties," and even their "feminine reserve" might make it difficult for women to vote or hold office, those restrictions did not make their participation impossible.[29]

Following this reasoning, some observers concluded that there was no sound rationale for excluding women from the franchise. The exclusion was customary rather than necessary. If society had created these customs, then society could also change them. As Paul Brown asserted in an 1828 lecture in Cincinnati, "Why has it been customary [to exclude women from the vote]? What is the reason this custom has always prevailed? We know of many customs that prevail, in favor of which no reason can be offered why they should prevail—and perhaps this is one of them." Similarly, an Ohio woman asserted in 1833, "If custom is to be the arbiter of laws and manners, then, all we will contend for, will be to make it customary for us to enjoy our privileges, and our object is accomplished." As long as women's exclusion was understood as a custom, there was hope for change. The day might soon come when women would be fully enfranchised.[30]

This possibility had been sustained by the Enlightenment theory that historians call "environmentalism." Traceable to John Locke's claim that the mind is a tabula rasa, or blank slate, this theory posited a view of human nature in which human capacities are not fixed and immutable but rather are susceptible to change according to circumstances. Following François Poulain de la Barre's declaration in 1673 that "The mind has no sex," the notion of women's intellectual equality gained increasing acceptance over the course of the eighteenth century. A main implication of the theory was to deemphasize the importance of physical strength and body size and to stress the similarities of the sexes in their mental capacities and moral faculties. Nonphysical attributes—the mind and the soul—were regarded as an individual's highest powers, while physical traits, such as anatomical differences between men and women, diminished in importance.[31]

The popularity of this notion contributed to a greater belief in women's potential. Diminishing the importance of physical attributes between the sexes expanded the scope of possibilities. It seemed possible that women one day might equal men's achievements in a wide variety of arenas. If mental characteristics were more important than body features in determining membership in the polity, then there seemed little reason to exclude women. In his novel *Alcuin*, Charles Brockden Brown focuses on this precise issue. Making the case for female suffrage, Brockden Brown's female protagonist, Mrs. Carter, insists that the differences between the sexes are so minor that they should not be an impediment to women's participation in government. "Mere sex," she declares, "is a circumstance so purely physical; has so little essential influence beyond what has flowed from the caprice of civil institutions on the qualities of mind or person, that I cannot think of it without impatience. If the law should exclude from all political functions every one who had a mole on his right cheek, or whose stature did not exceed six feet six inches, who would not condemn, without scruple, so unjust an institution? Yet in truth, the injustice would be less than in the case of women." Just as a person's height or facial features did not affect one's political rights, neither should a person's sex disqualify that person from political participation. "Mere sex," in her view, did not constitute sufficient grounds for exclusion. Women, in other words, should not be prohibited from voting simply because they were women.[32]

Such questions were not unique to the United States. Throughout the western world political thinkers on both sides of the Atlantic faced similar issues, trying to come to terms with the impact of liberal universalistic principles on their understanding of women's role and status. The emergence of democratic and egalitarian ideologies brought these issues to the fore throughout the nations of western Europe, especially in Britain and France.[33] However, the question was particularly pressing in the United States. Women's exclusion from governance raised disturbing doubts about the country's commitment to justice and fairness. As a young republic, the United States was in the very process of establishing its legitimacy and securing people's loyalty. If Americans chose to deny women equal political rights with men, then a more secure rationale for their disfranchisement would have to be found. This was not simply an academic exercise. The authority and legitimacy of the new republic were at stake.

The solution did not arise quickly or systematically. In fact, although the outlines had begun to appear by the late eighteenth century, the theory was not fully fleshed out until the middle decades of the nineteenth century. Participating in and borrowing from a broad transatlantic dialogue, Americans turned toward the newly emergent empirical sciences—biology, anatomy, and medicine—as a way of better understanding women's place in society. By selectively appropriating certain aspects of these ideas, they were able to create a rationale that satisfied them as to the grounds for women's exclusion from political rights.

Intellectual developments drawn from the transatlantic world of science shaped this new understanding of women. By the last quarter of the eighteenth century, developments in medicine and human anatomy, along with the rise of experimental science, led to an increased focus on men's and women's reproductive systems. Observers recorded, described, and analyzed the precise differences in genitalia, sexual impulses, and roles in procreation and childbirth between men and women. The more they examined these features, the more they highlighted the importance of physical attributes in defining human capacity. Whereas Enlightenment thinkers had stressed the essential similarities in men's and women's intellectual abilities and moral faculties, early nineteenth-century scientists emphasized the essential differences in the sexes' physical makeups. These differences, grounded in biological nature, appeared to be inherent and immutable.[34]

The most important change was not in the scientific findings themselves but in how they were used and interpreted. Rather than incidental and unimportant, physiological differences between the sexes came to represent what the historian Thomas Laqueur has called "the foundation of incommensurable difference." The female reproductive system was said to impose inherent limitations on women's abilities and capacities for a wide range of tasks. Women's menstrual cycles, pregnancies, and orgasms purportedly affected not only their physical strength but their mental ability as well. Not only were women doomed to be weaker and less robust than men, but in addition women's more vivid emotional life constricted their intellect. Female physiology created a heightened sensitivity to feelings, both physical and emotional. This greater "sensibility," as it was called, made women less logical and less rational than men. These changes were not understood in a neutral or value-free manner. Instead, they formed the basis for making moral and cultural judgments about women's place in society. Women's bodies came to be seen not simply as different from men's but also as inferior.[35]

American scholars and physicians who were educated in Europe transmitted these theories to the United States. Trained in Scotland, Dr. Benjamin Rush of Philadelphia became one of the foremost proponents of these new scientific ideas. Although a strong supporter of female education, he also believed in inherent biological differences between the sexes. In his lectures on medicine, he emphasized the impact of physical differences on women's abilities and potential. In contrast to the dictum, "The mind has no sex," Rush maintained that there was "a natural and original difference between the mind of a woman and [that of] a man, as certainly as there is between their bodies." This approach had significant consequences. Although women had greater "sensibility" and moral authority than men, they lacked men's full capacity for reason and understanding. They would never be capable of the same intellectual achievements. The physical differences between men and women mattered more than any other aspects of their personalities.[36]

From Rush's base in Philadelphia, these ideas spread throughout the scientific community and to a larger popular audience. Periodicals took up such ideas with enthusiasm. "Nature," noted the *New-York Weekly Magazine*, "seconded by reason and custom, had presumed to point out . . . the sphere of female duties and female obligations." Theology blended with science to sanction women's subordination and inferiority. "There is an admirable partition of qualities between the sexes," an article called "Parallel of the Sexes" noted, "which the Great Author of being has distributed to each, with a wisdom which calls for our admiration." Any effort to alter the gender hierarchy thus represented not only a crime against nature but also a challenge to the divine prerogative. "She who would invert the order of this system," declaimed a Philadelphia magazine, "not only betrays a pitiable ignorance of her own weakness but a spirit of rebellion against the ordinance of heaven."[37]

Naturalized sex differences had the appearance of irrevocable fact. Although "natural facts," says the historian Nancy Leys Stepan, "are always social facts, imbued with the values of the society in which they are produced, and unstable in their social meanings," it is much harder to resist "social claims made in the name of neutral science and inexorable nature."[38] If sexual differences were inscribed in nature, they could be seen as inherent, immutable, and unchangeable. Once biology became the markers not just of difference but also of inferiority, women's bodies provided a convenient explanation for excluding them from the same rights and privileges that men enjoyed.

This was particularly true with regard to politics and governance. A series of essays published in the *Virginia Gazette* in 1790 reveals an early American effort to use nature to justify women's exclusion. A thoughtful correspondent posed a provocative question to the editor of the *Virginia Gazette*. Why, he asked, if the Virginia Constitution of 1776 declared that "all mankind are born equal," did this phrase not extend to women, allowing them to vote and hold public office? Another author, who called himself "Philanthropos," responded and jumped into the fray. Equality, he said, could be applied in "too extensive a sense," producing, he feared, a tendency "to destroy those degrees of subordination which nature seems to point out as indispensable for the regulation of society." Turning specifically to the question of women, the author noted that God had made the world in such a fashion that "woman was originally created in subordination to man." This subordination, he suggested, should also extend to the political realm. Like Adams and *The Essex Result*, he pointed to the practical constraints on women's ability to participate in governance. "The relative duties of women in private life," he observed, were incompatible with "the perplexity and tumult of political life." Seeing the need for further explanation, however, he pushed his argument harder. "Nature (the surest guide)," he said, "has pointed out for [women] a course of duties and employments totally inconsistent with a life of political bustle and anxiety." Nature, not custom, provided the "surest guide" for excluding women from government.[39]

Retreating from the universalistic implications of their revolutionary ideals, Americans solidified a sexual division of political labor. Women's bodies, it was said, were inadequate for the purposes of governing. "Although perhaps even on the subject of law, politics or religion, [women] may form good judgment," said Hannah Mather Crocker, "it would be morally improper and *physically very incorrect*, for the female character to claim the statesman's berth, or ascend the rostrum to gain the loud applause of men." Men, it was said, governed not because of an accident of history but because of their inherent biological attributes. "The men who were to be guardians and law-givers," said *The Female Friend*, "had not only the greater share of bodily strength bestowed on them, but those also of reason and resolution." The consequences were profound. While customary restrictions could be changed, physiology could not. In an 1818 poem by Thomas Fessenden, a female character asks how it can be that men "esteem our sex so good and great" while at the same time preventing women from becoming "female warriors," "lady-legislators," or "hold[ing] offices in Church and State." Mentor, the male figure, supplies a succinct, but devastating, response:

Dame Nature tells us Mary's [Wollstonecraft] rights are wrong,
Her female freedom is a syren-song.

"Female freedom," then, should be understood as nothing more than a "syren-song" that lured women down a fallacious path. No law could alter what "Dame Nature" had decreed: women were not fit political actors.[40]

Women who stepped into the male realm of politics, it was said, not only acted like men but also became masculine. "Warlike women, learned women, and women who are politicians," proclaimed a Boston magazine, "equally abandon the circle which nature and institutions have traced round their sex; they convert themselves into men. They renounce the empire which they inevitably exercised by their weakness, to run vainly after the more equivocal empire of force." Violating these roles would open women to moral, legal, and even divine sanctions. A "female politician," then, could be seen as a deviant, an oxymoron, a "manly woman." Women who "so rule," warned a New Jersey newspaper, "are no longer women; but abortions." If domesticity was deemed "naturally" feminine, then governance could be seen as "naturally" masculine.[41]

In practice, biological essentialism meant that women's biological nature would prevent them from ever claiming the political rights and privileges that men enjoyed. Whereas customs and traditions could be changed, biology could not. This formulation deflected charges of a contradiction between a commitment to the universal principles of equality and natural rights and the exclusion of women. If sex roles were inscribed in nature, then no human being could alter them. As a result, according to an author writing in 1828, "The constitution of nature, ordained by no human conventions, recorded in no fundamental charter of government or petition of rights, but written over the face of the universe, and stamped indelibly upon the very organization of our race, has, we conceive, settled the question, whether the female sex should exercise political franchises equally with man." Although human constitutions might be modified, the "constitution of nature," which was "stamped indelibly upon the very organization of our race" could not be altered. A Virginia woman made a similar claim, also in 1828. "Even if men were disposed to admit women to an equality of rights and privileges," said Mrs. Virginia Cary, "both the laws of nature and of God, forbid them to accept such a concession." Nature, then, was invoked to help circumscribe women's natural rights. The political system was off the hook—at least temporarily. Nature had been harnessed to constrain women's natural rights.[42]

Not coincidentally, at the same time that gender boundaries were hardening, racial barriers were solidifying as well. Approaching the study of human beings more empirically, scientists grouped the peoples of the earth into different categories based on their physical, bodily characteristics, including skin color. Enlightenment thinkers, such as Johann Blumenbach, Samuel Stanhope Smith, and Georges-Louis Leclerc de Buffon, had attributed the condition of blacks to their circumstances or environment. Although in most typologies, darker peoples were ranked lower than other groups in the hierarchy of races, racial characteristics could be modified by changes in climate, environment, or access to opportunity.

By the late eighteenth century, however, a new generation of scientific empiricists had begun to suggest that racial characteristics were innate. Thinkers such as Germany's Samuel Thomas von Soemmerring in the 1780s and Britain's Charles White in the 1790s began to examine skulls, skeletons, and other physical characteristics, including facial features and skin color, in order to differentiate the various "races" of human beings. In their view, each race possessed distinctive qualities that were grounded in its particular anatomy and physiology. These physical characteristics determined a race's capacity for civilization, culture, and intellectual achievement. Such thinkers created their own racial hierarchies which, like earlier versions, placed black people at the bottom of the human scale. In the newer version, however, biology determined the rankings, on a scale that could not change. These ideas spread to the United States. Thomas Jefferson incorporated the concept of a biological basis for black inferiority into his *Notes on the State of Virginia*. In key areas such as reason, intellect, and beauty, Jefferson said, black people could never equal whites. By 1815, American physicians such as Charles Caldwell of Philadelphia had begun to use their scientific authority to bolster claims about the inherent differences between the races. By the 1820s, Tench Coxe, who had been an early supporter of abolition, had become a vehement racist. His writings, disseminated through Democratic newspapers, suggested that black people were so innately inferior to whites that they were incapable of being civilized. By the middle decades of the nineteenth century, the idea of innate black inferiority had become entrenched in scholarly circles and popular among the masses.[43]

Many of the same forces that led to a closing of political opportunities for white women also led to the elimination of political possibilities for free blacks. As politics became more focused on voting, electioneering, and party organization, both free blacks and white women became less significant in electoral politics. Whereas earlier political activities that were held in public spaces often included black participants, by the first decades of the nineteenth century these gatherings were often racially segregated. Towns and cities throughout the country often prohibited black people—even free blacks—from celebrating Independence Day along with whites or prohibited their public festivities. At the same time, as more states abolished property qualifications for voting, black men were explicitly excluded from the franchise. Inherent differences located in their bodies were said to justify their exclusion. Every state that entered the union after 1819 limited suffrage to "free, white males." By 1840 even states that had once enfranchised free black men, including New Jersey, Maryland, Connecticut, Pennsylvania, North Carolina, and Tennessee, had reversed course and disenfranchised them. Blackness came to be a marker not just of difference, but of inherent and ineradicable subordinate status. Those who attended the New York State Constitutional Convention of 1846 would cite these theories to justify their refusal to enfranchise free black males. "We are informed by physiologists," said John A. Kennedy, "that the human family was divided into five races, all of which had distinctive characteristics. Those two which had the fewest points of resemblance were the Caucasion and Ethiopian. Indeed, in their purity, they were almost antipodes to each other, as well in habits and manners, as in complexion and physical organization. These variations were not made by man, nor by human government. It was the work of nature." Race and gender essentialism thus replaced an environmentalist understanding of racial and sexual distinctions.[44]

Naturalizing Natural Rights

The invocation of essentialized sex roles went a long way in justifying women's exclusion from political rights. Yet lingering concerns remained. If women's biological incapacity precluded women from attaining the rights that men enjoyed, what then did it mean for women to have natural rights? Why was it even necessary to acknowledge their status as rights bearers? The answer goes beyond the relationship between the sexes and speaks to the function of women in maintaining a society predicated on white superiority.

Unlike slaves, whose status put them entirely outside the social compact, or free blacks, whose race was invoked to prevent them from claiming equal rights, white women were widely considered to possess natural rights. As a "Plan for the Emancipation of the Fair Sex" published in 1802 in a ladies' periodical put it, it was necessary to "re-establish" women "in their rights . . . [and] natural equality." The key term here is "re-establish." If women's rights were indeed "natural," they were inherent in women's status as human beings. Such rights could not be denied or disparaged. American society thus needed to clarify the nature of women's rights in order to "re-establish" them. In order to do so, they drew on a complex set of natural rights traditions. The most familiar tradition came by way of John Locke's *Second Treatise on Government*. According to Locke, in a state of nature all men were equal. In order to protect their life, liberty, and property, they joined together in a social compact. In relinquishing some of their personal freedom, they gained the protection of the state. If the state violated this contract, members could withdraw from the compact, renegotiate its terms, or in extreme cases assert their ultimate right to revolution. In Locke's original formulation, all rights carried a moral component. Rights could not be understood without reference to duties, or the mutual obligations that members of society owed to one another. Expressing one's rights carried the obligation to fulfill one's duties.[45]

Yet over time, especially in the United States, the Lockean notion came to be understood primarily in terms of individual autonomy and freedom of choice, with decreasing attention to the role of duties. Rights became individual entitlements rather than part of a network of mutual obligations. Accordingly, Lockean rights theory allowed individuals to claim certain privileges as "natural rights." Conservatives had long resisted the radical implications of this theory. "It is the fashion with all modern philosophers," remarked an author writing in a Federalist journal, the *Port Folio*, "to lay down, as the basis of their systems, rights which they assert to have existed in a state of nature, before any societies were formed amongst mankind." Such notions, he warned, led to social unrest, moral upheaval, and political chaos. "Upon these natural rights they build their pretensions to annul the most revered establishments of past times, and to overthrow at pleasure, governments that have been the work of ages, whenever the people can be brought to think fit to exert the authority that is inherent in them." Lockean rights, then, had a radical potential. Open-ended and expansive, they were capable of reinterpretation and renegotiation. By claiming their natural rights, individuals or groups might force society to explain why their rights were being denied or disparaged. Otherwise society had the duty to acknowledge their rights. Such claims had the potential to destabilize, or even overthrow, the existing order.[46]

Despite the prominence of Lockean rights theory, another rights tradition also circulated in early America. This theory, derived especially from thinkers of the Scottish Enlightenment, emphasized the close, even intimate relationship between individual rights and individual duties. Based on the earlier works of legal jurists such as Hugo Grotius and Samuel Pufendorf, Scots such as Francis Hutcheson, Thomas Reid, and others wished to stress the moral obligations and communal nature of rights claims. In their view, the social compact consisted not of an agreement among equals but of a hierarchy in which inequality was a given. Each person in society had an assigned station, role, or office consisting of one's social class, gender, or vocation. At the top of the hierarchy, God represented "the ultimate obligator," who put individuals under the obligation to do their duty and conferred benefits, which were known as rights. These rights consisted of the moral powers exerted over oneself and others. Mutual obligations and the preservation of social harmony took precedence over individual prerogatives and freedom of choice. Hence in doing their duties, people exercised their rights.[47]

This notion of rights as duties allowed for an understanding of rights entirely different from that of the Lockean view, especially as understood in America. It was not nearly as elastic, susceptible to expansion, or threatening to a hierarchical society. Expressing one's rights meant fulfilling the duties of one's existing station, role, or office in society, not claiming new privileges. As one American legal commentator explained it, "The RIGHT of any person to do an action, or possess a thing, is nothing more than the power to do that action, or possess that thing." People secured their rights, in other words, by fulfilling the duties that God had assigned them. In practice the two theories had vastly different implications. Whereas Lockean rights created the potential for social upheaval, the Scottish tradition tended to reinforce the status quo, preserve the existing social order, and insure political stability. The duty-bound theory of rights thus was as conservative in its implications as the Lockean view was radical.[48]

The problems of applying an open-ended, expansive notion of natural rights to women quickly became apparent. Shortly after the publication of Wollstonecraft's *A Vindication of the Rights of Woman*, a New York author, calling himself "A real friend of the fair sex," announced his "concern to see the papers so generally silent about the RIGHTS OF WOMEN." To alleviate this problem, he (and it is clear from the context that the "real friend" was a "he") wished to describe the rights of women and show how females made important contributions to "good strong, energetic family government." The author then attempted to equate the rights of women with the rights of men. He began by comparing the social compact to the marriage contract. Just as men sacrifice certain rights when they assent to the social contract, so women, "by entering upon the marriage state, renounce some of their natural rights (as men do, when they enter into civil society)." Pursuing the analogy further, he argued, "As the men, living under a free constitution of their own framing are entitled to the protection of laws, so likewise has a woman a right to be protected by the man of her choice." Like men, women choose or reject the compact. Furthermore, just as men could petition or protest against an unjust government, women too could express their grievances. "In family broils," he said, "the wife has a right to expostulate with temper."[49]

Then "A real friend" encountered problems with his analogy. According to Lockean theory, if a government became tyrannical, the people possessed the ultimate right—the right to revolution. The author, however, refused to acknowledge the possibility that a husband might turn into a tyrant or that a woman might need to rebel. He chose to depict the family only in terms of a fair, constitutional regime. "If rebellion, insurrection, or any other opposition to a just, mild, and free political government is odious," he said, "it is not less so to oppose good family administration." The author failed to acknowledge another flaw in the analogy. Whereas citizens could alter the fundamental articles of agreement in a constitutional government, a wife had no procedural outlet. In most states she could not get a divorce or afford the economic costs of ending the relationship. Submission remained her lot. "When entreaty is unavailing," "A real friend" said, "it is her duty to submit to the controul of that government she has voluntarily chosen." Thus, despite an apparently good-faith commitment to the principle of natural rights for women, the author refused to follow his analogy to its logical conclusion. For careful readers, the piece was disturbing. Natural rights talk led, seemingly inevitably, to unanswerable questions about women's consent, obligation, and choice. Instead of demonstrating the equivalence between the rights of man and those of woman, the exercise had exposed the fundamental differences between the two.[50]

Selectively drawing on these various rights traditions, Americans consistently began to make a distinction. They applied the more open-ended concept of rights, associated with Locke, to men and the more duty-bound theory, associated with the Scots, to women. Not only was there a gendered division of labor, but there was also a gendered division of rights. If nature determined men's and women's essential natures, then men and women could not deviate from their assigned roles. While men's rights involved liberties that allowed choices, women's rights consisted of benefits that imposed duties. In a Fourth of July toast offered in 1804, the young men of Harrisburg, Pennsylvania, captured the distinction succinctly. They toasted to: "The rights of man, and the rights of women—may the former never be infringed; nor the latter curtailed."[51]

Commentators deliberately distanced themselves from Wollstonecraft's—and Locke's—formulation for women. "You will not consult a Wollstonecraft for a code of 'Rights of Women,'" warned a Maine orator. "Do not usurp the rights of man; they are essentially distinct." For women, rights represented both an expression of and a confirmation of women's duties as wives and mothers. An article called, significantly, "Second Vindication of the Rights of Women" insisted that parents should "impress [their] daughters with a knowledge of the dignified sphere they were intended to move in, and the performances of such duties as naturally devolve on them." In fact, women's duties became so closely identified with their rights that the two became almost identical. "Let [girls] see that [their] very duties are the real source of all their pleasures, and the foundation of all their rights," urged the *Charleston Spectator*. "How engaging, how respectable are those rights! how sacred to the human heart, when a woman knows how to assert them properly." Understood "properly," then, women's rights led not to an expansion of their political privileges but to an affirmation of their duties as wives and mothers.[52]

This approach allowed Americans to acknowledge women's status as rights bearers but to preclude the possibility that they might claim political rights. In 1793 a male author presented a list of twelve rights belonging to women, including: "[a woman's] undoubted right to choose a husband"; "a right, in common with her husband, to instruct her children"; "a right to promote frugality, industry, and economy"; and "a right . . . to be neat and decent in her person and family." No mention was made of the right to vote or hold public office. Speaking to an audience of South Carolina women, William Loughton Smith waxed eloquent about women's rights, which explicitly excluded political rights. "Tho' you are excluded from a participation in our political institutions," he said, "nature has also assigned to you valuable and salutary rights. To delight, to civilize, and to ameliorate mankind—to exercise unlimited sway over obedient hearts, *these are the precious rights of woman!*" John Cosens Ogden of New Hampshire disposed of the question even more neatly: "Every man, by the constitution, is born with an equal right to be elected to the highest office. And every woman, is born with an equal right to be the wife of the most eminent man." Sex thus became determinative of rather than incidental to rights claims.[53]

Mutual acceptance of this understanding of women's rights imposed certain responsibilities on men. As long as women exercised rights consistent with their feminine duties, men would protect those rights from usurpation or abuse. Men had a responsibility to all women to guard their "natural rights" by protecting their chastity, purity, and virtue. Husbands, in particular, could show their respect for women's "rights" by not drinking, gambling, or being unfaithful. However, only those prerogatives associated with women's feminine nature would be acknowledged or protected. As "Morpheus" put it in 1802, women "have rights to tenderness, delicate treatment, and refined consideration. Men have no such rights. When women leave their character, and assume the character and rights, of men, they relinquish their own rights, and are to be regarded, and treated, as men." It was clear, then, that any woman who sought political rights would be on her own.[54]

Rather than accidental, the choice of the duty-bound version of rights for women seems deliberate and self-conscious. In 1802, a Miss M. Warner published a poem, "Rights of Woman," in which she defended an understanding of rights that was different for men than for women. Listing what she considered to be a woman's rights, Warner included items such as the right to cook delicious meals, to share in her husband's grief, and to nurse him when he is sick. Then the author addressed those who would criticize her apparently limited understanding of women's rights:

These are our rights: those rights who dares dispute
Let him speak now. No answer, what all mute?
But soft, methinks some discontented fair

Cries, 'These are duties, miss.' Agreed, they are
But know ye not that Woman's proper sphere
Is the domestic walk? To interfere
With politics, divinity, or law,
A much deserv'd ridicule would draw
On Woman—.

Women who sought a role in "politics, divinity, or law" were said to
"interfere" where they did not belong. By acting like men and trans-
gressing the boundaries of their "proper sphere," they brought upon
themselves "a much deserv'd ridicule." Hence the "discontented
fair['s]" criticism of rights as duties was duly considered—and sum-
marily dismissed. Far from blundering into the notion, Warner made it
clear that a different notion of rights applied to each sex.[55]

This understanding of rights would allow American women and men
to have it both ways: they could acknowledge women's status as rights
bearers but prevent them from using that status in the same way as men.
When white men demanded universal suffrage, they claimed that voting
was a natural right belonging to all people regardless of whether or not
they owned property. As we have seen, although men conveniently
excluded women and free blacks from these demands, this did not deter
them from making the claim to universality. Their strategy paid off.
They were able to gain the concessions from the state that opened up
the franchise to virtually all white males. When the issue of women's
rights arose, however, the question of political rights was quickly foreclosed. By invoking the Scottish notion, women's rights were defined in
terms of the exercise of women's traditional duties as wives and mothers.
There was no possibility that women might claim the vote as long as
their rights were understood as operating within the duty-bound tradition. Although both Lockean and Scottish traditions drew on existing
schools of thought, the one claimed by men opened up the possibility
of political change while the one applied to women defused or deflected
any opportunity to alter the status quo.

The recognition of women's inherent biological traits as different
from those of men, along with a belief in a duty-based understanding of
women's rights, proved to be a boon to defenders of the gender status
quo. It staved off charges of inconsistency or self-contradiction against
American society. It refuted criticisms of injustice and hypocrisy against
the American government. It even gave Americans bragging rights
about the status of women. "Thrice blessed are we," commented the
novelist Hannah Foster, "the happy daughters of this land of liberty,
where the female mind is unshackled by the restraints of tyrannical custom, in which many other regions confine the exertions of genius to the

usurped powers of lordly man! Here, virtue, merit, and abilities are properly estimated under whatever form they appear." Unlike women elsewhere throughout much of the world, American women enjoyed certain rights and had a modicum of equality in many areas. "Where shall we find women more enlightened, than the women of America?" asked Ebenezer French of Boston. "And is not the reason obvious? In some countries they are treated as slaves; in others, as inferiors, but in America as equals." Their elevated status was proof of the superiority of the American system. "We may with safety assert," said a Massachusetts author, "that in no country on the surface of the globe, are women in a more happy condition than in these United States." Because the comparison was with other women, rather than with white American men, women did indeed appear privileged.[56]

As if to reassure themselves, Americans continually congratulated themselves on their beneficence toward women. "You are blessed with existence in a land of liberty," Gardner Child told a female audience in Vermont, "where the rights of women are understood and regarded. While the man protects, labors, and accumulates wealth, you have to preside over domestic affairs, to cultivate civilization, soften manners, and correct morals." The implication was clear: American women should feel grateful for what they had rather than contemplate demanding more. "Under the mild influence of Christianity and the easy subsistence to be procured in our republican states," said Samuel L. Mitchill, "the condition of women is undoubtedly preferable to that of their sex in any part of the globe. [Women] ought to know that Fredonia [the United States] is a woman's terrestrial Paradise. Here they are the rational companions of men, not their playthings or slaves." How could a woman who lived in a "terrestrial Paradise" even think of demanding political rights?[57]

This understanding of women's roles and rights also reinforced the growing belief in white supremacy. It presumed the existence of a racial hierarchy in which all white women occupied a higher place in the order of things than any black person, free or slave.[58] Unlike black people, white women shared with white men certain inalienable natural rights. Acknowledging women's status as rights bearers differentiated among the nonfranchised population; it created a hierarchy among those who lacked political rights. Although white women might not be able to vote or hold public office, they possessed many civil rights and liberties that black people, free or slave, did not have. The possession of natural rights affirmed white women's privileged place in the racial hierarchy and, in effect, buttressed the existence of a social order that presumed white superiority. Once biological essentialism justified the distinctions between the sexes and the dominance of whites over blacks, a selective

appropriation of different rights traditions allowed Americans to trans-
late the universal imperatives of equality and natural rights into sex-
specific and race-particular prerogatives. In the early republic, scientific
racism and gender essentialism forged racial and gender hierarchies
that reinforced and complemented one another.

Even before women organized in the 1840s to demand political rights,
American society mounted a preemptive strike to prevent them from
doing so. The backlash was the result of both real and imagined threats
to the gender hierarchy. The specter of Mary Wollstonecraft, female suffrage in New Jersey, and the activities of "female politicians" confirmed
the possibility that even if American women were not yet demanding
political rights, it would be only a matter of time before they would do
so. For a few decades after the American Revolution an open debate
occurred in which both supporters and opponents of the proposition
expressed their views. However, the divisiveness of party conflict, the
growth of universal male suffrage, and the institutionalization of party
politics all led to the increasing marginalization of women from the electoral process. The passage of laws that limited the franchise to "free
white males" solidified women's exclusion from government and gave
that prohibition the force of law. Emerging at the same time were new
scientific theories that both justified women's exclusion and preserved
white women's claim to be rights-bearing individuals.

The Republicans' success in achieving virtually universal suffrage for
white males is typically portrayed as the quintessential expression of the
process of democratization. It is clear, however, that white men gained
while women and free black men lost—not the actual right to vote
(except in New Jersey) but in terms of the popular understanding of
what was possible. Universal male suffrage was increasingly defined
against—even predicated on—women's and blacks' exclusion from governance. While a given individual might change his wealth status and
enter the ranks of voters, a woman or a black person could never change
sex or race and thus could never hope to become a full member of the
polity. "Ascriptive" qualities, as the political scientist Rogers Smith calls
them, such as race and gender, replaced property and wealth as the pre-
requisites for full citizenship.[59] Whereas previously women had been
excluded from governance primarily by custom and tradition, now their
exclusion was legally required, scientifically mandated, and culturally
determined. Ironically, the triumph of democracy for white males
closed down the political possibilities for women that the Revolution
had opened up—and in some important ways made the barriers for
their reentry into politics more formidable than ever.

Epilogue
Memory and Forgetting

When Frances Trollope, a British visitor, toured the United States in 1828, she found few women in evidence at public celebrations and gatherings. Recalling her attendance at a Fourth of July festival in Cincinnati, she observed that women had "but little to do with the pageantry, the splendour, or the gaiety of [Independence] day." Visiting the country in 1830, Frenchman Alexis de Tocqueville made a similar observation. "Confined within the narrow circle of domestic life," he said, women did not "manage the outward concerns of the family, or conduct a business, or take a part in political life." In Trollope's judgment, American women were "guarded by a seven-fold shield of habitual insignificance," making them little more than "domestic slaves."[1]

By the late 1820s, women seemed to have entered a new era of political invisibility. In 1828 a Virginia woman stridently proclaimed that the specter of women's rights had been successfully thwarted. "Mrs. Wolstonecraft's book made a great noise about twenty-five years ago," said Virginia Cary. "Some unfortunate young women were destroyed by the literal adoption of her tenets; but there was not half as much mischief done as might have been predicted." A collective amnesia seemed to set in. Although women lost the vote in New Jersey only in 1807, popular knowledge of women's voting evaporated within decades. "It is a fact not generally known," noted a female author less than two decades later, "that by the Constitution of the State of New Jersey, females possessing the requisite qualification, [were] allowed the right of voting at elections." Women themselves became unwilling to acknowledge the political dimensions of their behavior and disavowed their connection with political parties or partisan causes. It became hard to remember a time when women had openly embraced politics. When Mrs. E. F. L. Ellet penned her *Domestic History of the American Revolution* in 1850, she spoke to an audience who appeared to be totally unfamiliar with the events she recounted. "It is almost impossible now," she said, "to appreciate the vast influence of women's patriotism upon the destinies of the infant republic."[2]

The American Revolution opened up a brief window of opportunity for women. New venues arose in which women might participate informally in politics. Some women embraced politics with a vigor that earned them the designation "female politicians." The triumph of equality and natural rights as foundational principles of American society and government also changed women's status. Women gained recognition as the possessors of rights that put them, in certain respects, on an equal footing with men. A lively popular debate erupted over the precise nature of women's rights, including whether women had the right to vote and hold public office. Within a few decades, however, a backlash ensued, resulting in the closing of many of the political opportunities that the Revolution had opened up. The specter of Mary Wollstonecraft, the experience of women voting in New Jersey, and the visibility of female politicians provoked fears of a larger transformation in gender roles and relations. Although most women were not yet demanding political rights for themselves, it was clear that they might one day do so.

Other circumstances conspired against women as well. The intensity of partisan conflict between the Federalists and Democratic Republicans, the narrowing of politics to focus on male voting and electioneering, and the growing hegemony of essentialized gender roles converged to make the political arena less hospitable to women. The tendency toward women's exclusion gained momentum after Thomas Jefferson's election in 1800, accelerated after the War of 1812, and was firmly in place by the time of Andrew Jackson's election as president. Lest the actual changes in women's status seem insufficient to provoke such an overwrought response, it is only necessary to look at recent history when the passage of gay marriage laws in a tiny number of states has produced a tidal wave of reaction in many more. People react not just against what has actually happened but in anticipation of the direction of social change. In the case of women's involvement in politics in the early republic, many American women and men wished to foreclose the most extreme possibilities before they could ever occur.

Yet the story is not all bleak. Some forms of women's political participation persisted. In the informal political realm, women continued to read and write about political matters, to influence their husbands' and sons' political choices, and to have a say in the national political debate. In civil society, the growth of benevolent activities, charitable organizations, and social reform societies offered women a whole new host of opportunities to work through the political system using their own methods. More significantly, by establishing the proposition that women as well as men possessed natural, God-given rights, the Revolution had actually given women the means to combat their own exclusion.

By the 1830s and 1840s a tiny group of radical female reformers had begun to understand the full meaning of their revolutionary legacy.

Unable to vote or hold public office, the women had depended on men to enact temperance legislation, pass antiprostitution statutes, and bring about an end to slavery. Seeing a comparison between the status of slaves and their own disenfranchisement, they concluded that they must embrace politics and promote the cause of women's rights. As abolitionist and woman's rights activist Sarah Grimké put it, "[Woman] has surrendered her dearest RIGHTS, and been satisfied with privileges which man has assumed to grant her. . . . Men and women were CREATED EQUAL; they are both moral and accountable beings, and whatever is right for man to do, is right for woman to do."[3]

These early feminists, however, confronted a radically different environment from that of the "female politicians" of the postrevolutionary era. In place of earlier possibilities and the hope for change, women reformers faced an implacable wall of hostility and the widespread belief that there was no place for women in party and electoral politics. Frustrated with these attitudes, Lucretia Mott and Elizabeth Cady Stanton placed an advertisement in an upstate New York newspaper calling for a meeting to be held on the subject of women's rights. In preparation for the gathering, Mott and Stanton met with other local women, including Mott's sister, Martha Wright, as well as Jane Hunt and Mary Ann McClintock, to prepare proposals for discussion. On July 19, 1848, almost three hundred women and men gathered together for two days at the Wesleyan Methodist Church in Seneca Falls, New York, for the nation's first meeting organized specifically to discuss the question of women's rights. Those attending the Seneca Falls convention voted on a variety of measures and resolutions concerning the status of women. In the end they published a "Declaration of Sentiments," modeled on the Declaration of Independence, that listed their grievances and issued a call to action. In addition to opposing women's exclusion from the rights of citizenship, the document rejected women's second-class legal position; objected to the moral double standard; and inveighed against women's inability to obtain the same educational and professional opportunities that men enjoyed. Perhaps most controversially, the declaration demanded that each woman be permitted to exercise "her inalienable right to the elective franchise." Sixty-eight women and thirty-two men signed the convention's final statement. Unlike the women of New Jersey who had voted in earlier decades, the women at Seneca Falls claimed the franchise not as a privilege but as a right.[4]

In a broader sense, American women's ongoing struggle for political inclusion can be understood as part of a larger contest occurring throughout the western world. Ever since the late eighteenth century, the nations that represent leading western democracies—France, Britain, and the United States—have confronted this tension. In none of

these countries has the path to women's full political participation proceeded easily, quickly, or in a straight line of development. There have
been many false starts, many twists, and convoluted turns along the way
to women's full acceptance. Why did it take so long to rectify the injus-
tices against women? Why has the path to women's rights been so tor-
tured and twisted?

Perhaps surprisingly, Louis Hartz's classic work, *The Liberal Tradition
in America*, may provide a fruitful point of departure for addressing these
questions. Written in 1955, Hartz's work did not consider the exclusion
of either women or black people as part of the revolutionary legacy.
Instead, he was interested in examining the sources of what he believed
was the troubling emphasis in the United States on individual rights and
the pursuit of self-interest at the expense of the common good. He
called this the country's "liberal tradition." In Hartz's rather idiosyn-
cratic view, the absence of a feudal past and lack of true social classes
had robbed the United States of a useful clash between opposing political ideologies. Except among southern slaveholders, he said, the country lacked an indigenous conservative tradition that would promote a
sense of mutual obligation between social classes and foster community.
At the other end of the spectrum, there was also no strong socialist tradition that would preserve the common good in a different way, through
social leveling and the abolition of distinctions based on wealth and
property. Both alternatives nurtured social relationships, strengthened
the bonds of mutuality, and shielded individuals from the vagaries of a
solitary existence. Instead, Americans faced society as isolated individuals, without protection from the impact of unfettered individualism. In
Hartz's terms, "The master assumption of American political thought
[became] . . . the reality of atomistic social freedom."[5]

Lacking the insights of postmodernism, Hartz did not understand
that race and gender might be considered as social constructs, analo-
gous to the category he was most concerned with, class. But what if he
had? As we have seen, during the Enlightenment, differences between
the sexes and races tended to be attributed to custom, habit, and tradition rather than to innate characteristics. With sufficient education and
opportunity, it was said, women might accomplish as much as men
could. The proposition was often held for black people as well. By the
early nineteenth century, however, biological essentialism was replacing
environmentalism. In a variety of venues, ranging from scientific literature to medical textbooks to popular periodicals, distinctions between
sexes and races came to be seen as the result of innate, biological differences. As the site of ineradicable differences, the body became the basis
for exclusion from the polity. Even if women were educated, it was said,
they could never function in the same capacities as men; they would

never be as rational or capable as men. Similarly, even if black people were given more opportunities, their inherent limitations would prevent them from achieving as much as whites could. Rather than custom or tradition, biological differences between the sexes and the races would preclude women's and blacks' full inclusion in the polity.

The liberal tradition thus offers a bifurcated legacy. The universalistic promises of equality and natural rights appeared to be offered to all people. However, certain groups were excluded from its promises because of their unchangeable, physical attributes. As the historian Nancy Leys Stepan puts it, "The embodiment of sex and racial differences [in biology] . . . differentiated [other groups] from an implicit white, male norm. By being embodied as qualitatively different in their substantial natures—by creating group identities in difference—communities of individuals were placed outside the liberal universe of freedom, equality and rights. In effect, a theory of politics and rights was transformed into an argument about nature; equality under liberalism was taken to be a matter not of ethics, but of anatomy."[6]

This notion suggests that in the United States, where class tensions were less important than they were in Europe at the time, the categories of race and gender, along with the cultural work they performed, functioned as a collectivist and hierarchical political ideology. If this is true, then what implications can we draw? First of all, there may after all have been a Thermidorean reaction to the American Revolution.[7] While in France the reaction occurred primarily in the realm of politics, and resulted in mass executions and the Terror, in America the backlash occurred primarily in the realms of culture and society. American leaders did not overthrow the political settlement of the Revolution. They did, however, reject the full implications of equality and natural rights, with a resultant hardening of boundaries between the races and the sexes. The legacy of the Revolution was redefined and circumscribed so as to limit its full benefits to white males.

A second implication speaks to the function of racial and gender hierarchies in the United States. Understanding race and gender as countervailing tendencies to the liberal tradition suggests one reason why racial and sexual prejudices have been so hard to eradicate in this country. The battle for equal rights has for a long time been fought on unwinnable territory: equality under liberalism was taken to be a matter not of ethics but of anatomy. The American Revolution did not eliminate all social hierarchy; it reconfigured the character of that hierarchy. In place of birth and wealth, supposedly inherent bodily characteristics became the most salient markers of difference and created the basis for social and political exclusion. All males became more equal while women and blacks were consigned to a permanent lower status. In this scenario, white men, contrary to Hartz's supposition, did actually have a refuge against the excesses of unfettered individualism. Although white men may have been in conflict with other white men, they stood at the peak of both the racial and the gender hierarchies. They were deeply enmeshed in various forms of community. As the heads of families and masters of slaves, they participated in an extensive network of mutual obligations and enjoyed numerous social relationships. They were not atomistic individuals at all. By virtue of their domestic connection with women, and their presumed superiority over black people, white men could enjoy the benefits of the liberal tradition while being protected from its most alienating social and emotional consequences.

This understanding of the revolutionary legacy does not suggest that liberal polities can never fully enfranchise blacks and women. However, because specific assumptions about gender and race were, and are, so deeply embedded in the political system, any change in the relationship between the sexes or races also threatens the very foundations of the social and political hierarchy. For women and black people to gain true equality, society must abolish the remnants of racial and gender essentialism. Doing so requires a fundamental transformation not just in governmental institutions but in the ordering of society itself. Yet because of the triumph of equality and natural rights as foundational principles of American society and government, the question of inclusion and exclusion is now subject to debate and open to contestation. Ironically, the explicit acknowledgment of exclusion may represent the first step toward ultimate inclusion.

Notes

Introduction

1. *Maryland Gazette and Political Intelligencer* (Annapolis), October 21, 1819; Judith Sargent Murray, *The Gleaner*, ed. Nina Baym (Schenectady, N.Y.: Union College Press, 1992 [orig. pub. 1798]), 702–3. See also Sheila Skemp, *Judith Sargent Murray: A Brief Biography with Documents* (Boston: Bedford Books, 1998).

2. *Columbian Centinel/ Massachusetts Federalist* (Boston), January 24, 1801; Hannah Adams, *A Memoir of Miss Hannah Adams, Written by herself: With Additional Notices by a Friend* (Boston: Gray & Bowen, 1832), 86.

3. Linda K. Kerber, *Women of the Republic: Intellect and Ideology in Revolutionary America* (Chapel Hill: University of North Carolina Press, 1980); Mary Beth Norton, *Liberty's Daughters: The Revolutionary Experience of American Women, 1750–1800* (Glenview, Ill.: Little, Brown, & Co., 1980). For the view that women had no revolution, see Joan Hoff-Wilson, "The Illusion of Change: Women and the American Revolution," in *The American Revolution: Explorations in the History of American Radicalism*, ed. A. Young (DeKalb: Northern Illinois University Press, 1976), 383–445.

4. Joan Wallach Scott's *Gender and Politics of History* (New York: Columbia University Press, 1996) provides a discussion of the theoretical framework for this approach.

5. Catherine Allgor, *Parlor Politics in Which the Ladies of Washington Help Build a City and a Government* (Charlottesville: University Press of Virginia, 2000); Susan Branson, *These Fiery Frenchified Dames: Women and Political Culture in Early National Philadelphia* (Philadelphia: University of Pennsylvania Press, 2001); Cynthia A. Kierner, *Beyond the Household: Women's Place in the Early South, 1700–1835* (Ithaca, N.Y.: Cornell University Press, 1998); Simon P. Newman, *Parades and the Politics of the Street: Festive Culture in the Early American Republic* (Philadelphia: University of Pennsylvania Press, 1997); David Waldstreicher, *In the Midst of Perpetual Fetes: The Making of American Nationalism, 1776 1820* (Chapel Hill: University of North Carolina Press, 1997); Jan Lewis, "'Of Every Age Sex & Condition': The Representation of Women in the Constitution," *Journal of the Early Republic* 15 (Fall 1995): 359–87; Jan Lewis, "Politics and the Ambivalence of the Private Sphere: Women in Early Washington, D.C.," in *A Republic for the Ages: The United States Capitol and the Political Culture of the Early Republic*, ed. Donald R. Kennon (Charlottesville: University Press of Virginia, 1999), 122–51. Other groundbreaking works relating to women and politics in this period include Paula Baker, "The Domestication of Politics: Women and American Political Society, 1780–1920," *American Historical Review* 89 (1984): 620–47; and Ruth H. Bloch, "The Gendered Meanings of Virtue in Revolutionary America," *Signs: Journal of Women in Culture and Society* 13 (1987): 37–58.

6. Sean Wilentz, *The Rise of American Democracy: Jefferson to Lincoln* (New York: W. W. Norton, 2005).

7. Kerber, *Women of the Republic*, 269–88; Jan Lewis, "The Republican Wife: Virtue and Seduction in the Early Republic," *William & Mary Quarterly* 3rd ser., 44 (October 1987): 689–721. Linda Kerber explores some of the contradictions in the trope of republican motherhood in "Making Republicanism Useful," *Yale Law Journal* 97 (July 1988): 1663–72; and in "Separate Spheres, Female Worlds, Woman's Place: The Rhetoric of Women's History," *Journal of American History* 75 (1988): 9–39.

8. Scott, *Gender and the Politics of History*, 26; Mary Kelley, *Learning to Stand and Speak: Women, Education and Public Life in America's Republic* (Chapel Hill: University of North Carolina Press, 2006), 5; John L. Brooke, "Consent, Civil Society, and the Public Sphere in the Age of Revolution and the Early American Republic," in *Beyond the Founders: New Approaches to the Political History of the Early American Republic*, ed. Jeffrey L. Pasley, Andrew W. Robertson, and David Waldstreicher (Chapel Hill: University of North Carolina Press, 2004), 207–50.

9. Mary P. Ryan, *Women in Public: Between Banners and Ballots, 1825–1880* (Baltimore: Johns Hopkins University Press, 1990), 19–57; Ronald Zboray and Mary Saracino Zboray, "Political News and Female Readership in Antebellum Boston and Its Region," *Journalism History* 22 (Spring 1996): 2–14; Ronald Zboray and Mary Saracino Zboray, "Whig Women, Politics, and Culture in the Campaign of 1840: Three Perspectives from Massachusetts," *Journal of the Early Republic* 17 (Summer 1997): 278–315; Janet L. Coryell, "Superseding Gender: The Role of the Woman Politico in Antebellum Partisan Politics," in *Women and the Unstable State in Nineteenth-Century America*, ed. Alison M. Parker and Sarah Barringer Gordon (College Station: Texas A&M Press, 2000), 84–112; Elizabeth R. Varon, *We Mean to Be Counted: White Women and Politics in Antebellum Virginia* (Chapel Hill: University of North Carolina Press, 1998); Amy S. Greenberg, *Manifest Manhood and the Antebellum American Empire* (New York: Cambridge University Press, 2005); Lori D. Ginzberg, *Women and the Work of Benevolence: Morality, Politics, and Class in the Nineteenth-Century United States* (New Haven, Conn.: Yale University Press, 1990); Anne M. Boylan, *The Origins of Women's Activism: New York and Boston, 1797–1840* (Chapel Hill: University of North Carolina Press, 2002); Julie Roy Jeffrey, *The Great Silent Army of Abolitionism: Ordinary Women in the Antislavery Movement* (Chapel Hill: University of North Carolina Press, 1998); Susan Zaeske, *Signatures of Citizenship: Petitioning, Antislavery, and Women's Political Identity* (Chapel Hill: University of North Carolina Press, 2003).

Chapter 1

1. The piece was one installment in a series called "Rights of Women: A Dialogue," originally published in the *Weekly Magazine of Original Essays, Fugitive Pieces, and Interesting Intelligence* 1 (Philadelphia), March 10, 1798; March 17, 1798; March 24, 1798; and April 7, 1798. The quoted section appears in the April 7, 1798, issue. The series constituted parts 1 and 2 of Brown's novel *Alcuin* and was published anonymously that same year as a pamphlet: [Charles Brockden Brown], *Alcuin: A Dialogue* (New York: T. & J. Swords, 1798). Parts 3 and 4, which contained additional material that was even more incendiary than that in the first sections, celebrated the notion of free love and challenged the institution of marriage. These parts were published in 1815, five years after Brown died. Quotations are from a modern edition of the entire novel: Charles Brock-

den Brown, *Alcuin: A Dialogue*, ed. Lee R. Edwards (New York: Grossman Publishers, 1971), 29–30.

2. Judith Sargent Murray, *The Gleaner*, ed. Nina Baym (Schenectady, N.Y.: Union College Press, 1992 [orig. pub. 1798]), 705.

3. Lieselotte Steinbrügge, *The Moral Sex: Woman's Nature in the French Enlightenment*, trans. Pamela F. Selwyn (New York: Oxford University Press, 1995), 10–18; Siep Stuurman, "The Deconstruction of Gender: Seventeenth-Century Feminism and Modern Equality," in *Women, Gender and Enlightenment*, ed. Sarah Knott and Barbara Taylor (Hampshire: Palgrave-Macmillan, 2005), 371–88; Melissa A. Butler, "Early Liberal Roots of Feminism: John Locke and the Attack on Patriarchy," *American Political Science Review* 72 (March 1978): 135–50; Mary Astell, *A Serious Proposal to the Ladies, for the Advancement of their True and Greatest Interest* (1694), in *Women in the Eighteenth Century: Constructions of Femininity*, ed. Vivien Jones (London: Routledge, 1990), 198–99.

4. D. R. Woolf, "A Feminist Past?: Gender, Genre, and Historical Knowledge," *American Historical Review* 102 (June 1997): 645–79; Philip Hicks, "The Roman Matron in Britain: Female Political Influence and Republican Response, ca. 1750–1800," *Journal of Modern History* 77 (March 2005): 35–69; Sylvana Tomaselli, "Civilization, Patriotism, and Enlightened Histories of Women," in *Women, Gender and Enlightenment*, 117–35; William Alexander, *History of Women, From the Earliest Antiquity, to the Present Time; Giving an Account of Almost Every Interesting Particular Concerning that Sex, Among All Nations, Ancient and Modern* (Philadelphia: H. Dobelbower, 1796), front-page advertisement; John Shirley, *The Illustrious History of Women, or A Compendium of the many virtues that adorn the Fair Sex* (London: John Harris, 1686); Nahum Tate, *A Present for the Ladies: Being An Historical Account of Several Illustrious Persons of the Female Sex*, 2nd ed. (London: F. Saunders, 1693), 1. For a later period in the development of women's history, see Nina Baym, *American Women Writers and the Work of History, 1790–1860* (New Brunswick, N.J.: Rutgers University Press, 1995).

5. Woolf, "A Feminist Past?," 645–79; Julia Cherry Spruill, *Women's Life and Work in the Southern Colonies* (New York: W. W. Norton, 1998 [orig. pub. 1938]), 228n35; Kevin J. Hayes, *A Colonial Woman's Bookshelf* (Knoxville: University of Tennessee Press, 1996), 72–73.

6. Antoine-Léonard Thomas, *Essay on the Character, Manners, and Genius of Women in Different Ages*, trans. William Russell, 2 vols. (Philadelphia: R. Aitken, 1774); [By a Friend to the Sex], *Sketches of the History, Genius, Disposition, Accomplishments, Employments, Customs and Importance of the Fair Sex in All Parts of the World* (Philadelphia: Samuel Sanson, 1796); *The American Lady's Preceptor*, 9th ed. (Baltimore: Edward J. Coale, 1821), 26.

7. William Alexander, *History of Women*, 2 vols. (London: W. Stahan, 1779; Dublin: J. A. Husband, 1779; Philadelphia: J. Turner & J. H. Dobelbower, 1795; Philadelphia: J. H. Dobelbower, 1796)—subscribers' list is at the end of the 1796 edition; Murray, *Gleaner*, 709–26; Hannah Mather Crocker, *Observations on the Real Rights of Women, with their Appropriate Duties, agreeable to Scripture, Reason and Common Sense* (Boston: privately printed, 1818), 22–64; Kate Davies, *Catharine Macaulay and Mercy Otis Warren: The Revolutionary Atlantic and the Politics of Gender* (Oxford: Oxford University Press, 2005), 233.

8. *Literary Magazine & American Register* (Philadelphia), February 1806, 87; ibid., July 1805, 57; *New-York Weekly Museum*, August 8, 1812; *Mrs. A. S. Colvin's Weekly Messenger* (Washington City, D.C.), June 16, 1827, 320.

9. *Weekly Museum* (New York), February 9, 1805; ibid., August 10, 1816; *Port*

Folio (Philadelphia), June 22, 1805, 187–88; *Independent Chronicle and the Universal Advertiser* (Boston), March 10, 1800; *New-York Weekly Museum, or Polite Repository of Amusement and Instruction*, March 19, 1816, 291.

10. [Written by a Lady], *The Female Advocate* (New Haven, Conn.: Thomas Green & Son, 1801), 12; Murray, *Gleaner*, 710; *Boston Monthly Magazine* 1 (August 1825), 129.

11. Alexander, *History of Women*, 2:336; *New-York Magazine*, February 1790, 90.

12. Murray, *Gleaner*, 710; *New-York Magazine; or Literary Repository*, February 1790, 90; Miss Laskey, "The Valedictory Oration," May 15, 1793, in *The Rise and Progress of the Young Ladies' Academy of Philadelphia: Containing An Account of a Number of Public Examinations & Commencements; the Charter and Bye-Laws; Likewise a Number of Orations delivered by the Young Ladies, And Several by the Trustees of said Institution* (Philadelphia: Stewart & Chochran, 1794), 98; *Gentleman & Lady's Town & Country Magazine; or, Repository of Instruction and Entertainment* (Boston), December 1784, 339.

13. For further discussion, see Rosemarie Zagarri, "Morals, Manners, and the Republican Mother," *American Quarterly* 44 (June 1992): 192–215; Sylvana Tomaselli, "The Enlightenment Debate on Women," *History Workshop* 20 (Autumn 1985): 101–24.

14. William Robertson, *The History of America* (1777) (Albany: E. Hosford, 1822), 1:255, 257; Henry Home, Lord Kames, *Six Sketches on the History of Man* (abridged version) (Philadelphia: R. Bell & R. Aitken, 1776), 195, 228; David Hume, "Of Polygamy and Divorces" (1742), in *Essays and Treatises on Several Subjects* (Edinburgh, 1825), 1:181; John Millar, *The Origin of the Distinction of Ranks; or, An Inquiry into the Circumstances which give Rise to Influence and Authority in the Different Members of Society* (1771), in *John Millar of Glasgow, 1735–1805*, ed. William C. Lehmann (New York: Arno Press, 1979), 225.

15. John Cosens Ogden, *The Female Guide: or, Thoughts on the Education of That Sex; Accommodated to the State of Society, Manners, and Government, in the United States* (Concord, N.H.: George Hough, 1793), 4; Samuel Miller, *A Brief Retrospect of the Eighteenth Century* (New York: T. & J. Swords, 1803), 2:280; *Weekly Museum* (New York), July 2, 1803.

16. James Tilton, M.D., "An Oration pronounced on the 5th July, 1790," *Universal Asylum & Columbian Magazine* 5 (December 1790), 372; James Wilson, "Lecture on the Study of the Law in the United States" (1790), in *The Works of James Wilson*, ed. Robert Green McCloskey (Cambridge: Harvard University Press, 1967), 1:88.

17. Miller, *Brief Retrospect of the Eighteenth Century*, 2:278–79.

18. Hilda L. Smith, *Reason's Disciples: Seventeenth-Century Feminists* (Urbana: University of Illinois Press, 1982), 57; Katherine M. Rogers, *Feminism in Eighteenth-Century England* (Urbana: University of Illinois Press, 1982), 2–20; Hayes, *Colonial Woman's Bookshelf*, 67–68; *The Hardship of English Laws in Relation to Wives with an Explanation of the Original Curse of Subjection passed upon the Woman. In An Humble Address to the Legislature* (London: W. Bowyer, 1735), 1–2; *Woman Not inferior to Man: Or, A Short and Modest Vindication of the Natural Right of the Fair-Sex to a Perfect Equality of Power, Dignity, and Esteem, with Men*, 2nd ed. (London: John Hankins, 1740), 55; [By a Lady], *Female Rights vindicated; or The Equality of the Sexes Morally and Physically Proved* (London: G. Burnet, 1758), 43, 67. Anna Clark, "Women in Eighteenth-Century British Politics," in *Women, Gender and Enlightenment*; and Arianne Chernock, "Extending the 'Right of Election': Men's Arguments for Women's Political Representation in Late Enlightenment Britain," in ibid., 570–609.

19. Hayes, *Colonial Woman's Bookshelf*, 67, 159n27; *Virginia Gazette* (Williamsburg), October 22, 1736; *South-Carolina Gazette* (Charles Town), August 15, 1743, November 21, 1743; *Columbian Magazine* (Philadelphia), January 1788, 22–27, February 1788, 61–65, March 1788, 126–29, April 1788, 186–89, May 1788, 243–46.

20. *New-York Weekly Journal*, August 19, 1734; Esther Edwards Burr to Sarah Prince Gill, November 29, 1755 (entry for December 20, 1755), in *The Journal of Esther Edwards Burr, 1754–1757*, ed. Laurie Crumpacker and Carol F. Karlsen (New Haven, Conn.: Yale University Press, 1984).

21. John Adams to Abigail Adams, November 4, 1775, *Adams Family Correspondence* (Cambridge: Harvard University Press, 1963), 1:320; Mercy Warren to John Adams, September 4, 1775, in *Warren-Adams Letters, Being chiefly a correspondence among John Adams, Samuel Adams, and James Warren* (Boston: Massachusetts Historical Society, 1917), 1:106–7.

22. Linda K. Kerber, *Women of the Republic: Intellect and Ideology in Revolutionary America* (Chapel Hill: University of North Carolina Press, 1980); Mary Beth Norton, *Liberty's Daughters: The Revolutionary Experience of American Women, 1750–1800* (Glenview, Ill.: Little, Brown, & Co., 1980); Joan R. Gundersen, *To Be Useful to the World: Women in Revolutionary America, 1740–1790* (New York: Twayne Publishers, 1996), 149–83; Carol Berkin, *Revolutionary Mothers: Women in the Struggle for America's Independence* (New York: Alfred A. Knopf, 2005), 12–49, 148–61; Alfred F. Young, "The Women of Boston: 'Persons of Consequence' in the Making of the American Revolution, 1765–76," in *Women and Politics in the Age of Democratic Revolution*, ed. Harriet B. Applewhite and Darline G. Levy (Ann Arbor: University of Michigan Press, 1990), 118–26.

23. Laurel Thatcher Ulrich, *Good Wives: Image and Reality in the Lives of Women in Northern New England, 1650–1750* (New York: Knopf, 1982), 9; "Narrative of Mrs. Abraham Brasher [Helen Kortright], Giving an Account of Her Experiences during the Revolutionary War" (1802) MS, 24, New York Historical Society, New York City.

24. Abigail Adams to Mercy Warren, August 27, 1775, in *Warren-Adams Letters*, 1:106; Edith B. Gelles, *Portia: The World of Abigail Adams* (Bloomington: Indiana University Press, 1992), 30–36; Rosemarie Zagarri, *A Woman's Dilemma: Mercy Otis Warren and the American Revolution* (Wheeling, Ill.: Harlan Davidson, Inc., 1995), 87–88.

25. Mercy Otis Warren to James Warren, March 12, 1780, Mercy Otis Warren Papers, Massachusetts Historical Society, Box 1 (1779); Zagarri, *Woman's Dilemma*, 104–8.

26. Mercy Otis Warren, "To the Hon. J. Winthrop, Esq.," in *Plays and Poems of Mercy Otis Warren*, ed. Benjamin Franklin V (Delmar, N.Y.: Scholars' Facsimiles & Reprints, 1980 [orig. pub. 1790]), 208; Milcah Martha Moore, "Patriotic Poesy," *William & Mary Quarterly*, 3rd ser., 34 (1977): 307; Mary Fish quoted in Joy Day Buel and Richard Buel, *The Way of Duty: A Woman and Her Family in Revolutionary America* (New York: W. W. Norton & Co., 1984), 129; Esther DeBerdt Reed, "Sentiments of an American Woman" (1780), supplement to *Columbian Magazine* 3 (Philadelphia), September 1789, 760.

27. John Fauchereaud Grimké, *An Oration Delivered in St. Philip's Church, before the Inhabitants of Charleston, South-Carolina, on Saturday, the Fourth of July, 1807* (Charleston: W. P. Young, 1807), 17; Keating Lewis Simon, *An Oration delivered in the Independent Circular Church, before the Inhabitants of Charleston, South-Carolina, on Friday, the Fourth of July, 1806* (Charleston: W. P. Young, 1806), 6; Reverend

Solomon Aiken, *An Oration, Delivered before the Republican Citizens of Newburyport, and its Vicinity, July 4, 1810* (Newburyport, Mass.: N. H. Wright, 1810), 13.

28. Kerber, *Women of the Republic,* 119–21; Norton, *Liberty's Daughters,* 45–50.

29. For contrasting portrayals of the postrevolutionary era, see Gordon S. Wood, *The Radicalism of the American Revolution* (New York: Vintage Books, 1991); Gary Nash, *The Unknown American Revolution: The Unruly Birth of Democracy and the Struggle to Create America* (New York: Viking, 2005).

30. Bernard Bailyn, *The Origins of American Politics* (New York: Vintage Books, 1967), 86–88; Robert J. Dinkin, *Voting in Provincial America: A Study of Elections in the Thirteen Colonies, 1689–1776* (Westport, Conn.: Greenwood Press, 1977), 28–49; Robert J. Dinkin, *Voting in Revolutionary America: A Study of Elections in the Original Thirteen States, 1776–1789* (Westport, Conn.: Greenwood Press, 1982), 27–43; Alexander Keyssar, *The Right to Vote: The Contested History of Democracy in the United States* (New York: Basic Books, 2000), 3–7.

31. Marc W. Kruman, *Between Authority and Liberty: State Constitution Making in Revolutionary America* (Chapel Hill: University of North Carolina Press, 1997), 87–108; Keyssar, *Right to Vote,* 8–25.

32. John Adams to James Sullivan, May 26, 1776, in *Works of John Adams, Second President of the United States,* ed. Charles Francis Adams (Boston: Little, Brown, & Co., 1854), 9:375–78.

33. Chilton Williamson, *American Suffrage from Property to Democracy, 1760–1860* (Princeton, N.J.: Princeton University Press, 1960), 181; Richard R. Beeman, *The Varieties of Political Experience in Eighteenth-Century America* (Philadelphia: University of Pennsylvania Press, 2004), 293–94; John G. Kolp and Terri L. Snyder, "Women and the Political Culture of Eighteenth-Century Virginia," in *The Many Legalities of Early America,* ed. Christopher L. Tomlins and Bruce H. Mann (Chapel Hill: University of North Carolina Press, 2001), 275–76. Even so, there were a few isolated reports that unmarried women with property may have cast ballots in the colonial period. See Robert J. Dinkin, *Before Equal Suffrage: Women in Partisan Politics from Colonial Times to 1920* (Westport, Conn.: Greenwood Press, 1995), 8–9.

34. [Thomas Paine], "An Occasional Letter on the Female Sex" (1775), in *The Complete Writings of Thomas Paine,* ed. Philip S. Foner (New York: Citadel Press, 1945), 1:34–38; James Otis, "The Rights of the British Colonies Asserted and Proved" (1764), in *The Debate on the American Revolution, 1761–1783,* ed. Max Beloff, 3rd ed. (New York: Sheridan House, 1949), 48–52; Judith Sargent Murray, "On the Equality of the Sexes," in *Judith Sargent Murray: A Brief Biography with Documents,* ed. Sheila Skemp (Boston: Bedford Books, 1998), 176–82; Richard Henry Lee to Mrs. Hannah Corbin, March 17, 1778, in *Letters of Richard Henry Lee,* ed. James Curtis Ballagh (New York: Macmillan Co., 1911), 1:392–93.

35. Abigail Adams to John Adams, March 31, 1776, in *Adams Family Correspondence,* 1:370; John Adams to Abigail Adams, April 14, 1776, in ibid., 1:382; Zagarri, *Woman's Dilemma,* 91–92; Gelles, *Portia,* 47–49.

36. "Copy of an Original Letter from Mr. John Adams, to a Gentleman in Massachusetts," *Universal Asylum & Columbian Magazine* (Philadelphia), April 1792, 219–22.

37. Constitution of New Jersey—1776, in *The Federal and State Constitutions, Colonial Charters, and Other Organic Laws of the States, Territories and Colonies Now or Heretofore Forming the United States of America* (Washington, D.C.: Government Printing Office, 1909), 5:2595; William Smith, *A Comparative View of the Constitutions of the Several States with Each Other, and with that of the United States* (Philadel-

phia, 1796; Washington, D.C., 1832); Keyssar, *Right to Vote*, 29–52, 55–56, Table A.1, 328–29.

38. Although some historians claim that women's enfranchisement in New Jersey was an accidental oversight, more careful students of the episode confirm the deliberate nature of the legislature's actions, at least by the 1790s. Prior election laws in 1777 and 1783 used only the male pronoun. In the 1790 and 1797 laws, the phrase "he and she" was used. See "Election Law of 1790," in *Acts of the 15th New Jersey General Assembly, Nov. 18, 1790*, 670; and "An Act to Regulate an election of members of the legislative council and general assembly, sheriffs, and coroners, in this State," in *Laws of New Jersey*, 1797, for the precise wording. See also Judith Apter Klinghoffer and Lois Elkis, "'The Petticoat Electors': Women's Suffrage in New Jersey, 1776–1807," *Journal of the Early Republic* 12 (summer 1992): 159–93; Edward Raymond Turner, "Women's Suffrage in New Jersey: 1790–1807," *Smith College Studies in History* 1 (July 1916): 156–87; Kruman, *Between Authority and Liberty*, 191n85; Carl Prince, *New Jersey's Jeffersonian Republicans: The Genesis of an Early Party Machine, 1789–1817* (Chapel Hill: University of North Carolina Press, 1964), 134n7; Irwin N. Gertzog, "Female Suffrage in New Jersey, 1790–1907," in *Women, Politics, and the Constitution*, ed. Naomi B. Lynn (New York: Haworth Press, 1990), 47–58.

39. It is difficult to get accurate estimates of how many women actually voted. A poll list from Burlington in 1787 lists two women voters; see Henry C. Shinn, "An Early New Jersey Poll List," *Pennsylvania Magazine of History and Biography* 44 (January 1920): 77–81. To my knowledge, other poll lists have not been systematically examined for women voters. Other evidence is impressionistic. The *Centinel of Freedom* (Newark) of October 18, 1797, states, "no less than seventy-five women were *polled* at the late election in a neighboring borough." Presumably, more women voted throughout the entire state. The *Boston Independent Chronicle* of October 27, 1800, reporting on "female electors" in New Jersey, simply claimed that at the last election "there were many [who] exercised this privilege."

40. *Trenton True American* (New Jersey), October 18, 1802; *Centinel of Freedom* (Newark), November 7, 11, 1800; Neale McGoldrick and Margaret Crocco, *Reclaiming Lost Ground: The Struggle for Woman Suffrage in New Jersey* (Trenton: New Jersey Council for the Humanities, 1994), 2–5.

41. *Independent Chronicle* (Boston), October 27, 1800; Abigail Adams to Mary Cranch, November 15, 1797, in *The New Letters of Abigail Adams*, ed. Stewart Mitchell (Boston: Houghton Mifflin Co., 1947), 112.

42. Henry Ford, *An Oration, Delivered in the Presbyterian Church at Morris-Town, July 4, 1806* (Morris-Town, N.J.: Henry P. Russell, 1806), 11; William Griffith, *Eumenes: Being a Collection of Papers written for the Purpose of Exhibiting Some of the More Prominent Errors and Omissions of the Constitution of New-Jersey* (Trenton, N.J.: G. Kraft, 1799), 33; *Centinel of Freedom* (Newark, N.J.), October 18, 1797.

43. *Centinel of Freedom* (Newark, N.J.), October 18, 1797.

44. John Lambert, *Travels throughout Canada, and the United States of North America, in the Years 1806, 1807 & 1808*, 2nd ed. (London: C. Cradock and W. Joy, 1813), 2:315.

45. Edward Raymond Turner, "Women's Suffrage in New Jersey: 1790–1807," in *Smith College Studies in History* 1, ed. John S. Bassett and Sidney B. Fay (July 1916): 165–87; Klinghoffer and Elkis, "Petticoat Electors," 186–91; Gertzog, "Female Suffrage in New Jersey," in *Women, Politics, and the Constitution*, 47–58.

46. "Conducting an Election in Virginia: The Contested Election of Congressman Francis Preston, 1793," in *The Early Republic, 1789–1828*, ed. Noble E. Cunningham, Jr. (New York: Harper and Row, 1968), 214; Lambert, *Travels throughout Canada, and the U.S.*, 2:314; Richard Henry Lee to Mrs. Hannah Corbin, March 17, 1778, in *Letters of Richard Henry Lee*, 1:392–93.

47. Allan Greer, *The Patriots and the People: The Rebellion of 1837 in Rural Lower Canada* (Toronto: University of Toronto Press, 1993), 203–10.

48. Linda K. Kerber, "'Ourselves and Our Daughters Forever': Women and the Constitution, 1787–1876," in *One Woman, One Vote: Rediscovering the Woman Suffrage Movement*, ed. Marjorie Spruill Wheeler (Troutdale, Oreg.: NewSage Press, 1995), 21–36; James H. Kettner, *The Development of American Citizenship, 1608–1870* (Chapel Hill: University of North Carolina Press, 1978), 287–88; Rogers M. Smith, *Civic Ideals: Conflicting Visions of Citizenship in U.S. History* (New Haven, Conn.: Yale University Press, 1997), 115–36; Linda K. Kerber, *No Constitutional Right to Be Ladies: Women and the Obligations of Citizenship* (New York: Hill & Wang, 1998), 36–37, 128–36.

49. Samuel L. Mitchill to Catharine Mitchill, December 8, 1804, Mitchill Papers, Library of Congress.

50. John Thornton Kirkland, *An Oration, Delivered at the Request of the Society of Phi Beta Kappa, in the Chapel of Harvard College, on the Day of their Anniversary, July 19, 1798* (Boston: John Russell, 1798), 10; Jan Lewis, "'Of Every Age Sex & Condition': The Representation of Women in the Constitution," *Journal of the Early Republic* 15 (fall 1995): 382n76.

51. Nancy Cott, "Divorce and the Changing Status of Women in Eighteenth-Century Massachusetts," *William & Mary Quarterly*, 3rd ser., 33 (October 1976): 586–614; Cynthia A. Kierner, ed., *Southern Women in Revolution, 1776–1800: Personal and Political Narratives* (Columbia: University of South Carolina Press, 1998), xix–xxviii, 231–32; Ruth Bogin, "Petitioning and the New Moral Economy of Post-Revolutionary America," *William & Mary Quarterly*, 3rd ser. (July 1988): 391–425; Alison G. Olson, "Eighteenth-Century Colonial Legislatures and Their Constituents," *Journal of American History* 79 (September 1992): 557–59; Linda Burch, "1789–1820: The Republican Mother Exercises Her Right to Petition," unpublished research paper, George Mason University, May 2, 1997; Kerber, *Women of the Republic*, 93–99.

52. Petition of Janet Spurgin to the North Carolina Assembly, November 28, 1791 in *Southern Women in Revolution*, 180–81; Cynthia A. Kierner, *Beyond the Household: Women's Place in the Early South, 1700–1835* (Ithaca, N.Y.: Cornell University Press, 1998), 124–29.

53. Mary Wollstonecraft, *A Vindication of the Rights of Woman*, ed. M. Brody (London: Penguin Books, 1975 [orig. pub. 1792]); Thomas Paine, *Rights of Man, Common Sense, and Other Political Writings* (Oxford: Oxford University Press, 1995 [orig. pub. 1791–92]). Useful interpretations of Wollstonecraft include Barbara Taylor, *Mary Wollstonecraft and the Feminist Imagination* (Cambridge: Cambridge University Press, 2003); Mary Poovey, *The Proper Lady and the Woman Writer: Ideology as Style in the Works of Mary Wollstonecraft, Mary Shelley, and Jane Austen* (Chicago: University of Chicago Press, 1984); Virginia Sapiro, *A Vindication of Political Virtue: The Political Theory of Mary Wollstonecraft* (Chicago: University of Chicago Press, 1992); Garry Kelly, *Revolutionary Feminism: The Mind and Career of Mary Wollstonecraft* (New York: St. Martin's Press, 1992).

54. Wollstonecraft, *Vindication*, 87, 88, 188, 326.

55. Ibid., 265.

56. *New-York Magazine, or Literary Repository* (February 1793), 77. For early excerpts from *A Vindication*, see *Ladies Magazine* (Philadelphia), September 1792, 189–98; and *Massachusetts Magazine* (Boston), October 1792, 598–99. See also Marcelle Thiébaux, "Mary Wollstonecraft in Federalist America, 1791–1802," in *The Evidence of the Imagination: Studies of Interactions between Life and Art in English Romantic Literature*, ed. D. H. Reiman, M. C. Jaye, and B. T. Bennett (New York: New York University Press, 1978), 195–235; R. M. Janes, "On the Reception of Mary Wollstonecraft's *A Vindication of the Rights of Woman*," *Journal of the History of Ideas* 39 (1978): 293–302; David Lundberg and Henry F. May, "The Enlightened Reader in America," *American Quarterly* 28 (summer 1976): 262–71 and graphs following.

57. Miller, *Brief Retrospect of the Eighteenth Century*, 2:284. On Wollstonecraft's changing reputation, see William St. Clair, *The Godwins and the Shelleys: The Biography of a Family* (New York: Norton, 1989); Chandos Michael Brown, "Mary Wollstonecraft, or, The Female Illuminati: The Campaign against Women and 'Modern Philosophy' in the Early Republic," *Journal of the Early Republic* 15 (1995): 389–424; Patricia Jewell McAlexander, "The Creation of the American Eve: The Cultural Dialogue on the Nature and Role of Women in Late Eighteenth-Century America," *Early American Literature* 9 (1975): 262–64.

58. *Weekly Museum* (New York), April 15, 1795; reprinted in *Philadelphia Minerva*, October 1795.

59. Elias Boudinot, *An Oration Delivered at Elizabeth-Town, New-Jersey, Agreeably to a Resolution of the State Society of Cincinnati on the Fourth of July DCCXCIII* (Elizabethtown, N.J., 1793), 24; *Weekly Magazine of Original Essays, Fugitive Pieces, and Interesting Intelligence* 4 (April 13, 1799): 19; *Philadelphia Magazine, or Weekly Repository of Polite Literature*, May 2, 1818, 89.

60. *Ladies' Monitor* (New York), August 10, 15, 1801, 19–20; Jeremiah Perley, *An Anniversary Oration, Delivered before the Federal Republicans of Hallowell and Its Vicinity* (Augusta, Maine: Peter Edes, 1807), 23; Crocker, *Observations on the Real Rights of Women*; Miller, *Brief Retrospect of the Eighteenth Century*, 2:284.

61. Wollstonecraft, *Vindication*, 328. On "rights bearers," see Mary Ann Glendon, *Rights Talk: The Impoverishment of Political Discourse* (New York: Macmillan, 1991); Richard Tuck, *Natural Rights Theories: Their Origin and Development* (Cambridge: Cambridge University Press, 1979); Knud Haakonssen, "From Natural Law to the Rights of Man: A European Perspective on American Debates," in *A Culture of Rights: The Bill of Rights in Philosophy, Politics, and Law—1791 and 1991*, ed. Michael J. Lacey and Knud Haakonssen (Cambridge: Cambridge University Press, 1991); Thomas L. Haskell, "The Curious Persistence of Rights Talk in the 'Age of Interpretation,'" in *The Constitution and American Life*, ed. David Thelen (Ithaca, N.Y.: Cornell University Press, 1988), 324–52; Daniel T. Rodgers, *Contested Truths: Keywords in American Politics Since Independence* (New York: Basic Books, 1987).

62. *National Magazine, or, A Political, Historical, Biographical, and Literary Repository* 2 (1800): 206; William Boyd, *Woman: A Poem, Delivered at a Public Exhibition, April 19, at Harvard University; in the College Chapel* (Boston: John W. Folsom, 1796), 13; *Columbian Phenix and Boston Review* (May 1800): 267; *Philadelphia Repository, and Weekly Register*, May 21, 1803, 165.

63. *New-York Weekly Museum, or Polite Repository*, March 2, 1816, 276; *Philadelphia Repository and Weekly Register*, March 14, 1801, 5; *Mercury and New-England*

Palladium (Boston), September 15, 1801. Originally from a London publication, "The Rights of Both Sexes" was published numerous times in the United States, including in *Lady's Monitor* (New York), October 31, 1801, 88; *Mercury and New-England Palladium* (Boston), August 17, 1802; *Weekly Visitor, or, Ladies' Miscellany* (New York), October 16, 1802, 12; and *Weekly Magazine* (New York), April 13, 1799, 19. Multiple reprintings of the same article, which occurred frequently at this time, indicate how ideas about women's rights were circulated and spread throughout the transatlantic world. Although I have found several printings of many articles that I cite, I do not list every source, unless it helps substantiate a particular point.

Chapter 2

1. John Adams to his grandson, November 26, 1821, John Adams Papers, Letterbook (August 18, 1819–February 20, 1825), microfilm reel 124, Massachusetts Historical Society, Boston. I am grateful to Richard Samuelson for directing me to this reference.

2. *Columbian Magazine*, September 1787, 643; Catherine A. Brekus, "Restoring the Divine Order to the World: Religion and the Family in the Antebellum Woman's Rights Movement," in *Religion, Feminism, and the Family*, ed. Anne Carr and Mary Stewart Van Leeuwen (Louisville: University of Kentucky Press, 1996), 166–82.

3. *American Spectator, or Matrimonial Preceptor* (Boston: Manning & Lorring, 1797), vi; Rosemarie Zagarri, "Morals, Manners, and the Republican Mother," *American Quarterly* 44 (June 1992): 192–215.

4. *Boston Monthly Magazine* 1 (August 1825), 131, 135; *Mercury and New-England Palladium* (Boston), July 10, 1801; Mary Kelley, *Learning to Stand and Speak: Women, Education, and Public Life in America's Republic* (Chapel Hill: University of North Carolina Press, 2006), 34–111.

5. "The Salutatory Oration," delivered by Miss [Priscilla] Mason, in *The Rise and Progress of the Young Ladies' Academy of Philadelphia: Containing an Account of a Number of Public Examinations & Commencements; the Charter and Bye-Laws; Likewise; a Number of Orations delivered by the Young Ladies and Several by the Trustees of said Institution* (Philadelphia: Stewart & Cochran, 1794), 93, 94–95; *Philadelphia Repository and Weekly Register*, November 22, 1800, 4.

6. Franklin B. Dexter, ed., *The Literary Diary of Ezra Stiles, D.D., L.L.D.* (New York: Charles Scribner's Sons, 1901), 2:490; 3:15; Brothers in Unity, Secretary's Records, Yale University Archives, Book 2, Box 8, 64, 87, 114; Belles-Lettres Society, Minutes, Dickinson College Archives, vols. 1 (1786–91) and 2 (1792–1806); Dialectic Society, University of North Carolina—Chapel Hill Archives, ser. 1 (Minutes), vol. 3, September 22, 1803; May 11, 1804; May 17, 1804. For contemporaneous debates in England, see Barbara Taylor, *Mary Wollstonecraft and the Feminist Imagination* (Cambridge: Cambridge University Press, 2003), 176–78. I thank David W. Robson for providing the references to the Dickinson College debates.

7. *New-York Daily Advertiser*, January 19, 1790; *New-York Weekly Museum, or Polite Repository*, March 2, 1816, 276.

8. Charles Brockden Brown, *Alcuin: A Dialogue*, ed. Lee R. Edwards (New York: Grossman Publishers, 1971 [orig. pub. 1798, 1815]), 29, 37, 38.

9. John Thornton Kirkland, *An Oration, Delivered at the Request of the Society of Phi Beta Kappa, in the Chapel of Harvard College, on the Day of their Anniversary, July*

19, 1798 (Boston: John Russell, 1798), 10; reprinted in *Monthly Magazine and American Review* 2 (January 1800).

10. *Port-Folio* (Philadelphia), January 31, 1801, 38; *Mercury and New-England Palladium* (Boston), May 17, 1801; David Hackett Fischer, *The Revolution of American Conservatism: The Federalist Party in the Era of Jeffersonian Democracy* (New York: Harper & Row, 1965); Jeffrey L. Pasley, *"The Tyranny of Printers": Newspaper Politics in the Early American Republic* (Charlottesville: University Press of Virginia, 2001).

11. For the satire on illiterate women, see *Ladies Literary Museum, or Weekly Repository* (Philadelphia), January 17, 1818, and *Weekly Visitor, and Ladies' Museum* (New York), February 28, 1818, 281. For literacy rates, see Joel Perlmann and Dennis Shirley, "When Did New England Women Acquire Literacy?," *William & Mary Quarterly*, 3rd ser., 48 (January 1991): 50–67; William J. Gilmore, *Reading Becomes a Necessity of Life: Material and Cultural Life in Rural New England, 1780–1835* (Knoxville: University of Tennessee Press, 1989), 116–21, 221; Robert E. Gallman, "Changes in the Level of Literacy in a New Community of Early America," *Journal of Economic History* 48 (September 1988): 567–82; E. Jennifer Monaghan, "Literacy Instruction and Gender in Colonial New England," in *Reading in America: Literature and Social History*, ed. Cathy N. Davidson (Baltimore: Johns Hopkins University Press, 1989), 53–80; "Literacy," in Darrett B. Rutman and Anita H. Rutman, *A Place in Time: Explicatus* (New York: W. W. Norton & Co., 1984), 165–700.

12. *Boston Weekly Magazine: or, Ladies' and Gentleman's Miscellany*, October 29, 1803, 2; *Euterpeiad: or, Musical Intelligencer, and Ladies' Gazette* (Boston), September 15, 1821, 101; Linda K. Kerber, *Women of the Republic: Intellect and Ideology in Revolutionary America* (Chapel Hill: University of North Carolina Press, 1980), 189–231; Mary Beth Norton, *Liberty's Daughters: The Revolutionary Experience of American Women, 1750–1800* (Glenview, Ill.: Little, Brown, & Co., 1980), 256–99; Patricia Cline Cohen, *A Calculating People: The Spread of Numeracy in Early America* (Chicago: University of Chicago Press, 1982); Kelley, *Learning to Stand and Speak*, 66–111.

13. Pasley, *Tyranny of Printers*, 403–5; Richard D. Brown, *Knowledge Is Power: The Diffusion of Information in Early America, 1700–1865* (New York: Oxford University Press, 1989), 160–96; David A. Copeland, *Colonial American Newspapers: Character and Content* (Newark: University of Delaware Press, 1997), 151–73.

14. *Intellectual Regale, or, Ladies Tea Tray* (Philadelphia), 1814–15; Bertha Monica Stearns, "Before Godey's," *American Literature* 2 (1930): 248–55; Bertha Monica Stearns, "Early Philadelphia Magazines for Ladies," *Pennsylvania Magazine of History and Biography* 64 (1940): 479–91; Margaret Beetham, *A Magazine of Her Own? Domesticity and Desire in the Woman's Magazine, 1800–1914* (London: Routledge, 1996), 18–30; Kelley, *Learning to Stand and Speak*, 57–58.

15. Mrs. Mehatable Mumford to John R. Parker, August 10, 1821, Mehatable Mumford Papers, Southern Historical Collection, University of North Carolina, Chapel Hill, Collection 2953-Z; Cynthia A. Kierner, *Beyond the Household: Women's Place in the Early South, 1700–1835* (Ithaca, N.Y.: Cornell University Press, 1998), 103–5; Susan Branson, *These Fiery Frenchified Dames: Women and Political Culture in Early National Philadelphia* (Philadelphia: University of Pennsylvania Press, 2001), 21–53; David Paul Nord, "Magazine Reading and Readers in Late-Eighteenth-Century New York," in *Reading in America*, 114–39. For subscribers' lists, see *Port-Folio* (Philadelphia), May 21, 1803, 176; *Intellectual Regale, or Ladies' Tea Tray* 2

(Philadelphia), May 1815, pages preceding 417; *Parlour Companion*, December 6, 1817, 201–4.

16. Kevin J. Hayes, *A Colonial Woman's Bookshelf* (Knoxville: University of Tennessee Press, 1996), 11–16; James Raven, *London Booksellers and American Customers: Transatlantic Literary Community and the Charleston Library Society, 1748–1811* (Columbia: University of South Carolina Press, 2002), 69–71.

17. *Ladies Visitor* (Boston), December 4, 1806; *New York Magazine; or, Literary Repository* (October 1791), 571–72; *Mrs. A. S. Colvin's Weekly Messenger* (Washington, D.C.), June 15, 1822, 1; *Lady's Miscellany; or, the Weekly Visitor* (New York), August 10, 1811, 254; *Lady's Miscellany*, April 4, 1812, 380–81.

18. Margaret Bayard to Samuel Harrison Smith, September 5, 1800, Margaret Bayard Smith Papers, Library of Congress, microfilm reel 1 (container 10); Carol Berkin, *Revolutionary Mothers: Women in the Struggle for America's Independence* (New York: Alfred A. Knopf, 2005), 120–34.

19. Joan R. Gundersen, *To Be Useful to the World: Women in Revolutionary America, 1740–1790* (New York: Twayne Publishers, 1996), 77–93; Brown, *Knowledge Is Power*, 160–96.

20. "Books Read by Maria Margaret DeRieux," Commonplace Book, 1806–23, MSS 5:5D4454, Virginia Historical Society, Richmond.

21. Kelley, *Learning to Stand and Speak*, 112–90.

22. Barbara E. Lacey, "Women in the Era of the American Revolution: The Case of Norwich, Connecticut," *New England Quarterly* 53 (1980): 527–43; quotes on 541. For a discussion of women's literary societies, see Kelley, *Learning to Stand and Speak*, 112–53.

23. Susan Branson, "Elizabeth Drinker: Quaker Values and Federalist Support in the 1790s," *Pennsylvania History: A Journal of Mid-Atlantic Studies* 68 (Autumn 2001): 467; A. G. Roeber, ed., "A New England Woman's Perspective on Norfolk, Virginia, 1801–1802: Excerpts from the Diary of Ruth Henshaw Bascom," *Proceedings of the American Antiquarian Society* 88, part 2 (1979): 277–325; Rachel Mordecai to Samuel Mordecai, January 17, 1808, Mordecai Papers, #847, Folder 3, Southern Historical Collection, University of North Carolina—Chapel Hill (hereinafter referred to as UNC); Catherine Byles to Mrs. Elizabeth H., May 1795, Letters of Catherine and Mary Byles, Houghton Library, Harvard University, 1:42; Julia Anne Hieronymus Tevis, "Autobiography—1878," in *Recollections of the Early Republic: Selected Autobiographies*, ed. Joyce Appleby (Boston: Northeastern University Press, 1997), 85; Noble E. Cunningham, Jr., ed., "The Diary of Frances Few, 1808–1809," *Journal of Southern History* 29 (August 1963): 353.

24. Pamela Dwight Sedgwick to Theodore Sedgwick, July 8, 1790, in *The First Federal Congress, 1789–1791*, ed. Margaret Christman (Washington, D.C.: Smithsonian Institution Press, 1789), 321; Susana P. Robson to Thomas Jefferson, December 29, 1803, in *To His Excellency, Thomas Jefferson: Letters to a President*, ed. Jack McLaughlin (New York: W. W. Norton & Co., 1991), 106.

25. Ann Steele to John Steele, February 11, 1801, June 2, 1801, John Steele Papers, #689, Ser. 1.2, Folders 19 and 21, UNC; Rosalie Stier Calvert to H. J. Stier, April 27, 1807, in *Mistress of Riversdale: The Plantation Letters of Rosalie Stier Calvert, 1795–1821*, ed. Margaret Law Callcott (Baltimore: Johns Hopkins University Press, 1991), 166.

26. *Ariel and Ladies' Literary Gazette* (Philadelphia), April 14, 1827, 1.

27. Rosemarie Zagarri, *A Woman's Dilemma: Mercy Otis Warren and the American Revolution* (Wheeling, Ill.: Harlan Davidson, Inc., 1995), 48–77; John Adams to James Warren, December 22, 1773, in *Works of John Adams*, ed. Charles Francis

Adams (Boston: Little, Brown and Co., 1854), 9:335; [A Columbian Patriot], "Observations on the New Constitution, and on the Federal and State Conventions" (February 1788), in *The Complete Anti-Federalist*, ed. Herbert J. Storing (Chicago: University of Chicago Press, 1981), 4:270–87; Alexander Hamilton to Mercy Warren, July 1, 1791, in *Warren-Adams Letters, Being Chiefly a Correspondence among John Adams, Samuel Adams, and James Warren* (Boston: Massachusetts Historical Society, 1917), 2:326; Mercy Otis Warren, *History of the Rise, Progress and Termination of the American Revolution Interspersed with Biographical, Political and Moral Observations*, 2 vols. (Indianapolis: Liberty Press, 1988 [orig. pub. 1805]).

28. Mercy Warren to John Adams, September 4, 1775, in *Warren-Adams Letters*, 1:106–7; Warren, *History of the . . . American Revolution*, 1:xlii–xliii; Mercy Warren to John Adams, August 16, 1807, in *Correspondence between John Adams and Mercy Warren*, ed. Charles Francis Adams (New York: Arno Press, 1972 [orig. pub. 1878]), 454.

29. Judith Sargent Murray, *The Gleaner*, ed. Nina Baym (Schenectady, N.Y.: Union College Press, 1992 [orig. pub. 1798]), 698; Sheila Skemp, *Judith Sargent Murray: A Brief Biography with Documents* (Boston: Bedford Books, 1998), 95–107.

30. Murray, *Gleaner*, 804; *The Panoplist; or, The Christian's Armory*, 2 (Boston), January 1807, 380.

31. *Lady's Weekly Miscellany* (New York), October 21, 1809, 412; Kierner, *Beyond the Household*, 20; Julia Cherry Spruill, *Women's Life and Work in the Southern Colonies* (New York: W. W. Norton, 1998 [orig. pub. 1938]), 263–67.

32. Charles A. Kromkowski, *Recreating the American Republic: Rules of Apportionment, Constitutional Change, and American Political Development, 1700–1870* (Cambridge: Cambridge University Press, 2002), 380.

33. James Sterling Young, *The Washington Community, 1800–1828* (New York: Harcourt, Brace & World, Inc., 1966), 87–109; H. Douglas Price, "Congress and the Evolution of Legislative 'Professionalism,'" and Morris P. Fiorina, David W. Rohde, and Peter Wissel, "Historical Change in House Turnover," in *Congress in Change*, ed. Norman J. Ornstein (New York: Praeger Publishers, 1975), 3–57; Samuel Kernell, "Toward Understanding 19th Century Congressional Careers: Ambition, Competition, and Rotation," *American Journal of Political Science* 21 (November 1977): 669–93; Nelson W. Polsby, "The Institutionalization of the U.S. House of Representatives," *American Political Science Review* 62 (1968): 144–68. On average, members served between 4.12 and 5.24 years in Congress. These statistics are derived from my original analysis of data on the first through the twentieth Congresses found in the Roster of United States Congressional Officeholders and Biographical Characteristics of Members of the United States Congress, 1789–1996: Merged Data (ICPSR 7803) in the database from the Inter-University Consortium for Political and Social Research, 10th ed. (1997).

34. Martha Jefferson Randolph, November 23, 1807, in *The Family Letters of Thomas Jefferson*, ed. Edwin Morris Betts and James Adam Bear, Jr. (Charlottesville: University Press of Virginia, 1966), 315–16; Dolley Payne Madison to Martha Jefferson Randolph, January 9, 1814, in *The Selected Letters of Dolley Payne Madison*, ed. David B. Mattern and Holly C. Shulman (Charlottesville: University of Virginia Press, 2003), 183; Catherine Allgor, *Parlor Politics in Which the Ladies of Washington Help Build a City and a Government* (Charlottesville: University Press of Virginia, 2000); Jan Lewis, "Politics and the Ambivalence of the Private Sphere: Women in Early Washington, D.C.," in *A Republic for the Ages: The United States Capitol and the Political Culture of the Early Republic*, ed. Donald R. Kennon (Charlottesville: University Press of Virginia, 1999), 122–51. In *Parlor Politics*,

Allgor chooses to concentrate on the impact of the women who were present rather than those who were absent. For the more conventional view discussing the paucity of women in early Washington, see Constance McLaughlin Green, *Washington: A History of the Capital, 1800–1950* (Princeton, N.J.: Princeton University Press, 1962), 21, 108, 148–51.

35. *The Debates and Proceedings in the Congress of the United States*, 14th Congress (Washington, D.C.: Gales and Seaton, 1854), 1158; Young, *Washington Community*, 71, 89, 101, 268n44; Karen Kauffman, "James and Rebecca Hillhouse: Public and Private Commitments in the Early Republic," *Connecticut History* 8 (fall 1999): 105–26.

36. Mary Stanford to Richard Stanford, January 25, 1804, Richard Stanford Papers, UNC; John Steele to Mary Steele, October 8, 1798, John Steele Papers, UNC; Abijah Bigelow to Hannah Bigelow, December 26, 1813, Bigelow Family Papers, Folio 1, American Antiquarian Society (hereinafter referred to as AAS).

37. Hannah Bigelow to Abijah Bigelow, December 27, 1812, Bigelow Family Papers, Box 1, AAS; Catherine Few to Mrs. Albert Gallatin, July 1, 1798, Mrs. Edmund C. Genêt Papers, Misc. Mss., New York Historical Society, New York City; Rebecca Faulkner Foster to Dwight Foster, February 6, 1792, Foster Family Papers, Box 4, AAS.

38. Jeremiah Mason to Mary Mason, in *Memoir and Correspondence of Jeremiah Mason* (Cambridge, Mass.: Riverside Press, 1873), 78, 103–4, 109; Elijah Brigham to Sarah Brigham, February 8, 1814, Elijah Brigham Papers, Library of Congress, Manuscript Room (hereinafter referred to as LC); Thomas H. Hubbard to Phebe Hubbard, January 31, 1818, Thomas Hubbard Papers, LC.

39. Rebecca Faulkner Foster to Dwight Foster, May 2, 1796, Foster Family Papers, Box 4, AAS; Catharine Carroll Harper to Robert Goodloe Harper, March 1, 1814, Harper-Pennington Papers, MS 431, reel 2, Maryland Historical Society, Baltimore; Catherine McLane to Louis McLane, May 20, 1824, Louis McLane Papers, LC; Jeremiah Mason to Mary Mason, January 29, 1814, in *Memoir and Correspondence of Jeremiah Mason*, 79. In *Parlor Politics*, p. 125, Allgor describes similar functions for politicians' wives who were resident in Washington.

40. Catharine Carroll Harper to Robert Goodloe Harper, March 5, 1810, Harper-Pennington Papers, MS 431, reel 2, Maryland Historical Society, Baltimore; Hannah Gaston to William Gaston, July 2, 1810, William Gaston Papers, UNC; Mary Polk to George Badger, Polk, Badger and McGeher Family Papers, #3979, UNC. See also Kierner, *Beyond the Household*, 123.

41. Louis McLane to Kitty McLane, April 19, 1822, Louis McLane Papers, LC; Jeremiah Mason to Mary Mason, December 11, 1814, in *Memoir and Correspondence of Jeremiah Mason*, 109; John Steele to Mary Steele, November 21, 1801, John Steele Papers, #689, Ser. 1.2, UNC; Rebecca Faulkner Foster to Dwight Foster, January 13, 1801, Foster Family Papers, Box 4, AAS.

42. *Mrs. A. S. Colvin's Weekly Messenger* (Washington City, D.C.), September 22, 1827, 71; Edith B. Gelles, "'Splendid Misery': Abigail Adams as First Lady," in *John Adams and the Founding of the Republic*, ed. Richard Ryerson (Boston: Massachusetts Historical Society, 2001), 190–93; Hannah Mather Crocker, *Observations on the Real Rights of Women, with their Appropriate Duties, agreeable to Scripture, Reason and Common Sense* (Boston: privately printed, 1818), 47–48.

43. David Waldstreicher, *In the Midst of Perpetual Fetes: The Making of American Nationalism, 1776–1820* (Chapel Hill: University of North Carolina Press, 1997). See also Simon P. Newman, *Parades and the Politics of the Street: Festive Culture in the Early American Republic* (Philadelphia: University of Pennsylvania Press, 1997);

Len Travers, *Celebrating the Fourth: Independence Day and the Rites of Nationalism in the Early Republic* (Amherst: University of Massachusetts Press, 1997); Geneviève Fabre, Jürgen Heideking, and Kai Dreisbach, eds., *Celebrating Ethnicity and Nation: American Festive Culture from the Revolution to the Early Twentieth Century* (New York: Berghahn Books, 2001), 25–89.

44. Crocker, *Real Rights of Women*, 62; Abigail Adams to John Adams, June 17, 1782, in *Adams Family Correspondence*, ed. L. H. Butterfield (Cambridge, Mass.: Harvard University Press, 1963), 4:328.

45. Jane Ewing to her brother, April 23, 1789, Jane Ewing Collection, Misc. Mss., LC; Jürgen Heideking, "The Federal Processions of 1788 and the Emergence of a Republican Festive Culture in the United States," in Fabre et al., *Celebrating Ethnicity and Nation*, 25–43.

46. Letters of Catherine and Mary Byles, Houghton Library, Harvard University, 1:42; Rebecca Faulkner Foster to Dwight Foster, May 30, 1798, Foster Family Papers, Box 4, AAS; Rosalie Stier Calvert to Charles J. Stier, October 30, 1809, in *Mistress of Riversdale*, 209; Roeber, "New England Woman's Perspective on Norfolk, Virginia, 1801–1802," 315–16; Maria Beckley to Lucy Southall, June 8, 1808, Cutts Family Correspondence, Folder 1802–9, LC.

47. *Centinel of Freedom* (Newark, N.J.), July 19, 1797; Travers, *Celebrating the Fourth*, 31–68, 135–41.

48. *Niles' Weekly Register* (Baltimore), July 26, 1817, 347; *Ladies' Literary Cabinet* (New York), July 3, 1819, 64; Elias Boudinot, *An Oration Delivered at Elizabeth-Town, New-Jersey, Agreeably to a Resolution of the State Society of Cincinnati on the Fourth of July DCCXCIII* (Elizabethtown, N.J.: Shepard Kollock, 1793), 23; Sarah J. Purcell, *Sealed with Blood: War, Sacrifice, and Memory in Revolutionary America* (Philadelphia: University of Pennsylvania Press, 2002), 82–86; Waldstreicher, *In the Midst of Perpetual Fetes*, 233–41; Kierner, *Beyond the Household*, 129–33; Travers, *Celebrating the Fourth*, 135–41.

49. Catherine A. Brekus, *Strangers & Pilgrims: Female Preaching in America, 1740–1845* (Chapel Hill: University of North Carolina Press, 1998), 18, 23–67; Alfred A. Young, *Masquerade: The Life and Times of Deborah Sampson Gannett, Continental Soldier* (New York: Alfred A. Knopf, 2004).

50. "Salutatory Oration," delivered by Miss [Priscilla] Mason, in *Rise and Progress of the Young Ladies' Academy of Philadelphia*, 91; *Port Folio* (Philadelphia), August 15, 1807; Waldstreicher, *In the Midst of Perpetual Fetes*, 155–73.

51. *New-England Palladium*, July 21, 1807; *Ladies' Visiter* (Marietta, Pa.), September 28, 1819, 29.

52. *American Mercury* (Hartford, Conn.), August 5, 1822.

53. Ibid.; *Mrs. A. S. Colvin's Weekly Messenger*, August 10, 1822, 34.

54. *The Courier* (Norwich, Conn.), July 10, 1799; Kerber, *Women of the Republic*, 189–231.

55. [Written by a Lady], *The Female Advocate* (New Haven, Conn.: Thomas Green & Son, 1801); [By a Citizen of the United States], *An Oration Delivered on the Fourth of July 1800* (Springfield, Mass.: Henry Brewer, 1808). The Springfield, Massachusetts, version reprints *The Female Advocate* as a supplement to *An Oration Delivered on the Fourth of July 1800* by the anonymous "Citizen of the United States." The original *Female Advocate* is written as if it were delivered as an Independence Day oration. There is no direct evidence as to the author's name or where the address was delivered. Quotes are from the 1808 edition, 11, 21, 25, 34.

56. Adams's 1755 letter is quoted in John Adams to Benjamin Rush, May 1,

1807, in *The Spur of Fame: Dialogues of John Adams and Benjamin Rush 1805–1813*, ed. John A. Schutz and Douglass Adair (Indianapolis: Liberty Fund, 1966), 88. *Monthly Magazine, and American Review*, December 1800, 418; reprinted in *Lady's Monitor*, May 29, 1802. I am suggesting not that the term "female politician" was invented in the postrevolutionary period but rather that it came into wider usage then. For a discussion of women's political influence in Britain during this same period, see Anna Clark, *Scandal: The Sexual Politics of the British Constitution* (Princeton, N.J.: Princeton University Press, 2004), 53–83; Arianne Chernock, "Extending the 'Right of Election': Men's Arguments for Women's Political Representation in Late Enlightenment Britain," in *Women, Gender and Enlightenment*, ed. Sarah Knott and Barbara Taylor (Hampshire: Palgrave-Macmillan, 2005), 587–609.

57. Jeremiah Mason to Mrs. Mary Mason, February 23, 1814, in *Memoir and Correspondence of Jeremiah Mason*, 87; Thomas Lee Shippen to Nancy Shippen, summer 1785, in *Nancy Shippen: Her Journal Book*, ed. Ethel Armes (New York: Benjamin Blom, 1968), 232; Bayard and Brown quoted in Fredrika J. Teute, "A 'Republic of Intellect': Conversation and Criticism among the Sexes in the 1790s in New York," in *Revising Charles Brockden Brown: Culture, Politics, and Sexuality in the Early Republic*, ed. Philip Barnard, Mark L. Kamrath, and Stephen Shapiro (Knoxville: University of Tennessee Press, 2003), 149–81, quote on 167.

58. Manigault quoted in Norton, *Liberty's Daughters*, 189; Eleanor Parke Custis to Elizabeth Bordley, May 14, 1798, in *George Washington's Beautiful Nelly: The Letters of Eleanor Parke Custis Lewis to Elizabeth Bordley Gibson, 1794–1851*, ed. Patricia Brady (Columbia: University of South Carolina Press, 1991), 52; Mercy Otis Warren to Catharine Macaulay, December 29, 1774, Mercy Otis Warren Papers, Letterbook 6 (microfilm reel 1), Massachusetts Historical Society, Boston.

59. Hannah Webster Foster, *The Coquette* (1797), in *Public Women, Public Words: A Documentary History of American Feminism*, ed. Dawn Keetley and John Pettegrew (Madison, Wis.: Madison House Publishers, 1997), 1:75.

60. *Monthly Magazine, and American Review* (December 1800), 417–18; reprinted in *Lady's Monitor*, May 29, 1802; Skemp, *Judith Sargent Murray*, 39, 43.

61. Thomas Jefferson to Elizabeth Trist, August 18, 1785, in *Papers of Thomas Jefferson*, ed. Julian P. Boyd et al. (Princeton, N.J.: Princeton University Press, 1950–), 8:404.

62. *Centinel of Freedom* (Newark, N.J.), October 18, 1797.

63. Ibid.

64. *Columbian Centinel* (Boston), March 2, 1822; *Euterpeiad, Musical Intelligencer, and Ladies' Gazette* (Boston), March 2, 1822.

65. *Euterpeiad*, March 2, 1822; *Columbian Centinel*, March 6, 1822.

66. Hilda L. Smith, *All Men and Both Sexes: Gender, Politics, and the False Universal in England, 1640–1832* (University Park: Pennsylvania State University Press, 2002), 125–27; Lois G. Schwoerer, "Women's Public Political Voice in England: 1640–1740," in *Women Writers and the Early Modern British Political Tradition*, ed. Hilda L. Smith (Cambridge: Cambridge University Press, 1998), 60.

67. *The Hive* (Lancaster, Pa.), February 15, 1804, 138; *The Key* (Frederick-Town, Md.), March 13, 1815, 98–99; *Port Folio* (Philadelphia), February 26, 1803, 65–66; *Lady's Weekly Miscellany* (New York), December 17, 1808, 124–25; *Lady's Miscellany; or, The Weekly Visitor* (Philadelphia), February 22, 1812, 280–81.

68. *Philadelphia Repository and Weekly Register*, June 25, 1803, 202; *Lady's Miscellany*, February 22, 1812, 280.

Chapter 3

1. [John Murdock], *Politicians; or, A State of Things: A Dramatic Piece* (Philadelphia: printed for the author, 1798), 4, 5.

2. Richard Hofstadter, *The Idea of a Party System: The Rise of Legitimate Opposition in the United States, 1780–1840* (Berkeley: University of California Press, 1969), 40–121; James Roger Sharp, *American Politics in the Early Republic: The New Nation in Crisis* (New Haven, Conn.: Yale University Press, 1993); Joyce Appleby, *Capitalism and a New Social Order: The Republican Vision of the 1790s* (New York: New York University Press, 1984); Stanley Elkins and Eric McKitrick, *The Age of Federalism: The Early American Republic, 1788–1800* (New York: Oxford University Press, 1993); David Hackett Fischer, *The Revolution of American Conservatism: The Federalist Party in the Era of Jeffersonian Democracy* (New York: Harper and Row, 1965); Linda K. Kerber, *Federalists in Dissent: Imagery and Ideology in Jeffersonian America* (Ithaca, N.Y.: Cornell University Press, 1970).

3. Alan Taylor, *Liberty Men and Great Proprietors: The Revolutionary Settlement on the Maine Frontier, 1760–1820* (Chapel Hill: University of North Carolina Press, 1990); Joanne B. Freeman, *Affairs of Honor: National Politics in the New Republic* (New Haven, Conn.: Yale University Press, 2001), 123–26, 181–87; John F. Hoadley, *Origins of American Political Parties, 1789–1803* (Lexington: University Press of Kentucky, 1986).

4. Jefferson quoted in Hofstadter, *Idea of a Party System*, 89; Elkins and McKitrick, *Age of Federalism*, 303–73; David Waldstreicher, *In the Midst of Perpetual Fetes: The Making of American Nationalism, 1776–1820* (Chapel Hill: University of North Carolina Press, 1997), 126–73; Simon P. Newman, *Parades and the Politics of the Street: Festive Culture in the Early American Republic* (Philadelphia: University of Pennsylvania Press, 1997), 120–85; Jeffrey L. Pasley, *"The Tyranny of Printers": Newspaper Politics in the Early American Republic* (Charlottesville: University Press of Virginia, 2001); Charles Downer Hazen, "Contemporary American Opinion of the French Revolution," *Johns Hopkins University Studies in History and Political Science* 16 (1964): 214–15; Andrew W. Robertson, "'Look on This Picture . . . And on This!': Nationalism, Localism, and Partisan Images of Otherness in the United States, 1787–1820," *American Historical Review* 106 (October 2001): 1263–80.

5. *Monthly Magazine, and American Review* (December 1800), 417; [A Lay Preacher], *A Political Catechism, Intended for the Use of Children of a Larger Growth, and Respectfully Dedicated to the Republicans of the Counties of Morris, Essex and Sussex, in the State of New-Jersey* (Morris-Town, N.J., 1812), 15.

6. Jeffrey L. Pasley, "1800 as a Revolution in Political Culture," in *The Revolution of 1800: Democracy, Race and the New Republic*, ed. James Horn, Jan Ellen Lewis, and Peter S. Onuf (Charlottesville: University Press of Virginia, 2002), 121–52; Jeffrey L. Pasley, "The Cheese and the Words," in *Beyond the Founders: New Approaches to the Political History of the Early American Republic* (Chapel Hill: University of North Carolina Press, 2004), 31–56; J. R. Pole, *Political Representation in England and the Origins of the American Republic* (Berkeley: University of California Press, 1971), 543–64; Ronald P. Formisano, *The Transformation of Political Culture: Massachusetts Parties, 1790s-1840s* (New York: Oxford University Press, 1983); Fischer, *Revolution in American Conservatism*, xiv–xv, 182–99.

7. *Centinel of Freedom* (Newark, N.J.), July 19, 1797; Len Travers, *Celebrating the Fourth: Independence Day and the Rites of Nationalism in the Early Republic* (Amherst:

University of Massachusetts Press, 1997), 88–106; Newman, *Parades and the Politics of the Street*, 83–119; Susan Branson, *These Fiery Frenchified Dames: Women and Political Culture in Early National Philadelphia* (Philadelphia: University of Pennsylvania Press, 2001), 82–87.

8. Julius Forrest, *Oration Delivered before the Republican Students of the Belles-Lettres and Union Philosophical Societies of Dickinson College, July 4, 1815* (Carlisle, Pa., 1815), 10; *Centinel of Freedom* (Newark, N.J.), July 10, 1798.

9. John Morin Scott, *Oration delivered before the Philadelphia Association for Celebrating the Fourth of July, without Distinction of Party (July 4, 1833)* (Philadelphia: William F. Geddes, 1833), 8; Alexander DeConde, *The Quasi-War: The Politics and Diplomacy of the Undeclared War with France 1797–1801* (New York: Charles Scribner's Sons, 1966), 82–83; Lynn Hunt, "Symbolic Forms of Political Practice," in *Politics, Class, and Culture in the French Revolution* (Berkeley: University of California Press, 1984), 52–86, quote on 56.

10. Cornelia Clinton to Edmund C. Genêt, January 1794, Mrs. Edmund C. Genêt Papers, Misc. Mss., New York Historical Society, New York City; Eleanor Parke Custis to Elizabeth Bordley, November 23, 1797, and May 14, 1798, in *George Washington's Beautiful Nelly*, ed. Patricia Brady (Columbia: University of South Carolina Press, 1991), 41, 52; Catharine Boudinot Atterbury to Elisha Boudinot, February 16, 1804, Mrs. Lewis Atterbury Papers, Misc. Mss., New York Historical Society, New York City.

11. Abigail Adams to John Adams, June 17, 1782, in *Adams Family Correspondence*, ed. L. H. Butterfield (Cambridge: Harvard University Press, 1963), 4:328.

12. [A Columbian Patriot], "Observations on the New Constitution, and on the Federal and State Conventions," in *The Complete Anti-Federalist*, ed. Herbert J. Storing (Chicago: University of Chicago Press, 1981); Mercy Otis Warren, *History of the Rise, Progress, and Termination of the American Revolution Interspersed with Biographical, Political, and Moral Observations*, ed. Lester H. Cohen (Indianapolis: Liberty Press, 1988 [orig. pub. 1805]), 2:624, 629, 670.

13. Judith Sargent Murray, *The Gleaner*, ed. Nina Baym (Schenectady, N.Y.: Union College Press, 1992 [orig. pub. 1798]), 214, 216, 636; Judith Sargent Murray to her brother, February 13, 1796, Letterbook 9:536 (microfilm reel 3), Mississippi Archives, Jackson. My deep thanks to Sheila Skemp for providing archival references for Judith Sargent Murray's letters.

14. For a fascinating discussion of political socialization in a later era, see Jean H. Baker, *Affairs of Party: The Political Culture of Northern Democrats in the Mid-Nineteenth Century* (Ithaca, N.Y.: Cornell University Press, 1983).

15. William W. Story, ed., *Life and Letters of Joseph Story* (Cambridge: Charles C. Little and James Brown, 1851), 1:96; John Moody to James Madison, January 7, 1798, in *The Papers of James Madison*, ed. David B. Mattern, J. C. A. Stagg, Jeanne K. Cross, and Susan H. Perdue (Charlottesville: University Press of Virginia, 1991), 17:198; Lucy Kenney, *Description of a Visit to Washington* (N.p., 1835), 4.

16. Catharine Maria Sedgwick, *The Power of Her Sympathy: The Autobiography and Journal of Catharine Maria Sedgwick*, ed. Mary Kelley (Boston: Northeastern University Press, 1993), 64, 80.

17. Catharine Maria Sedgwick, "A Reminiscence of Federalism," in *Tales and Sketches* (Philadelphia, 1835); Alan Taylor, *William Cooper's Town: Power and Persuasion on the Frontier of the Early American Republic* (New York: Knopf, 1995), 305; Joseph Story to Capt. Ichabod Nichols, March 24, 1801, and Joseph Story to Lydia Pierce, November 28, 1801, Joseph Story Papers, Harry Ransom Humani-

ties Research Center, University of Texas, Austin; R. Kent Newmyer, *Supreme Court Justice Joseph Story: Statesman of the Old Republic* (Chapel Hill: University of North Carolina Press, 1985), 45–47.

18. Cornelia Greene to Margaret Cooper, May 3, 1800, MacKay-Stiles Papers, #470, Ser. A, Folder 5, Southern Historical Collection, University of North Carolina, Chapel Hill; Sophia May to her sister, April 17, 1812, Sophia May Letters, American Antiquarian Society, Worcester, Mass. (hereinafter referred to as "AAS").

19. Cornelia Clinton to Edmund Genêt, December 18, 1793, Mrs. Edmund C. Genêt Papers, Misc. Mss., New York Historical Society, New York City; Norman K. Risjord, *Jefferson's America, 1760–1815* (Madison, Wis.: Madison House Publishers, 1991), 216–18.

20. Fortescue Cuming, *Sketches of a Tour to the Western Country* (Pittsburgh, 1810), 57; Sheila Skemp, *Judith Sargent Murray: A Brief Biography with Documents* (Boston: Bedford Books, 1998), 3–31, 44–55.

21. Rosemarie Zagarri, *A Woman's Dilemma: Mercy Otis Warren and the American Revolution* (Wheeling, Ill.: Harlan Davidson, Inc., 1995), 114–60. For other examples of husbands and wives with divergent political opinions, see Cynthia A. Kierner, *Beyond the Household: Women's Place in the Early South, 1700–1835* (Ithaca, N.Y.: Cornell University Press, 1998), 120–24.

22. Robert E. Shalhope, *A Tale of New England: The Diaries of Hiram Harwood, Vermont Farmer, 1810–1837* (Baltimore: Johns Hopkins University Press, 2003), 215; Mary Jackson Lee to Henry Lee, Folder 2.10 (microfilm reel 2), Lee Family Papers, Massachusetts Historical Society, Boston; William Stedman to Thomas Dwight, September 14, 1803, Dwight-Howard Papers, Massachusetts Historical Society, Boston; Frederick Tupper and Helen Tyler Brown, *Grandmother Tyler's Book: The Recollections of Mary Palmer Tyler (Mrs. Royall Tyler), 1775–1866* (New York: G. P. Putnam's Sons, 1925), 297. Thanks to Rob McDonald for providing the reference to the Dwight-Howard Papers.

23. Elaine Forman Crane, ed., *The Diary of Elizabeth Drinker* (Boston: Northeastern University Press, 1991), 1:700–701; Judith Sargent Murray to her brother, April 13, 1796, and May 8, 1796, Letterbook, 9:572, 583–84, Judith Sargent Murray Papers, Mississippi Archives, Jackson.

24. Eleanor Parke Custis to Elizabeth Bordley, May 14, 1798, in *George Washington's Beautiful Nelly*, 52; Catherine Few to Mrs. Albert Gallatin, July 1, 1798, Chrystie Family Papers, New York Historical Society, New York City.

25. Margaret Bayard Smith to Miss Susan B. Smith, March 4, 1801, in *The First Forty Years of Washington Society in the Family Letters of Margaret Bayard Smith*, ed. Gaillard Hunt (New York: Frederick Ungar Publishing Co., 1965), 25–26; James Warren to Thomas Jefferson, March 4, 1801 (microfilm reel 2), Mercy Otis Warren Papers, Massachusetts Historical Society, Boston.

26. Judith Sargent Murray to Col. H.—of Philadelphia, December 29, 1800, Letterbook 236, Judith Sargent Murray Papers (microfilm reel 3), Mississippi Archives, Jackson; Harriet Trumbull to Daniel Wadsworth, May 6, 1801, in *A Season in New York 1801: Letters of Harriet and Maria Trumbull*, ed. Helen M. Morgan (Pittsburgh: University of Pittsburgh Press, 1969), 137; Hillhouse quoted in Karen Kauffman, "James and Rebecca Hillhouse: Public and Private Commitments in the Early Republic," *Connecticut History* 28 (fall 1999): 116.

27. Risjord, *Jefferson's America*, 268–70; Louis Martin Sears, "The South and the Embargo," *South Atlantic Quarterly* 20 (July 1921): 254–65.

28. *The Embargo: A New Song—Tune 'Yankee Doodle'* (1808), Broadside, AAS;

Rosalie Stier Calvert to H. J. Stier, July 9, 1808, *Mistress of Riverdale: The Plantation Letters of Rosalie Stier Calvert, 1795–1821,* ed. Margaret Law Callcott (Baltimore: Johns Hopkins University Press, 1991), 190.

29. Orangeburg, South Carolina, quote from Kierner, *Beyond the Household,* 136; *The Enquirer* (Richmond), February 26, 1808; *New-England Palladium* (Boston), July 14, 1807, reprinted in *New-York Weekly Museum,* July 18, 1807, and *New-York Weekly Museum,* December 31, 1808; Diary, December 22, 1808, in *Diary of Sarah Connell Ayer* (Portland, Maine: Lefavor-Tower Co., 1910), 66.

30. Julia Anne Hieronymus Tevis in *Recollections of the Early Republic: Selected Autobiographies,* ed. Joyce Appleby (Boston: Northeastern University Press, 1997), 75; Sophia May to her sister, April 17, 1812, Sophia May Letters, AAS.

31. Solomon Aiken, *An Oration, Delivered before the Republican Citizens of Newburyport, and Its Vicinity, July 4, 1810* (Newburyport, Mass.: N. H. Wright, 1810), 13; Ebenezer French, *An Oration, Pronounced July 4th, 1805, Before the Young Democratic Republicans of the Town of Boston in Commemoration of the Anniversary of American Independence,* 2nd ed. (Boston: J. Ball, 1805), 22; Anthony Haswell, "The Voice of Liberty," in *Songs, Written for the Celebration of the 16th of August, 1810* (Bennington, Vt.: Anthony Haswell, 1810), 11; Philip Mathews, *An Oration, Delivered on the 5th of July, 1813, in the Episcopal Church of Saint Helen* (Charleston, S.C., 1813), 27–28; Elias Glover, *An Oration, Delivered at the Court-House in Cincinnati, on the Fourth of July 1806* (Cincinnati, 1806), 23–24.

32. *New-York Weekly Museum,* October 15, 1814, 191.

33. *Niles' Weekly Register* (Baltimore), July 2, 1814, 320, and November 19, 1814, 168; *Supplement to Volume the Eighth of Niles' Weekly Register* (Baltimore), 1814, 188; *The Enquirer* (Richmond), October 13, 1812; Stocking Society Proceedings, Letter of November 1, 1814, and Subscription List (Broadside), Papers of the Stocking Society, Luther Bradish Papers, New York Historical Society, New York City. For Esther DeBerdt Reed's efforts during the Revolution, see Norton, *Liberty's Daughters,* 178–88.

34. *Niles' Weekly Register* (Baltimore), August 22, 1812; reprinted in *Raleigh (N.C.) Register,* October 12, 1812.

35. M. Waldo to Debby A. Fisher, December 12, 1813, in "Familiar Letters written between 1813 and 1831 from Friends in Salem to a Salem School Girl removed to Ohio," *Historical Collections of the Essex Institute* 36 (April 1900): 119; Memoirs of Eliza Williams (Chotard) Gould, Mss 5:1G7317:1, Virginia Historical Society, Richmond; Diary of Hannah Apthorp Bulfinch, June 1813, in *Life and Letters of Charles Bulfinch* (Boston: Houghton, Mifflin & Co., 1896), 189.

36. Harriet Livermore, *A Narration of Religious Experience* (Concord, N.H.: Jacob B. Moore, 1826), 69.

37. Sally Ripley Diary, April 8, 1813, September 11, 1814, AAS.

38. Autobiography of Mrs. William C. Rives, William Cabell Rives Papers, Container 103, LC; Sally Ripley Diary, February 19, 1815, AAS.

39. Freeman, *Affairs of Honor,* 123–26, 181–87. For related discussions about the use of feminine imagery in political discourse, see Sharon Block, "Rape without Women: Print Culture and the Politicization of Rape," *Journal of American History* 89 (December 2002); Ronald J. Zboray and Mary Saracino Zboray, "Gender Slurs in Boston's Partisan Press during the 1840s," *Journal of American Studies* 34 (2000): 413–46.

40. David Hackett Fischer, *Liberty and Freedom* (Oxford: Oxford University Press, 2005), 233–42; Betsey Erkkila, "Revolutionary Women," *Tulsa Studies in*

Women's Literature 6 (fall 1987): 189–223; Carroll Smith-Rosenberg, "Discovering the Subject of the 'Great Constitutional Discussion,' 1786–1789," *Journal of American History* 79 (December 1992): 841–73; James Jasinski, "The Feminization of Liberty, Domesticated Virtue, and the Reconstitution of Power and Authority in Early American Political Discourse," *Quarterly Journal of Speech* 79 (1993): 146–64.

41. Peter Brown, *The Body and Society: Men, Women, and Sexual Renunciation in Early Christianity* (New York: Columbia University Press, 1988), 153.

42. Joan Landes, *Women and the Public Sphere in the Age of the French Revolution* (Ithaca, N.Y.: Cornell University Press, 1988), 93–129; Olwen H. Hufton, *Women and the Limits of Citizenship in the French Revolution* (Toronto: University of Toronto Press, 1989); Dena Goodman, *The Republic of Letters: A Cultural History of the French Enlightenment* (Ithaca, N.Y.: Cornell University Press, 1994).

43. *American Universal Magazine* 1 (January 9, 1798): 58; *Massachusetts Magazine, or Monthly Museum* (Boston), October 1793, 579–80. For further examples, see Patricia Leigh Riley Dunlap, "Constructing the Republican Woman: American Periodical Response to the Women of the French Revolution, 1789–1844" (D.A. diss., George Mason University, 1999), 62–129.

44. Branson, *Fiery Frenchified Dames*, 88–99, quote on 91.

45. Mary Wollstonecraft, *An Historical and Moral View of the Origin and Progress of the French Revolution; and the Effect it has Produced in Europe* (London: J. Johnson, 1794); *Columbian Centinel; Massachusetts Federalist* (Boston), January 14, 1801; *Mercury and New England Palladium*, February 17, 1801. In addition to being published in the *Columbian Centinel*, "The Enlightened Eighteenth Century" was also published in the *Mercury and New England Palladium* (Boston), the *Connecticut Courant* (Hartford), and the *Gazette of the United States* (Philadelphia). See also Burton R. Pollin, "A Federalist Farrago," *Satire Newsletter* 4 (fall 1966): 29–34.

46. *Time Piece*, October 20, 1797; *Port Folio*, December 24, 1803; *New-York Weekly Museum*, August 6, 1808.

47. *The Embargo* (1808), Broadside, AAS.

48. *The Sacred Refuge for Federalists* (1808), Broadside, AAS.

49. *A Song Composed in the Year Seventy Five, Transferred to 1812* (Boston), Broadside, AAS.

50. *General Advertiser and Political, Commercial and Literary Journal* (Philadelphia), January 20, 1791; reprinted *in New-York Packet*, January 29, 1791.

51. *General Advertiser*, January 24, 1791.

52. *Ladies Literary Museum or Weekly Repository* (Philadelphia), June 24, 1818.

53. Dana Nelson, *National Manhood: Capitalist Citizenship and the Imagined Fraternity of White Men* (Durham, N.C.: Duke University Press, 1998), 37.

54. James D. Hopkins, *An Oration pronounced before the Inhabitants of Portland, July 4th, 1805, in Commemoration of American Independence* (Portland, Maine, 1805), 22; *Monthly Register, Magazine, and Review of the U.S.*, March 1807, 263.

55. [Richard Alsop], *The Echo, with Other Poems* (New York: Pasquin Petronium, 1807), 76.

56. Henry Bliss, *The Genius of Federalism, A Poem in Three Cantos* (Pittsfield, Mass.: Pinneas Allen, 1813), 5, 16, 17.

57. Joanna De Groot, "Coexisting and Conflicting Identities: Women and Nationalisms in Twentieth-Century Iran," in *Nation, Empire, Colony: Historicizing Gender and Race*, ed. Ruth Roach Pierson and Nupur Chaudhuri (Bloomington: Indiana University Press, 1998), 144.

Chapter 4

1. Catharine Maria Sedgwick, *The Power of Her Sympathy: The Autobiography and Journal of Catharine Maria Sedgwick*, ed. Mary Kelley (Boston: Northeastern University Press, 1993), 64.
2. Catharine Maria Sedgwick, "A Reminiscence of Federalism," in *Tales and Sketches* (Philadelphia: Carey, Lea, & Blanchard, 1835), 24.
3. Ibid., 23–25.
4. *Mrs. A. S. Colvin's Weekly Messenger* (Washington City, D.C.), February 10, 1827, 174.
5. *American Moral and Sentimental Magazine* (New York), September 25, 1797, 217; Joseph Bartlett, *Aphorisms on Man, Manners, Principles, & Things* (Portsmouth, N.H.: Oracle Office, 1810), 136; David Hackett Fischer, *The Revolution of American Conservatism: The Federalist Party in the Era of Jeffersonian Democracy* (New York: Harper and Row, 1965), 182–87; Samuel Eliot Morison, *Harrison Gray Otis, 1765–1848: The Urbane Federalist* (Boston: Houghton Mifflin Company, 1969), 275; Minor Myers, Jr., *Liberty without Anarchy: A History of the Society of the Cincinnati* (Charlottesville: University Press of Virginia, 1983), 185–95. For the ties of affection binding the nation, see Melvin Yazawa, *From Colonies to Commonwealth: Familial Ideology and the Beginnings of the American Republic* (Baltimore: Johns Hopkins University Press, 1985), 141–98.
6. Deborah Norris Logan, *Memoir of Dr. George Logan of Stenton*, ed. Francis A. Logan (Philadelphia: Historical Society of Pennsylvania, 1899), 54; Thomas Jefferson to Edward Rutledge, June 24, 1797, in *Papers of Thomas Jefferson*, ed. Julian P. Boyd et al. (Princeton, N.J.: Princeton University Press, 1950–); William W. Story, ed., *Life and Letters of Joseph Story* (Cambridge: Charles C. Little and James Brown, 1851), 1:86.
7. *Monthly Magazine, and American Review*, December 1800, 418, reprinted in *Lady's Monitor*, May 29, 1802; *Mrs. A. S. Colvin's Weekly Messenger*, February 10, 1827, 174; Solomon Aiken, *The Rise and Progress of Political Dissension in the United States: A Sermon, Preached in Dracutt, May 11, 1811* (Haverhill, Mass.: William B. Allen, 1811), 14.
8. "Conducting an Election in Virginia: The Contested Election of Francis Preston, 1793," in *The Early Republic, 1789–1828*, ed. Noble E. Cunningham, Jr. (New York: Harper Torchbooks, 1968), 215.
9. Morison, *Harrison Gray Otis*, 110–11; John R. Howe, Jr., "Republican Thought and the Political Violence of the 1790s," *American Quarterly* 29 (autumn 1967): 147–65.
10. Logan, *Memoir of Dr. George Logan*, 54; Catherine Few to Mrs. Albert Gallatin, [1802?], Albert Gallatin Papers, #167, (microfilm reel 4), New York Historical Society, New York City; Morison, *Harrison Gray Otis*, 278; Fischer, *Revolution of American Conservatism*, 185; Joanne B. Freeman, *Affairs of Honor: National Politics in the New Republic* (New Haven, Conn.: Yale University Press, 2001), 159–98.
11. Bartlett, *Aphorisms on Man, Manners, Principles, & Things*, 136; *Balance, and Columbian Repository* (Hudson, N.Y.), April 24, 1804, 130–31; *Alexandria (Va.) Daily Advertiser*, March 29, 1808.
12. Rosalie Stier Calvert to Charles J. Stier, October 30, 1809, in *Mistress of Riverdale: The Plantation Letters of Rosalie Stier Calvert, 1795–1821*, ed. Margaret Law Callcott (Baltimore: Johns Hopkins University Press, 1991), 197; William Charles White, *Avowals of a Republican* (Worcester, Mass.: Isaac Sturtevant, 1813), 16; [By a Citizen of Vermont], *The Crisis: or The Origin and Consequences of our*

Political Dissensions (Albany, N.Y.: E. & E. Hosford, 1815), 7; *Connecticut Courant* (Hartford), May 18, 1808; James M. Banner, Jr., *To the Hartford Convention: The Federalists and the Origins of Party Politics in Massachusetts, 1789–1815* (New York: Alfred A. Knopf, 1970).

13. Richard Hofstadter, *The Idea of a Party System: The Rise of Legitimate Opposition in the United States, 1780–1840* (Berkeley, Calif.: University of California Press, 1969), 74–121; John Taylor, *A Definition of Parties; or the Political Effects of the Paper System Considered* (Philadelphia: Francis Bailey, 1794), 2.

14. *National Magazine; or, a Political, Historical, Biographical and Literary Repository* (Richmond, Va.) 1 (1799): 344–45; White, *Avowals of a Republican*, 16, 32; [A Lay Preacher], *A Political Catechism, Intended for the Use of Children of a Larger Growth, and Respectfully Dedicated to the Republicans of the Counties of Morris, Essex and Sussex, in the State of New-Jersey* (Morris-Town, N.J.: Henry P. Russell, 1812); Elhanan Winchester, *A Plain Political Catechism intended for the Use of Schools, in the United States of America* (Greenfield, Mass.: B. Dickman, 1796; Philadelphia, 1796; Norfolk, Va.: R. Folwell, 1806); Hezekiah Packard, *A Political Catechism, Designed to Lead Children into the Knowledge of Society and to train them to the Duties of Citizens* (Burlington, Vt.: S. Mills, 1811); Sedgwick, "Reminiscence of Federalism," 23; Jefferson quoted in Hofstadter, *Idea of a Party System*, 125; *Dialogue Between One of the Old School Party and a Federalist* (Philadelphia, 1817), iv.

15. Holloway W. Hunt, *A Discourse on the Necessity of Unity in America* (N.J., 1798); Aiken, *Rise and Progress of Political Dissension*, 19–20; *Dialogue Between One of the Old School Party and a Federalist*, v.

16. Hunt, *Discourse on the Necessity of Unity*; [Aristides], *A Political Essay Addressed to the People of Maryland, by a Farmer of Cecil County* (Baltimore, 1808), 7.

17. Thomas Jefferson, *Inaugural Address*; Hofstadter, *Idea of a Party System*, 152–55; Joseph Ellis, *American Sphinx: The Character of Thomas Jefferson* (New York: Vintage Books, 1996), 214–21.

18. *Harrisburg (Pa.) Republican*, July 9, 1819; *Connecticut Courant* (Hartford), July 18, 1819; *Columbian Centinel* (Boston), July 12, 1820; Philip J. Lampi and Andrew Robertson, "The Election of 1800 Revisited," paper presented at the American Historical Association Annual Meeting, Chicago, Ill., January 9, 2000; Major Wilson, "Republicanism and the Idea of Party in the Jacksonian Period," *Journal of the Early Republic* 8 (winter 1988): 419–40; Hofstadter, *Idea of a Party System*, 212–71; Shaw Livermore, *The Twilight of Federalism: The Disintegration of the Federalist Party, 1815–1830* (Princeton, N.J.: Princeton University Press, 1962), 265; C. Edward Skeen, *1816: America Rising* (Lexington: University of Kentucky Press, 2003), 211–36; Sean Wilentz, *The Rise of American Democracy: Jefferson to Lincoln* (New York: W. W. Norton & Co., 2005), 181–217.

19. Philip Hamburger, "Liberality," *Texas Law Review* 78 (May 2000): 1216–85, quote on 1237.

20. [John Murdock], *Politicians; or, A State of Things: A Dramatic Piece* (Philadelphia: printed for the author, 1798), 7; [Mason Locke Weems], *The Philanthropist; or, A Good Twenty-Five Cents Worth of Political Love Powder, for the Honest Adamites and Jeffersonians* and *The Philanthropist; or A Good Twelve Cents Worth of Political Love Powder, For the Fair Daughters and Patriotic Sons of Virginia* (Dumfries, Va., 1799), 27; [Donald Fraser], *Party-Spirit Exposed, or Remarks on the Times: to which is added Some Important Hints to the Ladies* (New York, 1799), 10; William Gaston, "Intemperance of Party" (1815), William Gaston Papers, Southern Historical Collection, #272, Folder 21, University of North Carolina, Chapel Hill; *The Olive Branch, or Faults on Both Sides, Federal and Democratic* (Philadelphia: M. Carey, 1814).

21. Samuel Putnam Waldo, *The tour of James Monroe, president of the United States, in the year 1817* (Hartford, Conn.: F. D. Bolles & Col., 1818), 269.

22. Ibid., 270. Interestingly, Waldo used quotation marks but did not explicitly mention the Virginia Statute for Religious Liberty, suggesting that the source was widely known and would be immediately identifiable. Jefferson's actual text reads: "that Truth is great and will prevail if left to herself . . . errors ceasing to be dangerous when it is permitted freely to contradict them."

23. [By a Citizen of Vermont], *Crisis*, 7; *Balance, and Columbian Repository*, April 24, 1804, 268; *Mrs. A. S. Colvin's Weekly Messenger*, February 10, 1827, 174.

24. *Lady's Weekly Miscellany* (New York), December 13, 1806, 53; *Lady's Magazine and Musical Repository* 3 (New York), January 1802, 43.

25. *Lady's Weekly Miscellany*, April 1, 1809, 359; *Gospel Palladium* (Boston), July 16, 1824.

26. For negative treatments of women's influence, see Ann Douglas, *The Feminization of American Culture* (New York: Noonday Press, 1977), 9, 69; Jeanne Boydston, *Home & Work: Housework, Wages, and the Ideology of Labor in the Early Republic* (New York: Oxford University Press, 1990), 149.

27. Robert A. Dahl, *Modern Political Analysis* (Englewood Cliffs, N.J.: Prentice Hall, 1991), 38–39.

28. Bernard Bailyn, *The Origins of American Politics* (New York: Vintage Books, 1967), 28–29, 78–80; Gordon S. Wood, *The Radicalism of the American Revolution* (New York: Vintage Books, 1991), 94–124.

29. James Madison to Thomas Jefferson, May 13, 1798, in *Papers of James Madison*, ed. David B. Mattern et al. (Charlottesville: University Press of Virginia, 1991), 17:130; Lance Banning, *Jeffersonian Persuasion: Evolution of a Party Ideology* (Ithaca, N.Y.: Cornell University Press, 1978), 42–69, 150–60; John M. Murrin, "Escaping Perfidious Albion: Federalism, Fear of Aristocracy, and the Democratization of Corruption in Postrevolutionary America," in *Virtue, Corruption, and Self-Interest: Political Values in the Eighteenth Century*, ed. Richard K. Matthews (Bethlehem, Pa.: Lehigh University Press, 1994), 103–47.

30. Speech, March 5, 1806, in *John Randolph of Roanoke: A Study in American Politics, with Selected Speeches and Letters*, ed. Russell Kirk (Indianapolis: Liberty Press, 1978), 323–55; Norman K. Risjord, *Jefferson's America, 1760–1815* (Madison, Wis.: Madison House Publishers, 1991), 258–61.

31. Thomas Jefferson to George Washington, December 1788, in *Papers of George Washington*, ed. W. W. Abbot Presidential Series (Charlottesville: University Press of Virginia, 1987), 1:155; Philip Hicks, "The Roman Matron in Britain: Female Political Influence and Republican Response, ca. 1750–1800," *Journal of Modern History* 77 (March 2005): 35–69; Tjitske Akkerman, *Women's Vices, Public Benefits: Women and Commerce in the French Enlightenment* (Amsterdam: Het Spinhuis, 1992), 45–53; Anna Clark, *Scandal: The Sexual Politics of the British Constitution* (Princeton, N.J.: Princeton University Press, 2004), 15–18.

32. *Euterpeiad: or; Musical Intelligence & Ladies' Gazette* (Boston), April 14, 1821, 13; *New-York Magazine, or Literary Repository* (June 1795): 304; *Rural Repository, or Bower of Literature* 5 (Hudson, N.Y.), October 11, 1828, 78; Emma Willard, *An Address to the Public Particularly to Members of the Legislature of New-York, Proposing a Plan for Improving Female Education* (Albany, N.Y.: I. W. Clark, 1819), 29; Rosemarie Zagarri, "Morals, Manners, and the Republican Mother," *American Quarterly* 44 (June 1992): 192–215.

33. [Fraser], *Party-Spirit Exposed*, 9, 16, 25.

34. *Juvenile Port-Folio*, June 3, 1815, 86; *Ladies' Magazine*, June 1831, 266,

268–69; *Literary Magazine and American Register* (Philadelphia), June 1806, 407; *Western Sun* (Vincennes, Indiana), March 18, 1809.

35. *Monthly Magazine, and American Review* (December 1800): 418, reprinted in *Lady's Monitor,* May 29, 1802; *Columbian Phenix or, Boston Review* (July 1800): 425.

36. *Ladies' Visiter* (Marietta, Pa.), May 27, 1819, 5; *Ladies' Magazine* (June 1831): 266.

37. Daniel Bryan, *Oration on Female Education, Delivered before the Visitors and Students of the Female Academy in Harrisonburg, August 4th, 1815* (Harrisonburg, Pa., 1816), 10; *American Moral and Sentimental Magazine* (New York), September 25, 1797, 217.

38. Asa Packard, *An Oration, on the Means of Perpetuating Independence, delivered at East-Sudbury, July 4th, 1815* (Boston, 1815), 14–15; *Western Sun* (Vicennes, Ind.), March 18, 1809.

39. Sally Hastings, *Poems on Different Subjects* (Lancaster, Pa.: William Dickson, 1808), 120–21; Saint Louis poem quoted in David Waldstreicher, *In the Midst of Perpetual Fetes: The Making of American Nationalism, 1776–1820* (Chapel Hill: University of North Carolina Press, 1997), 241. For a good discussion of the role of politics in the antebellum domestic realm, see Nina Baym, "At Home with History: History Books and Women's Sphere before the Civil War," *Proceedings of the American Antiquarian Society* 101 (1992): 275–95.

40. *Ladies' Magazine, and Literary Gazette* 4 (December 1831): 530; Catherine Allgor, *A Perfect Union: Dolley Madison and the Creation of the American Nation* (New York: Henry Holt and Company, 2006).

41. Catherine Allgor, *Parlor Politics In Which the Ladies of Washington Help Build a City and a Government* (Charlottesville: University Press of Virginia, 2000), 48–101; *Ladies' Literary Museum, or Weekly Repository* (Philadelphia), February 7, 1818, 34.

42. Nancy F. Cott, *The Bonds of Womanhood: 'Woman's Sphere' in New England, 1780–1835* (New Haven, Conn.: Yale University Press, 1977); Linda Kerber, "Separate Spheres, Female Worlds, Woman's Place: The Rhetoric of Women's History," *Journal of American History* 75 (1988): 9–39; Lawrence J. Friedman, *Inventors of the Promised Land* (New York: Alfred A. Knopf, 1975), 111–44.

43. *New York Mirror: A Repository of Polite Literature and the Arts*, September 25, 1830, 95.

44. Wilentz, *Rise of American Democracy*, 202–17; Murray N. Rothbard, *The Panic of 1819: Reactions and Policies* (New York: Columbia University Press, 1962), 1–14.

45. *Harrisburg (Pa.) Republican*, October 8, 1819; Rothbard, *Panic of 1819*, 21–23, 160–61.

46. Washington Irving, "The Wife," *Poulson's American Daily Advertiser* (Philadelphia), July 17, 1819.

47. *Harrisburg Republican,* July 9, 1819; *Richmond Enquirer,* July 14, 1818; *Ladies' Literary Cabinet* (New York), June 12, 1819; *Ladies' Port Folio* (Boston), June 3, 1820.

48. *Connecticut Courant* (Hartford), July 6, 1819, reprinted in *Poulson's American Daily Advertiser,* July 13, 1819; *National Advocate* (New York), October 2, 1818, reprinted in *Euterpeiad* (Boston), March 31, 1821, 6; *Ladies' Literary Cabinet,* June 12, 1819.

49. *Poulson's American Daily Advertiser,* June 11, 1819, reprinted in *New-York Daily Advertiser,* June 15, 1819 and *Ladies' Visiter* (Marietta, Pa.), June 21, 1819; *Pittsburgh (Pa.) Gazette,* July 9, 1819.

50. *Poulson's American Daily Advertiser,* June 14, 1819; *Philadelphia Aurora,* June 18, 1819.

51. *Ladies' Visiter,* September 28, 1819; *Democratic Press* (Philadelphia), June 30, 1819.

52. Boydston, *Home & Work,* 30–55; Lawrence A. Peskin, *Manufacturing Revolution: The Intellectual Origins of Early American Industry* (Baltimore: Johns Hopkins University Press, 2003), 179–81; Rothbard, *Panic of 1819,* 2.

53. Anne M. Boylan, *The Origins of Women's Activism: New York and Boston, 1797–1840* (Chapel Hill: University of North Carolina Press, 2002), 15–53, 219–26; Lori D. Ginzberg, *Women and the Work of Benevolence: Morality, Politics, and Class in the Nineteenth-Century United States* (New Haven, Conn.: Yale University Press, 1990), 11–66; Elizabeth R. Varon, *We Mean to Be Counted: White Women and Politics in Antebellum Virginia* (Chapel Hill: University of North Carolina Press, 1998), 11, 183n3; Betty Wood, *Gender, Race, and Rank in a Revolutionary Age: The Georgia Lowcountry, 1750–1820* (Athens: University of Georgia Press, 2000), 57–82.

54. *National Advocate* (New York), October 2, 1818, reprinted in *Euterpeiad,* March 31, 1821; *Democratic Press,* June 30, 1819.

55. Boylan, *Origins of Women's Activism,* 135–209; *Mrs. A. S. Colvin's Magazine,* September 8, 1827, 33.

56. Boylan, *Origins of Women's Activism,* 15–52, 135–69; Anne M. Boylan, "Women and Politics in the Era before Seneca Falls," *Journal of the Early Republic* 10 (fall 1990): 363–82; Hannah Kinney's Records of the Newark Female Charitable Society, at http:// www.scc.rutgers.edu/njwomenshistory/Period_2/newark charitable.htm.

57. Ginzberg, *Women and the Work of Benevolence,* 67–132; Bruce Dorsey, *Reforming Men & Women: Gender in the Antebellum City* (Ithaca, N.Y.: Cornell University Press, 2002), 90–194; Julie Roy Jeffrey, *The Great Silent Army of Abolitionism: Ordinary Women in the Antislavery Movement* (Chapel Hill: University of North Carolina Press, 1998), 53–133; Susan Zaeske, *Signatures of Citizenship: Petitioning, Antislavery, and Women's Political Identity* (Chapel Hill: University of North Carolina Press, 2003), 29–72.

58. *Ladies' Literary Museum, or Weekly Repository* (Philadelphia), September 20, 1817, 95.

59. Boston Female Asylum quoted in Boylan, *Origins of Women's Activism,* 169; *Ladies' Magazine* (November 1829): 516; Maria Weston Chapman quoted in Ginzberg, *Women and the Work of Benevolence,* 72.

60. Lydia Maria Child, *The History of the Condition of Women, in Various Ages and Nations* (Boston: J. Allen & Co., 1835), 2:265; Carolyn L. Karcher, *The First Woman in the Republic: A Cultural Biography of Lydia Maria Child* (Durham, N.C.: Duke University Press, 1994).

61. Alisse Theodore Portnoy, " 'Female Petitioners Can Lawfully Be Heard': Negotiating Female Decorum, United States Politics, and Political Agency, 1829–1831," *Journal of the Early Republic* 23 (winter 2003): 573–610, quote on 574; Zaeske, *Signatures of Citizenship,* 24–27, 115–18; Kathryn Kish Sklar, *Catharine Beecher: A Study in American Domesticity* (New York: W. W. Norton and Co., 1973), 98–99.

62. Catharine Beecher, selection from *Treatise on Domestic Economy* (1841, rev. 3rd ed.), in *Root of Bitterness: Documents of the Social History of American Women,* ed. Nancy F. Cott (Boston: Northeastern University Press, 1986), 173.

63. Mary Kelley, *Learning to Stand and Speak: Women, Education, and Public Life in America's Republic* (Chapel Hill: University of North Carolina Press, 2006), 5.

Chapter 5

1. *Ladies' Magazine* (July 1829): 299–307, quotes on 299, 303, 306.

2. Stone quoted in David Hackett Fischer, *The Revolution of American Conservatism: The Federalist Party in the Era of Jeffersonian Democracy* (New York: Harper and Row, 1965), 17; Linda K. Kerber, *Federalists in Dissent: Imagery and Ideology in Jeffersonian America* (Ithaca, N.Y.: Cornell University Press, 1970); Christopher Grasso, *A Speaking Aristocracy: Transforming Public Discourse in Eighteenth-Century Connecticut* (Chapel Hill: University of North Carolina Press, 1999).

3. Philip S. Foner, ed., *The Democratic-Republican Societies, 1790–1800: A Documentary Sourcebook of Constitutions, Declarations, Addresses, Resolutions, and Toasts* (Westport, Conn.: Greenwood Press, 1976), 219; Joyce Appleby, *Capitalism and a New Social Order: The Republican Vision of the 1790s* (New York: New York University Press, 1984); Alan Taylor, "From Fathers to Friends of the People: Political Personae in the Early Republic," in *Federalists Reconsidered*, ed. Doron Ben-Atar and Barbara B. Oberg (Charlottesville: University Press of Virginia, 1998), 225–45.

4. Chilton Williamson, *American Suffrage from Property to Democracy, 1760–1860* (Princeton, N.J.: Princeton University Press, 1960), 117–37; Alexander Keyssar, *The Right to Vote: The Contested History of Democracy in the United States* (New York: Basic Books, 2000), 26–42.

5. *Rights of Suffrage* (Hudson, N.Y.: Asbel Stoddard, 1792), 4; Keyssar, *Right to Vote*, 42–52; Rogers M. Smith, *Civic Ideals: Conflicting Visions of Citizenship in U.S. History* (New Haven, Conn.: Yale University Press, 1997), 165–73.

6. *Richmond Enquirer*, October 20, 1829; *Columbian Phenix and Boston Review* 1 (February 1800): 112.

7. Massachusetts Constitutional Convention, December 11, 1820, New York Constitutional Convention, October 8, 1821, in *Democracy, Liberty, and Property: The State Constitutional Conventions of the 1820s*, ed. Merrill D. Peterson (Indianapolis: Bobbs-Merrill Co., Inc., 1966), 64, 228; [Rhode Island], *Report of the Extension of Suffrage* (Providence, 1829), 5; *Proceedings and Debates of the Virginia State Convention of 1829–30* (Richmond, Va.: Samuel Shepherd & Co., 1830), 67–68.

8. New York delegate quoted in Rowland Berthoff, "Conventional Mentality: Free Blacks, Women, and Business Corporations as Unequal Persons, 1820–1870," *Journal of American History* 3 (December 1989): 753–84, quote on 763; Memorial of the Non-Freeholders of the City of Richmond, October 13, 1829, in *Proceedings and Debates of the Virginia State Convention by 1829–30*, 30; Doddridge quote in *Democracy, Liberty, and Property*, 401.

9. *Euterpeiad: Or, Musical Intelligencer & Ladies' Gazette*, September 29, 1821, 112.

10. *Richmond Enquirer*, October 20, 1829. For a discussion of the relationship between the campaign for married women's property rights and woman suffrage, see Norma Basch, "Equity vs. Equality: Emerging Concepts of Women's Political Status in the Age of Jackson," *Journal of the Early Republic* 3 (fall 1983): 297–317.

11. Petition is reprinted in Lori D. Ginzberg, *Untidy Origins: A Story of Woman's Rights in Antebellum New York* (Chapel Hill: University of North Carolina Press, 2005), 2–3.

12. *Columbian Centinel* (Boston), June 10, 1820; Keyssar, *Right to Vote*, 26–52, 55–56, tables A.1, A.2; Smith, *Civic Ideals*, 143, 170–73; Laura J. Scalia, "Who Deserves Political Influence? How Liberal Ideals Helped Justify Mid-Nineteenth

Century Exclusionary Policies," *American Journal of Political Science* 42 (April 1998): 349–76. For a contemporaneous listing of suffrage qualifications in the states, see William Smith, *A Comparative View of the Constitutions of the Several States with Each Other, and with that of the United States* (Philadelphia, 1796; Washington, D.C., 1832).

13. Carole Pateman, *The Disorder of Women: Democracy, Feminism and Political Theory* (Stanford, Calif.: Stanford University Press, 1989), 39, 43; Nancy J. Hirschmann, *Rethinking Obligation: A Feminist Method for Political Theory* (Ithaca, N.Y.: Cornell University Press, 1992), 12; Joan B. Landes, *Women and the Public Sphere in the Age of the French Revolution* (Ithaca, N.Y.: Cornell University Press, 1988), 202. Pateman develops this theory more fully in *The Sexual Contract* (Stanford, Calif.: Stanford University Press, 1988).

14. Hilda L. Smith, *All Men and Both Sexes: Gender, Politics, and the False Universal in England* (University Park: Pennsylvania State University Press, 2002).

15. Richard R. Beeman, *The Varieties of Political Experience in Eighteenth-Century America* (Philadelphia: University of Pennsylvania Press, 2004), 276–92; Simon P. Newman, *Parades and the Politics of the Street: Festive Culture in the Early American Republic* (Philadelphia: University of Pennsylvania Press, 1997), 186–92; Ronald P. Formisano, "Deferential-Participant Politics: The Early Republic's Political Culture, 1789–1840," *American Political Science Review* 68 (1974): 473–87; Fischer, *Revolution of American Conservatism*, 50–109; Seth Cotlar, "Reading the Foreign News, Imagining an American Public Sphere," in *Periodical Literature in Eighteenth-Century America*, ed. Mark L. Kamrath and Sharon M. Harris (Knoxville: University of Tennessee Press, 2004), 307–38; Seth Cotlar, "The Federalists' Transatlantic Culture Offensive of 1798 and the Moderation of American Democratic Discourse," in *Beyond the Founders: New Approaches to the Political History of the Early American Republic*, ed. Jeffrey L. Pasley, Andrew W. Robertson, and David Waldstreicher (Chapel Hill: University of North Carolina Press, 2004), 274–99; Andrew W. Robertson, "Voting Rites and Voting Acts: Electioneering Ritual, 1790–1820," in ibid., 57–78.

16. David Ramsay, *A Dissertation on the Manner of Acquiring the Character and Privileges of a Citizen of the United States* (Charleston, S.C., 1789), 3; Webster quoted in Jean H. Baker, *Affairs of Party: The Political Culture of the Northern Democrats in the Mid-Nineteenth Century* (Ithaca, N.Y.: Cornell University Press, 1983), 267; Jeffrey L. Pasley, "1800 as a Revolution in Political Culture," in *The Revolution of 1800: Democracy, Race and the New Republic*, ed. James Horn, Jan Ellen Lewis, and Peter S. Onuf (Charlottesville: University Press of Virginia, 2002), 121–52; Formisano, "Deferential-Participant Politics," 481–83; Fischer, *Revolution of American Conservatism*, 187–92.

17. Fischer, *Revolution of American Conservatism*, 110–28; Robertson, "Voting Rites and Voting Acts," 57–78; Desley Deacon, "Politicizing Gender," *Genders* 6 (fall 1989): 1–19.

18. Robert E. Shalhope, *A Tale of New England: The Diaries of Hiram Harwood, Vermont Farmer, 1810–1837* (Baltimore: Johns Hopkins University Press, 2003), 89–90, 108, 169.

19. Thomas Jefferson to N. Burwell (1818), in *The Jefferson Cyclopedia*, ed. John P. Foley (New York: Russell & Russell, 1967 [orig. pub. 1900]), 1:274.

20. Thomas Jefferson to Anne Willing Bingham, May 11, 1788, in *Papers of Thomas Jefferson*, ed. Julian P. Boyd et al. (Princeton: Princeton University Press, 1950–), 13:151; Jefferson's quote on postmistresses is in a letter to Albert Gallatin, January 13, 1807, in ibid. On Mary Catherine Goddard, see Richard R. John

and Christopher J. Young, "Rites of Passage: Postal Petitioning as a Tool of Governance in the Age of Federalism," in *The House and Senate in the 1790s: Petitioning, Lobbying, and Institutional Development* (Athens: Ohio University Press, 2002), 109–15. Jefferson was abroad at the time of Goddard's dismissal. Nonetheless, it is surprising, given the publicity surrounding the case, that Jefferson was unaware of the precedent.

21. Keating Lewis Simon, *An Oration delivered in the Independent Circular Church, before the Inhabitants of Charleston, South-Carolina, on Friday, The Fourth of July, 1806* (Charleston, S.C., 1806), 6; Richard Dinsmore, *A Long Talk, Delivered before the Tammany Society, of Alexandria, District of Columbia, at their First Anniversary Meeting, May 12, 1804* (Alexandria, Va., 1804), 12; Rev. Solomon Aiken, *An Oration, Delivered before the Republican Citizens of Newburyport, and Its Vicinity, July 4, 1801* (Newburyport, Mass.: N. H. Wright, 1810), 13–14; Rosemarie Zagarri, "Gender and the First Party System," in *Federalists Reconsidered*, 118–34.

22. *New-York Weekly Museum*, June 1, 1808; *The Patriotic Class Book: Containing Letters, Orations and Essays, on Various Subjects, Religious, Moral and Entertaining* (Hagers-Town, Md.: W. D. Bell, 1815), 195; Anthony Haswell, *An Oration, Delivered at Bennington, Vermont, August 16, 1799* (Bennington, Vt.: Anthony Haswell, 1799), 33. Paula Baker, "The Domestication of Politics: Women and American Political Society, 1780–1920," *American Historical Review* 89 (1984): 620–47; Jean Matthews, "Race, Sex, and the Dimensions of Liberty in Antebellum America," *Journal of the Early Republic* 6 (fall 1986): 275–91. For other discussions of norms of masculinity and femininity among early partisans, see Nancy Isenberg, "The 'Little Emperor': Aaron Burr, Dandyism, and the Sexual Politics of Treason," and Albrecht Koschnik, "Young Federalists, Masculinity, and Partisanship during the War of 1812," in *Beyond the Founders*, 129–79.

23. William C. Dowling, *Literary Federalism in the Age of Jefferson: Joseph Dennie and* The Port Folio, *1801–1812* (Columbia: University of South Carolina Press, 1999), 80–81.

24. Pauline Maier, "The Transforming Impact of Independence, Reaffirmed: 1776 and the Definition of American Social Structure," in *The Transformation of Early American History: Society, Authority, and Ideology*, ed. James A. Henretta, Michael Kammen, and Stanley N. Katz (New York: Knopf, 1991), 215; Samuel Johnson quoted by Judith Sargent Murray in *The Gleaner*, ed. Nina Baym (Schenectady, N.Y.: Union College Press, 1992 [orig. pub. 1798]), 216.

25. In 1816 Krimmel produced another painting of an election day. Although the two images are very similar, there are minor, but important, differences. The 1816 image includes more women—an additional two women and a female child appear on the right side of the canvas. Krimmel also did another, different election image in 1821. See Milo M. Naeve, *John Lewis Krimmel: An Artist in Federal America* (Newark: University of Delaware Press, 1987), 75–78, 100–101, 118–19.

26. Jonathan Weinberg, "The Artist and the Politician—Experience in Missouri Politics informed George Caleb Bingham's election paintings," *Art in America* 88 (October 2000): 138–46; Gail E. Husch, "George Caleb Bingham's *The County Election*: Whig Tribute to the Will of the People," in *Critical Issues in American Art: A Book of Readings*, ed. Mary Ann Calo (New York: Westview Press, 1998), 77–92.

27. Elizabeth R. Varon, *We Mean to Be Counted: White Women and Politics in Antebellum Virginia* (Chapel Hill: University of North Carolina Press, 1998), 71–102.

28. [Theophilus Parsons], *The Essex Result* (Newburyport, Mass., 1778), in

American Political Writing during the Founding Era, 1760–1805, ed. Charles S. Hyneman and Donald S. Lutz (Indianapolis: Liberty Press, 1983), 1:497; John Adams to James Sullivan, May 26, 1776, in *Works of John Adams, Second President of the United States*, ed. Charles Francis Adams (Boston: Little, Brown, & Co., 1854), 9:375–78.

29. William Alexander, *History of Women, From the Earliest Antiquity, to the Present Time; Giving an Account of Almost Every Interesting Particular Concerning that Sex, Among All Nations, Ancient and Modern* (Philadelphia: J. Turner & J. H. Dobelbower, 1795); Mary Beth Norton, *Liberty's Daughters: The Revolutionary Experience of American Women, 1750–1800* (Glenview, Ill.: Little, Brown, & Co., 1980); Linda K. Kerber, *Women of the Republic: Intellect and Ideology in Revolutionary America* (Chapel Hill: University of North Carolina Press, 1980); Rosemarie Zagarri, *A Woman's Dilemma: Mercy Otis Warren and the American Revolution* (Wheeling, Ill.: Harlan Davidson, Inc., 1995), 73–77.

30. Paul Brown, *A Lecture Concerning Marriage: Delivered February 10 1828 at Cincinnati—Re-delivered March 29th 1829, at Kendall, with emendations* (Rochester, N.Y.: R. Scranton, 1830), 21; *Literary Cabinet & Western Olive Branch* (St. Clairsville, Ohio), March 16, 1833, 20.

31. Lieselotte Steinbrügge, *The Moral Sex: Woman's Nature in the French Enlightenment*, trans. Pamela F. Selwyn (New York: Oxford University Press, 1995), 10–18; Siep Stuurman, "The Deconstruction of Gender: Seventeenth-Century Feminism and Modern Equality," in *Women, Gender and Enlightenment*, ed. Sarah Knott and Barbara Taylor (Hampshire: Palgrave-Macmillan, 2005), 371–88; Melissa A. Butler, "Early Liberal Roots of Feminism: John Locke and the Attack on Patriarchy," *American Political Science Review* 72 (March 1978): 135–50.

32. Charles Brockden Brown, *Alcuin: A Dialogue*, ed. Lee R. Edwards (New York: Grossman Publishers, 1971 [orig. pub., 1798, 1815]), 38.

33. Landes, *Women and the Public Sphere*, 201–6; Arianne Chernock, "Extending the 'Right of Election': Men's Arguments for Women's Political Representation in Late Enlightenment Britain," in *Women, Gender and Enlightenment*, 587–609.

34. Thomas Laqueur, *Making Sex: Body and Gender from the Greeks to Freud* (Cambridge, Mass.: Harvard University Press, 1990), 149–207.

35. Ibid., 149; G. J. Barker-Benfield, *The Culture of Sensibility: Sex and Society in Eighteenth-Century Britain* (Chicago: University of Chicago Press, 1992), 351–95.

36. Rush quoted in Sarah Knott, "Sensibility and Selfhood in Revolutionary America," in *Women, Gender and Enlightenment*, 649–66, quote on 659.

37. *New-York Weekly Magazine; or, Miscellaneous Repository*, April 13, 1799, 19; "Parallel of the Sexes," *Boston Spectator; Devoted to Politicks and Belles Lettres* (Boston), August 6, 1814, 127, reprinted in *New-York Weekly Museum, or Polite Repository of Amusement and Instruction*, June 15, 1816, 107; *Literary and Musical Magazine* (Philadelphia), May 3, 1819, 13. See also Beverly J. Reed, "Exhibiting the Fair Sex: The *Massachusetts Magazine* and the Bodily Order of the American Woman," in *Periodical Literature in Eighteenth-Century America*, ed. Mark L. Kamrath and Sharon M. Harris (Knoxville: University of Tennessee Press, 2005), 227–54.

38. Nancy Leys Stepan, "Race, Gender, Science, and Citizenship," *Gender & History* 10 (April 1998): 35.

39. *Virginia Gazette and Alexandria Advertiser*, April 22, 1790.

40. Hannah Mather Crocker, *Observations on the Real Rights of Women, with their Appropriate Duties, agreeable to Scripture, Reason and Common Sense* (Boston: pri-

vately printed, 1818), 15–16; *The Female Friend; or the Duties of Christian Virgins* (Baltimore: Henry S. Keatinge, 1809), 196; Thomas Fessenden, *The Ladies' Monitor, A Poem* (Bellows Falls, Vt., 1818), 58–59.

41. *Independent Chronicle and the Universal Advertiser* (Boston), March 10, 1800; *Euterpeiad: Or, Musical Intelligencer & Ladies' Gazette* (Boston), July 21, 1821, 71; *Mercury and New-England Palladium* (Boston), March 2, 1802; *Centinel of Freedom* (Newark, N.J.), December 11, 1798. The *Independent Chronicle* quote was from an article entitled "Woman: An Apologue" and was reprinted numerous times, including in *Columbian Phenix and Boston Review* (July 1800): 438–39; *Philadelphia Repository, and Weekly Register,* January 22, 1803, 26; *Lady's Weekly Miscellany* (New York), August 26, 1809; and *Ladies' Literary Cabinet* (New York), December 18, 1819. These reprintings confirm how often publications recycled previously printed materials.

42. *North American Review* 59 (April 1828): 318; Mrs. Virginia Cary, *Letters on Female Character* (Richmond, Va., 1828), 44.

43. Winthrop Jordan, *White over Black* (New York: W. W. Norton, 1968), 429–81; Gary B. Nash, *Forging Freedom: The Formation of the Philadelphia Black Community, 1720–1840* (Cambridge, Mass.: Harvard University Press, 1988), 181, 223–27; Londa Scheibinger, "The Anatomy of Difference: Race and Sex in Eighteenth-Century Science," *Eighteenth-Century Studies* 23 (summer 1990): 387–405; Alexander O. Boulton, "The American Paradox: Jeffersonian Equality and Racial Science," *American Quarterly* 47 (1995): 467–92; Roxann Wheeler, *The Complexion of Race: Categories of Difference in Eighteenth Century British Culture* (Philadelphia: University of Pennsylvania Press, 2000), 251–53, 280–99.

44. New York State Convention of 1846, *Jim Crow New York: A Documentary History of Race and Citizenship,* ed. David N. Gellman and David Quigley (New York: New York University Press, 2003), 255; Len Travers, *Celebrating the Fourth: Independence Day and the Rites of Nationalism in the Early Republic* (Amherst: University of Massachusetts Press, 1997), 141–53; Joanne Pope Melish, *Disowning Slavery: Gradual Emancipation and 'Race' in New England, 1780–1860* (Ithaca, N.Y.: Cornell University Press, 1998), 238–85; Keyssar, *Right to Vote,* 54–60, tables A.4, A.5; Smith, *Civic Ideals,* 170–73, 201–16. Free blacks were disenfranchised in Maryland in 1801, New Jersey in 1807, Connecticut in 1818, Tennessee in 1834, North Carolina in 1835, and Pennsylvania in 1838. By the Civil War, only six states—Maine, Vermont, New Hampshire, Massachusetts, Rhode Island, and New York—allowed free blacks to exercise some form of the franchise. Even then they did not enjoy the same civil rights as whites.

45. *Lady's Magazine and Musical Repository* 3 (New York), January–June 1802, 43. The classic formulation of the American understanding of Locke is found in Louis B. Hartz, *The Liberal Tradition in America: An Interpretation of American Political Thought since the Revolution* (New York: Harcourt, Brace, and World, 1955). More recent interpretations may be found in Jerome Huyler, *Locke in America: The Moral Philosophy of the Founding Era* (Lawrence: University of Kansas Press, 1995); Richard Tuck, *Natural Rights Theories: Their Origin and Development* (Cambridge: Cambridge University Press, 1979); Daniel T. Rodgers, *Contested Truths: Keywords in American Politics Since Independence* (New York: Oxford University Press, 1987); Mary Anne Glendon, *Rights Talk: The Impoverishment of Political Discourse* (New York: Oxford University Press, 1991); T. H. Breen, *The Lockean Moment: The Language of Rights on the Eve of the American Revolution* (Oxford: Oxford University Press, 2001); Knud Haakonssen, "From Natural Law to the Rights of Man: A European Perspective on American Debates," in *A Culture of*

Rights: The Bill of Rights in Philosophy, Politics, and Law—1791 and 1991, ed. M. J. Lacey and K. Haakonssen (Cambridge: Cambridge University Press, 1991); Thomas L. Haskell, "The Curious Persistence of Rights Talk in the 'Age of Interpretation,'" in *The Constitution and American Life,* ed. David Thelen (Ithaca, N.Y.: Cornell University Press, 1988), 324–52.

46. *Port Folio* (Philadelphia), November 20, 1802, 364.

47. Haakonssen, "From Natural Law to the Rights of Man," 29; J. G. A. Pocock, "Cambridge Paradigms and Scotch Philosophers: A Study of the Relations between the Civic Humanist and Civil Jurisprudential Interpretation of Eighteenth-Century Social Thought," in *Wealth and Virtue: The Shaping of Political Economy in the Scottish Enlightenment,* ed. Istvan Hont and Michael Ignatieff (Cambridge: Cambridge University Press, 1983), 235–52; Andrew Hook, "Philadelphia, Edinburgh, and the Scottish Enlightenment," in *Scotland and America in the Age of the Enlightenment,* ed. Richard B. Sher and Jeffry R. Smitten (Princeton, N.J.: Princeton University Press, 1990), 227–41. For a more detailed analysis of these issues, see Rosemarie Zagarri, "The Rights of Man and Woman in Post-Revolutionary America," *William & Mary Quarterly* 3rd ser., 60 (April 1998): 203–30.

48. Edward D. Mansfield, *The Legal Rights, Liabilities, and Duties of Women* (Salem, Mass.: John P. Jewett and Co., 1845), 120.

49. *Weekly Museum* (New York), March 16, 1793.

50. Ibid.

51. *Carlisle (Pa.) Gazette,* July 20, 1804.

52. Jeremiah Perley, *An Anniversary Oration, Delivered before the Federal Republicans of Hallowell and Its Vicinity* (Augusta, Maine: Peter Edes, 1807), 23; *Ladies' Monitor* (New York), August 10, 15, 1801, 19–20; *Charleston [S.C.] Spectator, and Ladies' Literary Port Folio,* August 16, 1806, 70.

53. *Weekly Museum* (New York), March 16, 1793, 10–11; William Loughton Smith, *An Oration, Delivered in St. Philip's Church, before the Inhabitants of Charleston, South-Carolina, on the Fourth of July, 1796, in commemoration of American Independence* (Charleston, S.C.: W. P. Young, 1796), 9; John Cosens Ogden, *The Female Guide: or, Thoughts on the Education of That Sex, Accommodated to the State of Society, Manners, and Government, in the United States* (Concord, N.H.: George Hough, 1793), 26.

54. Thomas Branagan, *The Excellency of the Female Character Vindicated; being an investigation relative to the cause and effects of the Encroachments of Men upon the Rights of Woman and the too frequent degradation and consequent misfortunes of the Fair Sex* (New York: Samuel Wood, 1807), ix, 139–40; Rev. J. Hanning, M.D., *Rights of Women Vindicated in the Following Sermon,* 2nd ed. (New York: T. Kirk, 1807), 2; *Mercury and New-England Palladium* (Boston), March 2, 1802.

55. *Boston Weekly Magazine,* October 30, 1802, 2.

56. Hannah Foster, *The Boarding School* (Boston, 1798), 31; Ebenezer French, *An Oration, Pronounced July 4th, 1805, Before the Young Democratic Republicans of the Town of Boston in Commemoration of the Anniversary of American Independence* (Boston: J. Ball, 1805), 20–21; *Columbian Centinel* (Boston), January 24, 1801.

57. Gardner Child, *An Oration, delivered at Richmond, Vermont, on the 31st Anniversary of American Independence, July 4th, 1807* (Bennington, Vt.: Anthony Haswell, 1807), 44; Samuel Latham Mitchill, *Address to the Fredes, or People of the United States on the 28th Anniversary of their Independence* (New York: G. & R. Waite, 1804), 7.

58. Pauline Schloesser, *The Fair Sex: White Women and Racial Hierarchy in the Early American Republic* (New York: New York University Press, 2002).

59. Smith, *Civic Ideals*, 5.

Epilogue

1. Frances Trollope, *Domestic Manners of the Americans*, ed. Donald Smalley (New York: Alfred A. Knopf, 1949 [orig. pub. 1832]), 86, 69, 118; Alexis de Tocqueville, *Democracy in America*, trans. Henry Reeve (New York, 1889), 2:290–313, 221–24.

2. Mrs. Virginia Cary, *Letters on Female Character* (Richmond, Va.: A. Werks, 1828), 106; *Literary Cabinet & Western Olive Branch* (St. Clairsville, Ohio), March 16, 1833, 20; Mrs. E. F. L. Ellet, *Domestic History of the American Revolution* (New York, 1850), 43. Women's rights activists rekindled the memory of the New Jersey experiment after the Civil War. See, for example, "An Address delivered by Lucy Stone, at a hearing before the New Jersey Legislature, March 6th, 1867," in *Votes for Women: Selections from the National American Woman Suffrage Association Collection, 1848–1921*, online at http://memory.loc.gov/cgi-bin/query/r?ammemem/nawbib; Eileen Hunt Botting and Christine Cavey, "Wolstonecraft's Philosophical Impact on Nineteenth Century Women's Rights Advocates," *American Journal of Political Science* 48 (October 2004): 70–22.

3. Nancy F. Cott, *The Bonds of Womanhood: 'Woman's Sphere' in New England, 1780–1835* (New Haven, Conn.: Yale University Press, 1977), 197–206; Lori D. Ginzberg, *Women and the Work of Benevolence: Morality, Politics, and Class in the Nineteenth-Century United States* (New Haven, Conn.: Yale University Press, 1990), 98–132; Sarah Grimké, "The Pastoral Letter of the General Association of Congressional Ministers of Massachusetts" (1837), in *Public Women, Public Words: A Documentary History of American Feminism*, ed. Dawn Keetley and John Pettegrew (Madison, Wis.: Madison House Press, 1997), 1:99.

4. Elizabeth Cady Stanton, Lucretia Mott, Martha C. Wright, Mary Ann McClintock, and Jane C. Hunt, "Declaration of Sentiments and Resolutions at the First Woman's Rights Convention in Seneca Falls" (1848), in *Public Women, Public Words*, 190–93; Linda K. Kerber, "'Ourselves and Our Daughters Forever': Women and the Constitution, 1787–1876" and "The Seneca Falls Convention," in *One Woman, One Vote: Rediscovering the Woman Suffrage Movement*, ed. Marjorie Spruill Wheeler (Troutdale, Oreg.: NewSage Press, 1995), 21–44.

5. Louis Hartz, *The Liberal Tradition in America* (New York: Harcourt, Brace, and World, 1955), 60. Hartz is enjoying something of a comeback in scholarly circles. See, for example, a forum on Hartz by Philip Abbott, Richard Iton, and Sean Wilentz in *Perspectives on Politics* 3 (March 2005): 93–120, and Alan Wolfe, "Nobody Here but Us Liberals," *New York Times Book Review*, July 3, 2005, 23. For a thoughtful critique of Hartz, see James T. Kloppenberg, "In Retrospect: Louis Hartz, *The Liberal Tradition in America*," *Reviews in American History* 29 (2001): 460–78. On the long-term relationship between slavery and universal rights, see Orlando Patterson, "Freedom, Slavery and the Modern Construction of Rights," in *Historical Change and Human Rights*, ed. Olwen Hufton (New York: Basic Books, 1995), 131–78.

6. Nancy Leys Stepan, "Race, Gender, Science, and Citizenship," *Gender & History* 10 (April 1998): 29–30.

7. The question of whether the United States witnessed a conservative backlash, similar to France's experience after their revolution, dates back at least to

Crane Brinton's *The Anatomy of Revolution* (New York: Vintage Books, 1965 [orig. pub. 1938]). More recent works that portray a retreat from revolutionary radicalism include Larry Tise, *American Counter-Revolution, 1783–1800* (Mechanicsburg, Pa.: Stackpole Books, 1995); Gary B. Nash, *Forging Freedom: The Formation of Philadelphia's Black Community, 1720–1840* (Cambridge, Mass.: Harvard University Press, 1988); James H. Hutson, "Women in the Era of the American Revolution: The Historian as Suffragist," *The Quarterly Journal of the Library of Congress* 32 (October 1975): 290–303; Seth Cotlar, "The Federalists' Transatlantic Cultural Offensive of 1798 and the Moderation of American Democratic Discourse," in *Beyond the Founders: New Approaches to the Political History of the Early American Republic*, ed. Jeffrey L. Pasley, Andrew W. Robertson, and David W. Waldstreicher (Chapel Hill: University of North Carolina Press, 2004), 274–99.

Index

134; and violence, 116–20, 157; women
as mediators in, 6, 116, 124–36, 148,
161, 162; women's influence in, 124–36,
146; women's participation in, 6, 60, 93–
97, 115–47; and women's rights, 180,
182. *See also* Democratic Republicans;
Federalists; liberality; political parties;
politics

Party-Spirit Exposed (Fraser), 129

Pateman, Carole, 155

patriotism, women's: in American Revolution, 23–25, 181; and inclusive politics,
69–73; of Dolley Madison, 133–34; and
nonpartisanship, 143–44; and Panic of
1819, 137, 138; and party conflict, 82–
114, 132, 133, 146; passive, 159–60; and
public speaking, 72, 73; and War of
1812, 98, 100

Peale, Charles Willson, 52

Pennsylvania, 150, 172

periodicals, popular, 80; on essentialism,
169, 184; ladies' magazines, 9, 14, 41,
53–54, 56, 125; and politics, 53–54, 55;
women's history in, 14–17; women writers for, 58–59

petitioning, 38, 65, 80, 145, 154; right of,
38–39; and social reform, 143, 144

Pettigru, Charles, 118

Pierce, Lydia, 89

political parties, 2, 82–114; acceptance of,
161, 163; and foreign policy, 95–97, 127;
and images of women, 105–6, 107–14;
institutionalization of, 6–7, 156, 157–58;
180; legitimacy of, 120–24; marginalization of women in, 155–64; in periodicals, 55; and political socialization,
88–93; as religion, 120–24; rise of,
82–88; and social reform, 143; and suffrage, 34, 36, 149, 150, 154, 160–61, 180;
women's participation in, 5, 84–85, 113.
See also Democratic Republicans; Federalists; liberality; party conflict; politics

Politicians; or, A State of Things (play), 82,
123

politics: celebratory, 68, 69–73, 84–85, 156;
and charitable organizations, 145–46;
definitions of, 2, 7–8; democratization
of, 2, 6, 10, 27–30, 46, 51, 149–51, 154,
160–61, 165, 180; encouragement of
women's participation in, 2, 4, 22–26,
76–77, 113, 137–38; and essentialism,

169–73; inclusive, 4, 6–7, 8, 46, 68–75,
156, 161–62, 164, 172; institutionalized,
6–7, 156, 157–58, 180; and literacy,
50–58; marginalization of women in,
155–64; and Panic of 1819, 137; and
periodicals, 55; popular participation in,
81, 85, 86, 156; and private societies,
117, 157; vs. social reform, 143–44; and
women as rights bearers, 44; in women's
education, 51; women's participation in,
2, 5, 6, 8–9, 19–20, 29, 40–41, 46, 57–61,
68–69, 70–75, 81, 84–85, 86, 93–97, 113,
115–47, 158–59, 163, 165–66; women's
rejection of, 140, 145–46, 147. *See also*
Democratic Republicans; Federalists;
influence, women's; party conflict; political parties

Polk, Mary, 66

Poulain de la Barre, François, 3, 12, 166

A Present for the Ladies (Tate), 13

Preston, Francis, 118

print culture, 8, 9; in American Revolution,
22, 26; and Embargo, 97; and politics,
50–58, 68, 83; and women as authors,
59–61; and women's political participation, 46, 57, 58–61, 81. *See also* literature,
women in; newspapers; periodicals, popular

property, 62, 178; and Federalists, 149, 160;
and female suffrage, 29, 31, 37, 46; and
suffrage, 27–30, 31, 33, 37, 38, 46, 149–
50, 153, 154, 172; women's rights to, 26,
29, 30, 38, 78, 153

prostitution, campaigns against, 142, 143,
145, 183

Pruitt, John, 99

Pruitt, Mary, 99

public office, 4, 62–68, 81, 182; expansion
of, 62; men's participation in, 62, 67–68;
women in, 77, 78, 159

public speaking by women, 71–75, 81,
135–36

Pufendorf, Samuel, 174

Quakers, 31–32, 109

Quasi-War with France (1798), 93–94, 140,
146–47, 148

Quincy, Josiah, 151

Ramsay, David, 56, 156

Randolph, John, 63, 127

Randolph, Martha Jefferson, 62

Acknowledgments

Perhaps the best thing—maybe the only good thing—about taking a long time to write a book is the ever-enlarging circle of people who have helped me in one way or another and who, in a sense, formed a community centered around the book. Making new friends and getting to know other scholars in the field have been among the most rewarding aspects of the project. A long genesis also means that I have acquired a long list of debts which a simple "thank you" can hardly repay. In any case, I will try.

First of all, I would like to thank the National Endowment for the Humanities, the Society for Eighteenth Century Studies, the American Antiquarian Society (AAS), and George Mason University for providing fellowships or financial support that allowed me to research and write the book. I am especially grateful to Joanne Chaison, John Hench, and Phil Lampi at the AAS, who played key roles in the early stages of the project and have made their institution a delightful haven for scholars of early America. I would also like to thank Dave Kelley of the Library of Congress for reference assistance that went above and beyond the call of duty. Because most of the research for this book was finished before the widespread availability of digital databases and web search engines, I had to rely on more old-fashioned methods. More than ten years ago, Dave showed me an obscure index to the American Periodical Series, printed on microprint cards (if anyone remembers what those are), that opened up whole new avenues of inquiry.

Many other individuals aided my research in ways both large and small. I would like to thank the staffs at the Library of Congress Manuscript Room and Rare Book Room, the Massachusetts Historical Society, the New York Historical Society, the Houghton Library at Harvard University, the Maryland Historical Society, the Virginia Historical Society, and the Southern Collection at the University of North Carolina, Chapel Hill, for help in uncovering the riches of their archives. I am grateful to the editors of the *William & Mary Quarterly* and the *American Quarterly* for giving me permission to reproduce portions of articles previously published in their journals. I would also like to acknowledge the assistance of my graduate students, Linda Burch, Pat Dunlap, Clayton Jewett, Stephanie Hurter, and Karen McPherson, who made useful contributions to my research. In addition, I thank Terry Ross, who provided timely advice of another sort that helped bring the project to fruition.

Many scholars have commented on papers related to this project or read sections of the work that appeared previously in article form. For useful comments and suggestions, I would like to thank Catherine Allgor, Doron Ben-Atar, Tim Breen, Pat Cohen, Seth Cotlar, Nancy Cott, Mary Kelley, Sarah Knott, Jan Lewis, Barbara Oberg, Peter Onuf, Jeff Pasley, Whit Ridgway, Andy Robertson, Barbara Taylor, David Waldstreicher, and Gordon Wood. I am especially grateful to Dan Richter, who read the entire manuscript and provided astute criticism that helped me sharpen and refine my argument. My editor at the University of Pennsylvania Press, Bob Lockhart, has been supportive and enthusiastic for as long as I have been working on the project. He has been the ideal person to shepherd the manuscript into print.

Sheila Skemp, Elaine Forman Crane, and Edie Gelles have been my intellectual companions throughout the entire journey. We have done so many conference sessions together that I am sure I don't know where my ideas end and theirs begin. They have read my papers, articles, and drafts and offered innumerable suggestions for improvement. I thank them for their intellectual generosity, their friendship, and their own significant contributions to the field of early American women's history.

The book has also benefited from discussions with other colleagues. My department at George Mason University has been a most congenial and dynamic place for a historian to work. Jack Censer, Jane Turner Censer, Marion Deshmukh, the late Larry Levine, Mike O'Malley, Roy Rosenzweig, Suzy Smith, and Jeffrey Stewart have all provided help, insight, or encouragement at key moments. I also thank Paula Petrik for her generous assistance in reproducing some of the digital images. Members of my history reading group have kept me abreast of developments in other fields and pushed my thinking about history in new directions. For their collegiality and intellectual stimulation, I thank Jim Gilbert, Mike Kazin, Nelson Lichtenstein, Melani McAlister, Joe McCartin, Tim Meagher, Terry Murphy, Adam Rothman, and Roy Rosenzweig.

During the years I worked on this project, there were a lot of ups and downs in my personal life. My friends and family offered the love and support that got me through it all. I especially thank Margarita Egan, Kim Gray, Susie Hogan, Laura Kalman, Stacy Moses, Nancy Pfenning, Jolene Reiter, Robin Chapman Stacey, Kathleen Trainor, Deborah Walther, and Ellen Warnock for helping me keep things in perspective. My children, Anthony Morley and Angela Rose Gormley, made sure that I had balance in my life. My husband, Bill Gormley, encouraged me, sustained me, and believed in me the whole time. He knows I probably would have finished the book a lot sooner had I not spent so many hours in my garden. But he also understands why it is important to stop and smell the roses.